SEXUALITY AND PSYCHOANALYSIS

PHILOSOPHICAL CRITICISMS

FIGURES OF THE UNCONSCIOUS 10

SEXUALITY AND PSYCHOANALYSIS

Philosophical Criticisms

Edited by
Jens De Vleminck and Eran Dorfman

LEUVEN UNIVERSITY PRESS

ISBN 978 90 5867 844 7
D/ 2010 / 1869 / 59
NUR: 777

Cover illustration: Louise Bourgeois *The Family I*, 2007
(gouache on paper, suite of 12 each 59.7 x 45.7 cm).
Courtesy Cheins & Reid, New York – Photo: Christopher Burke
Cover design: Griet Van Haute
Lay-out: Friedemann BVBA

Table of Contents

Acknowledgements

The editors want to thank Saskia Bultman, Andreas De Block, Isabelle Demortier, Corry Shores, Philippe Van Haute, and Mieke Van Rensbergen for their advice and assistance during the editing process.

Abbreviations

"Standard Edition", followed by a number from 1-24, refers to:

Freud, S. (1953-1974). *The Standard Edition of the Complete Psychological Works of Sigmund Freud.* 24 Vols. (J. Strachey, Ed. and Trans.). London: Hogarth Press.

Apart from this, the contributors' own references have been used, with bibliographies attached to each paper.

Sexuality, Psychoanalysis, and Philosophy – An Introduction

Jens De Vleminck

At the end of the nineteenth century, sexology emerged as a new sub-discipline within the biomedical sciences. The works of the first generation of sexologists, including Richard von Krafft-Ebing, Albert Moll, and Albert von Schrenck-Notzing, were a major source of inspiration for the "young" Sigmund Freud (Ellenberger, 1970; Sulloway, 1979). Although these sexologists certainly did inspire him, however, Freud went beyond the then prevailing sexological approach. Rather than limiting himself to the anatomy and physiology of the sexual apparatus, he explicitly tackled the issue of the place of sexuality in human life as such. This is most evident in his handling of the sexological tradition in his clinical work with hysterical patients. With Freud, the psychoanalytical account of human sexuality was elaborated with concepts articulating sexual reality from a different point of view. Psychoanalysis even produced some of the strongest criticisms of sexology, stressing the inevitable pains of sexuality. Against the idea that there are no inherent difficulties barring the full enjoyment of a *completely satisfactory* sexual life, Freud argues that there is something intrinsically lacking in sexuality that prevents complete pleasure. In one of his latest papers, Freud writes: "There is always something lacking for complete discharge and satisfaction – en attendant toujours quelque chose qui ne venait point – and this missing part, the reaction of orgasm, manifests itself in equivalents in other spheres, in *absences*, outbreaks of laughing, weeping, and perhaps other ways. – Once again infantile sexuality has fixed a model in this" (Freud, 1941, p. 300).

Hence, it comes as no surprise that some authors argue that Freud's most radical claims were not about the unconscious, but concerned the profoundly ambivalent nature of human sexuality and its omnipresence in human thought and behaviour (Laplanche, 1970, p. 27). From his earliest writings onward, psychoanalysis has been centrally involved with the complexity of human sexuality. In his *Fragment of an Analysis of a Case of Hysteria* (1905), Freud acknowledges: "I was further anxious to show that sexuality does not simply intervene, like a *deus ex machina*, on one single occasion, at some point in the working of the processes which characterize hysteria, but that it provides the motive power for every single symptom, and for every single manifestation of a symptom. The symptoms of the disease are nothing else than *the patient's sexual activity*. A single case can never be capable of proving a theorem as general as this one; but I can only repeat over and over again – for I never find it otherwise – that sexuality is the key to the problem of psychoneurosis and of the neuroses in general. No one who disdains the key will ever be able to unlock the door. I still await news of the investi gations which are to make it possible to contradict this theorem or to limit its scope. What I have hitherto heard against it have been expressions of personal dislike or disbelief. To these it is enough to reply in the words of Charcot: 'Ça n'empêche pas d'exister'" (Freud, 1905, p. 115).

Freud's most systematic account of human sexuality can be found in his *Three Essays on the Theory of Sexuality.* In this text, he sketches an impressive panorama of the vicissitudes of human sexuality and of sexual psychopathology in particular. Moreover, Freud sets out to overthrow contemporary conceptions of sexuality as exclusively biological, absent in childhood, and emerging after puberty. By broadening the concept of sexuality and extending human sexuality back into childhood, Freud also rejects the popular idea of a pre-given aim or object for the libido. Many of his critics accused him of trying to get a grip on human nature by reducing it to the seemingly animalistic aspect of sexuality. However, from the beginning Freud took into account the complex and distinctly human nature of our sexuality, confronting us with the all encompassing impact of the "goddess Libido" (McGuire, 1974, p. 400).

After Freud's death in 1939, Theodor Reik wrote: "Freud's death does not mean the beginning of the end of psychoanalysis, as his foes aver, but rather the end of the beginning" (Reik, 1940, p. 22). This is nowhere more true than in his psychoanalytical theorizing on human sexuality. Freud's work brought about a revolution in sexual education, behaviour and mores. Its impact is omnipresent in psychoanalytical authors such as Theodor Reik, Wilhelm Reich, Erich Fromm, Otto Fenichel, Françoise Dolto, Jacques Lacan and Herbert Marcuse. In recent years, however, many psychoanalytical theoreticians seem to have forgotten about sexuality. During the last few decades, the major theories of psychoanalysis have focused on other topics, such as object relations, borderline psychopathology and developmental observational research, thereby neglecting or even denying the importance of sexuality (Green, 1996; Spruiell, 1997; Green, 2000; Fonagy, 2008). Contrary to the "classical" view of the relation between sexuality and psychoanalysis as "an old love affair" (Levine & Schwartz, 1999), sexuality has become one of the blind spots of contemporary psychoanalysis. As indicated by a computer-assisted analysis of psychoanalytical literature, the contemporary psychoanalytical concern with sexuality has declined dramatically (Fonagy, 2008, pp. 14-15). In a certain sense, the publication of this collection of essays can be seen as a response to this remarkable trend and as a rebuttal of its implicit assumptions.

This collection of essays does more, however, than simply offer an alternative psychoanalytical account of sexuality. It also develops a wide range of philosophical reflections on sexuality as conceptualized by Freudo-Lacanian psychoanalysis. The unfolding of a philosophical perspective on the place of sexuality in psychoanalysis is far from evident for at least two reasons. First, both Freud and the post-Freudians share an ambivalent attitude towards the philosophical tradition, and vice versa. Second, the theme of sexuality has been largely ignored or marginalized by Western philosophy (Scruton, 2006). It is common knowledge that the history of Western thought has been at this impasse for over two thousand years (Soble, 2006). The abject character of sexuality has been linked to the depreciated status of the human body since Plato. Sexuality was seen as mysterious, paradoxical and, most of all, as a threatening and uncontrollable force, deeply embedded in our animal nature. Remnants of this Platonic view can be found in Ancient and Medieval philosophy. The depreciation of human sexuality – which is associated with sin, guilt, and the idea of "animality", and is considered to be opposed to our "true human nature", our rational capacities and our spiritual aspirations – survived in the philosophy of the neo-Platonists, Augustine and Aquinas. However, an equally depreciating view can be found in the work of many modern philosophers, such as Kant, Hegel and Schopenhauer, who developed what may be called a "pessimistic metaphysics of human sexuality". According to Kant, for example, sexuality "makes of the loved person an object of appetite. … Taken by itself it is a degradation of human nature" (Kant, 1963, p. 163). This pessimistic view goes together with the fact that, throughout the history of Western philosophy, questions related to sex and sexuality have been monopolized by such philosophical sub-disciplines as moral philosophy and ethics. Victorian morality relegated sexuality to the privacy of the bedroom, rendering it unavailable to the scrutiny of the physician, the scientist and the philosopher. It is precisely at the acme of the Victorian era that Freud and his collaborators, struggling with this pessimism, claimed that sexuality as such lies at the very heart of the human condition. In this sense, precisely because of its basic preoccupation with the theme of sexuality, psychoanalysis can make an important contribution to philosophical thought on sexuality, a domain of utmost importance for philosophical theorizing about human nature. Conversely, psychoanalysis may benefit from the philosophical input.

A philosophical approach can be used fruitfully as a critical tool for elucidating and analyzing the concepts and foundations of the psychoanalytical enterprise (Van Haute & Geyskens, 2004).

The history of the early relations between philosophy and psychoanalysis is characterized by many misconceptions and mutual misunderstanding. However, the large overlap between the two disciplines has ensured their mutual influence. A large number of the topics analytical and continental philosophers are interested in are closely tied to psychoanalysis. For the analytical context, for instance, one may think of Ludwig Wittgenstein, Richard Wollheim, Alisdair McIntyre, Sebastian Gardner, Stanley Cavell, Jonathan Lear, Jerome Neu and Donald Davidson. It is clear, however, that psychoanalysis impacted philosophy far more profoundly on the continent. This is illustrated by the work of Jean-Paul Sartre, Maurice Merleau-Ponty, Louis Althusser, Paul Ricoeur, Gilles Deleuze, Michel Foucault, Jacques Derrida and Alain Badiou. At the same time, psychoanalysis has often shown an interest in philosophy. Both psychoanalysts (e.g. Jacques Lacan, Daniel Lagache, Didier Anzieu, Serge Leclaire, André Green and Jean Laplanche) and psychoanalytically oriented phenomenological psychiatrists (e.g. Eugen Bleuler, Ludwig Binswanger, Karl Jaspers and Medard Boss) have been influenced by philosophy. G.W.F. Hegel, Friedrich Nietzsche, Arthur Schopenhauer, Henri Bergson, Edmund Husserl and Martin Heidegger are frequently mentioned as sources of inspiration.

Converging research initiated on several fronts by international colloquia in the United States, Brazil, Japan, the United Kingdom, France, the Netherlands and Belgium illustrates the diversity and increasing intellectual validity of the research field lying at the crossroads of psychoanalysis and philosophy. The international convergence of these intellectual interests over the past ten years has given a more distinct method and form to the currents of thought which have brought psychoanalysis to bear on philosophy, and – from another angle – have brought philosophy into psychoanalysis, in a variety of ways. The inauguration of the *International Society for Psychoanalysis and Philosophy* (ISPP) in 2008 was a response to these developments. This international society seeks to cultivate relations between psychoanalysts who are also philosophers by training or practice, and philosophers who find in the questions initiated by Freud and his successors a source for the renewal of contemporary thought.

For this tenth volume of the series *The Figures of the Unconscious*, a diverse group of philosophers and psychoanalysts were asked to reflect on the concept of sexuality in Freudo-Lacanian psychoanalysis. The result is a stimulating collection of essays where the role of sexuality in psychoanalysis is scrutinized from a philosophical point of view. It can be read as an invitation to a revitalization of sexuality as a central theme of both psychoanalytical and philosophical reflection.

This volume consists of four sections, and closes with an epilogue. The first section of this volume is entitled "Sexuality and Metaphysics". It looks at fundamental questions related to what, from the very beginning, Freud called his "metapsychology", a notion that has often been interpreted as an immediate allusion to metaphysics (Rado, 1949, p. 181). Freud's most systematic account of metapsychology can be found in a collection of papers published in 1915. The same meta-psychological preoccupation can also be found in later works, such as his *New Introductory Lectures* (1933). In the opening essay, Paul Moyaert explores the nature of sexual pleasure and, more in particular, questions what can be so frightening about it. The Freudian answer is criticized and confronted with the two standard answers provided by Plato and Aristotle. The Aristotelian account shows certain similarities with that of Lacan, who differentiates between two forms of pleasure, i.e. "*plaisir*" and "*jouissance*". This distinction is related to a question that is totally neglected by Freud, i.e. the relation between pleasure and the Good. In the following essay, Adrian Johnston points out how Freud posits many of the axiomatic ideas of impersonal metapsychology on the basis of realizations garnered through his personal self-analysis. Johnston claims that Freud's focus on sexual matters is, in part, a result of his incomplete self-analytic confrontation with his own death anxiety. Lacan's suggestions concerning how to re-read the textual fragments of Freud's self-analysis in relation to his other writings hint at the contention that sexuality enjoys a prominent place at the very centre of psychical life precisely because it contains something "in it more than itself", this "excess" being its incarnation of the human condition of inescapable condemnation to death. Vladimir Safatle discusses the ontological nature of the psychoanalytical theory of the death drive in Freud and Lacan. Safatle shows that this ontological nature can be understood only if we accept the claim that the concept of the death drive asks for a notion of ontological negation. It is contended that this intuition also propels a further elucidation of the concepts of libido and sexuality as major features of psychoanalytical theory. In her contribution, Ruth Ronen questions whether psychoanalysis is disengaged from the philosophical commitment to truth or whether psychoanalysis, just as much as philosophy, espouses a love of truth. Through a discussion of Lacan's reading of Plato's *Symposium* and Alain Badiou's re-addressing of the notion of truth in contemporary philosophy, the philosophical love of truth is viewed against the way truth is loved in analytical transference. Ronen holds that psychoanalysis does not replace the philosophical love of truth with an alternative notion of truth. It replaces the *love* of truth with a *desire* for truth, which is the only position from which the real power of truth can be produced as the effect of transference. Charles Shepherdson's paper explores the relation between Lacan and Derrida, focusing on their use of modal logic (the categories of possibility, impossibility, necessity and contingency). Shepherdson argues that, in Derrida's work, these four categories are largely absorbed by the logic of the aporia, whereas in Lacan they are distinguished and used to elaborate sexual difference and the "Other *jouissance*". Shepherdson shows how Lacan's elaboration of the four "modes of being", defined by the modal categories, also subjects them to a series of transformations. This complicates any attempt to understand sexual difference as a simple binary opposition, and produces a set of discursive transformations that brings Lacan's account closer to Foucault than most readers of Lacan have acknowledged.

Complementary to the first section, which is devoted to theoretical and "metaphysical" questions on the concept of sexuality, the second section attends to the vicissitudes of sexuality in clinical practice. In Freud, a tension always exists between the therapeutic endeavour in clinical practice and what he calls his "science of unconscious mental processes" (Freud, 1925d, p. 255). Freud refers to many different patients in the short illustrations and examples he gives in his theoretical papers. However, the best way to observe Freud as analyst at work is, no doubt, by reading his case studies. In this section, entitled "Sexuality in Practice", two essays each take one of Freud's most famous case studies as a point of departure. Both essays can be taken as prototypic examples showing the value of a renewed examination of Freud's case studies. Elissa Marder devotes an essay to Freud's famous and complex study *From the History of an Infantile Neurosis* (1918), better known as the Wolf Man case. In this paper, Freud grapples with the fact that the specificity of human subjectivity is grounded in a relation to sexuality that renders us simultaneously too close as well as too far from the realm of animals. The collapse between human and animal figures pervades the entire case history but has received surprisingly little critical attention. Most critics focus on the temporal status of the primal scene and the problem of sexual difference. Marder, however, argues that Freud posits the problem of the primal scene in order to circumvent an interrogation of the ways in which animality lies at the core of sexual difference and human subjectivity. Philippe Van Haute and Tomas Geyskens focus on one of Freud's first, and probably most famous patients, Dora (Ida Bauer). Through a reading of Freud's *Fragment of an Analysis of a Case of Hysteria* (1905), the authors show that the classical interpretation of the abandonment of the seduction theory cannot be maintained. Abandoning this theory did not mean that, from then on, Freud interpreted the stories of his patients as motivated by Oedipal fantasies. Rather, in his texts after 1897 Freud develops an alternative theory of the specific causes of hysteria (and pathology in general), in which trauma and an "organic disposition" are linked in an original way. In this theory there is no sign yet of the Oedipus complex as the nuclear complex of all neuroses. It is still bisexuality that plays a crucial role in the understanding of pathology.

The third section of the book, "Sexuality and Politics", brings together three essays that pay tribute to the work of Michel Foucault. His three volumes on *The History of Sexuality* can, of course, be seen as a milestone in philosophical thinking on sexuality. Foucault shows how the various "sciences of sexuality", including psychoanalysis, have an intimate association with the power structures of modern society. According to Foucault, sexuality is the result of a political discourse that has the power to create sexual identities. No doubt, Foucault's accomplishment is to have brought the "politics of sexuality" to the surface. Eran Dorfman's essay follows Foucault's claim in *The History of Sexuality* that psychoanalysis blindly pushes forth and enforces the discourse of sexuality. Dorfman argues that the Freudian accent on sexuality is subordinated to his discovery of the unconscious, and that sexuality is only one of the instances of the unconscious. From this perspective, he analyzes the similarities and differences between Freudian descriptions of the perceptual apparatus of the mind and the Foucaultian structure of power, in order to arrive at a clearer picture of the relationship between power, the unconscious, resistance and sexuality. Veronica Vasterling's paper triangulates between Foucault, Butler and Lacan. Since *Gender Trouble* (1990), Butler has used psychoanalytical theory to elaborate her critical analysis of hetero-normativity and gender binarity. Vasterling discusses Butler's attempt to join a Lacanian account of the psyche with a Foucaultian account of power. She argues that the aim of Butler's enterprise is to develop a theory of the sexed subject that, on the one hand, is politically more viable than the Lacanian subject and, on the other hand, provides insight into an aspect of power that Foucault's theory neglects, i.e. the psychic life of power. Cecilia Sjöholm's essay starts from the Foucaultian claim that the most important human practices should be considered as "technologies". Foucault's technologies of the self operate at the junction where *tekhne* becomes *poiesis*, thereby allowing the self to adhere to various possibilities of truth, rather than one particular truth. Although an adamant critic of psychoanalysis, Foucault's truth-concept has a lot in common with that of psychoanalysis. Sjöholm argues that psychoanalysis is a process, set in motion through forms of technology, or, techniques, a practice that helps to produce forms of truth, rather than discover a particular truth.

The fourth and last section, "Sexuality and Aesthetics", pays tribute to sexuality as one of the most important themes in the history of Western art (Lucie-Smith, 1997). Ari Hirvonen's contribution explores how Lacan presents sexual difference and feminine *jouissance* and their relationship to the concepts of the Real, the object *a*, the drive and the not-all in his *Seminar XX: Encore* (1975). Specific attention is given to the figure of the mystic, Saint Teresa, who seems to be the representative of the feminine *jouissance*. Moreover, Hirvonen asks whether Lacan is inscribed in the ontological and metaphysical tradition, as Lacoue-Labarthe and Nancy have argued. The thesis is that the feminine *jouissance* may be seen as Lacan's answer to this critique and as a new mode of the subversion of the subject. Tomas Geyskens' essay articulates a Deleuzian account of the paintings of the French painter Francis Bacon. The author argues that Deleuze's work on Francis Bacon is an aesthetic clinic of hysteria and an implicit critique of the psychoanalytical conception of hysteria. Bacon's paintings reveal what is at stake in hysteria: not the symbolic expression of unconscious representations, but the pure presence of the body, the experience of the body under the organism. Inspired by the work of the phenomenologist Henri Maldiney, Deleuze argues that Bacon's paintings become non-figurative without being abstract. In this way, painting shows the hysterical struggle of the body to escape from itself in the rhythm of its movement.

The philosophical discussions on the concept of sexuality in psychoanalysis make clear that the theme of sexuality gives rise to major psychoanalytical problems, including philosophical questions that go to the heart of the most important of the four central questions raised by Kant, namely, "What is man?" The goal of this volume is to provide an impetus to the revitalization of sexuality as a central theme of psychoanalytical theory and practice and to emphasize the importance of the psychoanalytical enterprise as a valuable contribution to philosophical anthropology.

References

Ellenberger, H. (1970). *The discovery of the unconscious: The history and evolution of dynamic psychiatry.* New York, NY: Basic Books.

Fonagy, P. (2008). A genuine developmental theory of sexual enjoyment and its implications for psychoanalytic technique. *Journal of the American Psychoanalytic Association, 56(1),* 11-36.

Freud, S. (1905). Fragment of an analysis of a case of hysteria. *Standard Edition 7,* pp. 7-122.

———. (1925). An autobiographical study. *Standard Edition 20,* pp. 1-74.

———. (1941). Findings, ideas, problems. *Standard Edition 23,* pp. 299-300.

Green, A. (1996). Has sexuality anything to do with psychoanalysis? *International Journal of Psychoanalysis, 76,* 871-883.

Green, A. (2000). *The chain of Eros: The sexual in psychoanalysis.* London: Rebus Press.

Jones, E. (1953-1957). *The life and work of Sigmund Freud.* New York, NY: Basic Books.

Kant, I. (1963). *Lectures on ethics.* New York, NY: Harper and Row.

Laplanche, J. (1985). *Life and death in psychoanalysis.* (J. Mehlman, Trans.). London/ Baltimore, MD: Johns Hopkins University Press. (Original work published 1970).

Lucie-Smith, E. (1997). *Sexuality in Western art.* London: Thames and Hudson.

McGuire, W. (1974). *The Freud/Jung letters: The correspondence between Sigmund Freud and C. G. Jung (1906-1923).* Princeton: Princeton University Press.

Rado, S. (1955). Mind, unconscious mind, and brain. In *Psychoanalysis of behavior: Vol. I* (pp. 181-182). New York, NY: Grune and Stratton. (Original work published 1949).

Reik, T. (1940). *From thirty years with Freud.* Toronto/New York, NY: Farrar & Rinehart.

Scruton, R. (2006). *Sexual desire: A philosophical investigation.* London/New York, NY: Continuum.

Soble, A. (Ed.) (2006). *Sex from Plato to Paglia: A philosophical encyclopedia.* 2 Vols. Westport: Greenwood Press.

Spruiell, V. (1997). Review of the psychoanalytic theory of sexuality: Comments on the assault against it. *International Journal of Psychoanalysis, 78,* 357-361.

Sulloway, F. (1979). *Freud, biologist of the mind: Beyond the psychoanalytic legend.* New York, NY: Basic Books.

Van Haute, P., & Geyskens, T. (2004). *Confusion of tongues: The primacy of sexuality in Freud, Ferenczi, and Laplanche.* New York, NY: Other Press.

Section I
Sexuality and Metaphysics

What is Frightening about Sexual Pleasure? – Introducing Lacan's *Jouissance* into Freudian Psychoanalysis via Plato and Aristotle

Paul Moyaert

We know that sexual pleasure is exciting. But Freud ascertains that, for some people, excitement does not add to the pleasure. In fact, they find the excitement of arousal so oppressive that they cannot enjoy sex. This is a curious finding. For how can sexual pleasure be rendered joyless by fear of excitement? Pleasure is something that has preoccupied Western philosophers since ancient times, and without much exaggeration one could say that the innumerable answers to the question "What is pleasure?" are variations on the two standard answers provided by Plato in the *Philebus* and by Aristotle in *The Nicomachean Ethics*. According to Plato, pleasure is the fulfilment of a lack or the satisfaction of a need, while for Aristotle pleasure is the unhindered unfolding or expression of an activity. For both of these philosophers, the ontological question is related to what, in their eyes, is the far more important question of the moral value of pleasure. Is pleasure as such a good, or are only certain enjoyments under certain conditions good? Or might pleasure even qualify as the highest good? Is pleasure the most valuable thing, to which all of life's other affairs are subordinate, and from which they derive their relative value? Here, too, the answers diverge. Plato is far more reticent than Aristotle with regard to the moral value of pleasure.

If these ancient questions have recurred throughout the history of Western philosophy, it is only recently that attention has been given to the fact that sexual pleasure is not without its anxieties. But even here, Freud is not the only one to pay attention to this combination. While Levinas generally had little sympathy for Freudian ideas, he, too, notices the connection of pleasure and anxiety in the description of *jouissance* that he provides in the unsurpassed phenomenology of Eros in *Totality and Infinity* (Levinas, 1969, pp. 256-266).

Freud's finding that sexual enjoyment is not without fear is interesting in itself, but even more remarkable is that Freud himself could not quite place his own observation. He can understand what anxiety is and how it goes together with sexual object drives: in the Freudian scheme, anxiety is unbounded physical excitation, i.e. an accumulation of energy that has no release. But this notion of anxiety does not explain why sexual *pleasure* can be frightening. Freud has trouble with the frightening nature of sexual pleasure for at least two reasons. First, because of his definition of pleasure, and second, because he neglects the question that Plato and Aristotle considered the more important one. This is the question of the value of pleasure in a good life, a life that is worth living. According to Plato, gods experience neither pleasure (joy), nor its opposite (Plato, *Phil.*, 33b). This is why, at least for the later Plato, the life of the gods is not always very appealing to humans. A life entirely without pleasure has little attraction, but just how important is that element in life as a whole? Some philosophers, again including Plato, have seriously questioned whether pleasure is in itself really a good thing. For Lacan, too, the moral value of pleasure is by no means a foregone conclusion. The hedonistic component of utilitarianism, in which pleasure is presented as a good, he characterized as fraud. Whoever maintains that pleasure is good, says Lacan in *The Ethics of Psychoanalysis*, first has to explain what is so good about it, or of what the goodness of pleasure consists. And because hedonists fail to do so, their theories are a swindle. "In truth, it isn't because they have emphasized the beneficial effects of pleasure that we criticize the so-called hedonist tradition. It is rather because they haven't stated what the good consisted of. That's where the fraud is" (Lacan, 1992, pp. 185-188). I would suggest that, had Freud given more consideration to this moral question, he would have been better able to understand why pleasure may be frightening.

Let me first investigate Freud's definition of pleasure and demonstrate how, as his definition largely corresponds to Plato's, it prevented him from understanding his own observation. Then, we will look for a better definition, inspired by the views of Aristotle. It appears to me that Lacan's view of *jouissance* comes closer to Aristotle's definition of the appetites, even though Lacan himself was drawn to the dark sides of pleasure. He saw these dark sides not only in the most sensual desires of the flesh, but also in what are traditionally considered the higher pleasures, such as the search for truth. Aristotle was less sensitive to these because in his eyes nature is spontaneously self-limiting and directed towards the golden mean from within.

Freud

Pleasure as Satisfaction – What is pleasure? According to Freud, it is the perception of a change in one's own body. More specifically, pleasure is feeling the satisfaction of a drive or a need. Freud's view seems self-evident. Whenever you experience pleasure, you *know* that you are experiencing pleasure, and you know this because your enjoyment puts you in touch with your own corporeal sensations. Pleasure makes you return to your own body. To speak of an unconscious pleasure would make no sense. Despite its apparent self-evidence, however, this definition immediately presents Freud with a problem. It is not clear, for instance, how it applies to more intellectual and aesthetic pleasures. Freud acknowledges this difficulty in *Civilization and its Discontents* (1930), where he says:

> A satisfaction of this kind, such as an artist's joy in creating, in giving his phantasies body, or a scientist's in solving problems or discovering truths, has a special quality which we shall certainly one day be able to characterize in metapsychological terms. At present we can only say figuratively that such satisfactions seem "finer and higher". But their intensity is mild as compared with that derived from the sating of crude and primary instinctual impulses; it does not convulse our physical being. (pp. 79-80)

What is more important is that this definition raises difficult issues even with regard to pleasures that are not so very "fine and high". I would argue, following Aristotle, that enjoyment is something other than becoming aware of changes in one's body. Of course, the body continually undergoes changes and these processes do not stop while a person is experiencing enjoyment. But that does not mean that pleasure consists of the perception of bodily changes.

Freud understands pleasure as satisfaction, much as does Plato. Freud, however, is quite aware that this is not the only possible definition of pleasure. In *Three Essays on the Theory of Sexuality* (1905) Freud twice remarks in a footnote that "in the German language, '*Lust*', is unfortunately ambiguous, and is used to denote the experience both of a need and of a gratification" (Freud, 1905, p. 135, note 2). And in a footnote in the third essay he says: "'*Lust*' has two meanings, and is used to describe the sensation of sexual tension ('*Ich habe Lust*' = 'I should like to', 'I feel an impulse to') as well as the feeling of satisfaction" (ibid., p. 212, note 1). Freud regrets this conceptual ambiguity, but sees no reason to call his own definition into question. This was a missed opportunity. First there is the need, the discomfort of hunger and thirst, of the full bladder, or of the tense restlessness of the sexual organs. And then, after certain goal-oriented actions, restfulness returns. Thus, pleasure is a draining of tension. The excess of excitation is evacuated, and this draining is experienced as pleasure. The return of the equilibrium that stimuli have disturbed, we are aware of as pleasure. Plato reaches the same conclusion in the *Philebus*. Just like Freud, he begins with examples that Socrates sees as beyond argument: eating and drinking (Plato, *Phil.*, 31e). To be sure, Plato does not speak of pleasure as an evacuation of tension in the sense of blowing off steam, but about the filling of a lack, an emptiness, a deficiency. However, this difference is entirely irrelevant. Whether the process is described as the filling of a lack or the draining off of an excess, in either case pleasure is the restoration of a disturbed balance, a return to what is represented as a more natural and more stable state. Pleasure is the *unstable* and *fleeting transition* from empty to full, or the reduction of tension from excess to normalcy. Plato strongly emphasizes that pleasure only takes place in the transitional process itself, or in the process of the reduction of the lack. Pleasure does not possess the stability of a substantial reality, but is characterized by the inconstancy of becoming. Pleasure does not endure, nor can it stand on its own. It is a reality that disappears at the moment that it arises. Plato is perfectly clear about the state that follows a pleasurable filling of an emptiness. This state is often mistakenly presented as pleasure. However, there is no pleasure without an awareness of a transition. Perhaps Freud is less accurate here, for it is not entirely clear whether he is of the opinion that the state wherein no lowering of tension is felt – that is, the absence of excitation – can be called pleasurable in the same way that the reduction or the disappearance of tension can be. Either way, Freud as much as Plato has difficulty in fixing a sense of physical well-being that is not a transition from a state of discomfort.

Unlike Freud, Plato directs his attention towards the question of what to think of a life that is directed only towards the maximization of sensual enjoyment. A person for whom pleasure were the highest goal would, in Plato's view, desire only the constant repetition of the fleeting transition from emptiness to satisfaction. This would be a restless life, mainly consisting of being constantly shunted back and forth from empty to full and from full to empty. Is this not comparable to repeatedly having long bouts of hiccups? In Plato's view, pleasure, in spite of its calming effects, takes on the appearance of an insatiable hunger or thirst. Freud, by contrast, describes the human organism not so much in terms of a *vain* desire to eternalize the fleeting transition, but in terms of the state that follows upon satisfaction. That is, he describes pleasure from the perspective of the state of equilibrium that follows it. Freud's perspective is not that of an organism seeking to maximize pleasure, but of one desiring to minimize unpleasant excitation to the greatest possible extent.

Pleasure, in Freud's definition, is satisfaction. What follows from this simple definition? Defined in these terms, pleasure is a very meagre reality. Even physical enjoyment is relatively unsubstantial. The definitions provided by Freud and Plato are negative: pleasure is the disappearance or reduction of discomfort. It is no coincidence that, in *The Interpretation of Dreams*, Freud initially designated the pleasure principle by the term *the unpleasure principle* (Freud, 1900, p. 574). In his view, the sole motivation of the drives subject to the pleasure principle is the voidance of unpleasure. Pleasure is not the presence of something, but the disappearance of its opposite. Freud may quickly have come to prefer the term *pleasure principle*, but the change of name did nothing to alter his conceptualization of pleasure as the voidance of unpleasure. Comparing this definition of pleasure to a definition of beauty suggests some of its shortcomings. To define beauty as the absence of ugliness is simply to fail to define beauty, for beauty is not an absence, but a presence. This shortcoming is not unrelated to the fact that there is no place in Freud's thought for a moral life that would refine and cultivate pleasure, for such a way of life is only possible if pleasure is a positive reality.

For both Plato and Freud, pleasure primarily resembles something like recovery from illness or the restoration of equilibrium. However, one has to ask, is pleasure not rather the expression of health and vitality? Is pleasure not, in essence, an activity? This is, as we shall see, precisely how Aristotle approaches the question of pleasure. Freud's model of pleasure is orgastic. Pleasure is what ends the activity, completes and closes it. We only get out of bed because getting up is the quickest route to lying down again. We do not live to enjoy, but to rest from our exertions. After-pleasure is more important than pleasure. In Freud's view, the aim of the drives is to bring to as quick an end as possible the activities that will release the tension that activated them.

Freud's characterization of the drives associated with the pleasure principle applies not only to eating, drinking and lovemaking, but also to more intellectual activities, although these are not the examples that are the first to occur to him. The mind comes into play when we are presented with problems that cannot be solved by instinctual action. Specifically, it is negative experiences that set the mind working. Without pain, no thought. As thoughts are produced because the organism is frustrated, the immediate satisfaction of needs is the death of mental life. In this view, the negative is the motor of mental life. However, even if we grant that the mind is only set in motion by negative experiences, it does not follow that the only pleasure in thinking comes from the problem-solving action.

According to Freud, drives desire their own end, preferably as quickly as possible. They have no aim to conquer the world and make their mark on their surroundings. Drives, in Freud's view, are no will to power. They come into action only because action is the shortest way to inaction. While Freud does recognize the existence of a *Bemächtigungstrieb,* the aim of this drive is the mastering or controlling of hostile stimuli, and not self-expansion. According to Nietzsche, by contrast, drives that aim for satisfaction are weak and sickly. Strong drives affirm themselves and make use of their environment, not to exhaust themselves, but to feed, to increase their self-affirmation to the full. Hence, in Nietzsche's view, self-affirmation does not regret opposition. Rather, it regrets the weakness of the opposition, for without strong opposition one's powers are not stretched to the full. Healthy drives long for contradiction.

In any case, to define pleasure in terms of satisfaction is to present it as something that is reassuring. With this approach it is indeed hard to understand what could be frightening about pleasure. Nevertheless, Freud, too, knows that as far as the *sexual drives* are concerned, not only arousal but even an increase in excitation can, under certain conditions, be pleasurable. "If, however, the tension of sexual excitement is counted as an unpleasurable feeling, we are at once brought up against the fact that it is also undoubtedly felt as pleasurable. In every case in which tension is produced by sexual processes, it is accompanied by pleasure; even in the preparatory changes in the genitals a feeling of satisfaction of some kind is plainly to be observed. How, then, are this unpleasurable tension and this feeling of pleasure to be reconciled?" (Freud, 1905, p. 209) It has not escaped Freud that sexual arousal can be pleasurable, but given his definition of pleasure there is little that he can do with this observation. For Freud, fore-pleasure is a *conceptual* mystery and a physiological puzzle. Sexual foreplay that finds enjoyment in increasing rather than satisfying arousal cannot, in Freud's view, really be pleasurable in itself, except to the overpopulated category of masochists.

Autoerotism: A Missed Opportunity – But it is not only sexual arousal that presents Freud with problems. Take eating and drinking. Everybody, even Freud, knows that there is more to the pleasures of the table than the satisfaction of hunger and thirst: the enjoyment of a fine wine, for instance. While eating and drinking are not pleasurable without hunger and thirst, it does not follow that what is being enjoyed is an awareness of the diminution of hunger and thirst.

In his famous analysis of the oral drive of the nursing child, Freud indicates that the child enjoys sucking at the nipple of the mother's breast. Freud speaks of this as *autoerotic pleasure*, meaning pleasure found in the activity itself. This pleasure, too, does not fit into his standard definition. Had Freud not been the prisoner of his own definition, his observations on autoerotism could have been given wider bearing in a number of ways. (a) The concept of autoerotism could free pleasure from its subjection to satisfaction. Freud has surely missed an opportunity here. He claims that autoerotism comes about as an unintended side-effect of satisfaction. This makes it a surplus pleasure, a pleasure beyond the limits of satisfaction. But should autoerotism not also be seen as a *condition* for being interested in satisfaction? A child who takes no pleasure in the breast, nor, by extension, in eating and drinking, will not be interested in satisfying the need. So can needs really be the driving force of life? Does life not begin with the enjoyment of life, and what is that if not taking pleasure in one's activities? (b) Autoerotism could, moreover, have shown Freud the way to an understanding of pleasure that is not solely based on the search for an adequate object. Autoerotic drives have a different relation to their objects than do drives seeking satisfaction. Because the object is no longer required to provide satisfaction, drives can use objects as an opportunity to develop their own activity. This enables them to extend their activity. The object is no longer that in which drives find their end or fulfilment; it is transformed into an occasion for the drive's operation. (c) The way in which autoerotism and pleasure stand in relation to excitation also deserves a closer look. Autoerotism is pleasure found in the movement – the rhythmic development – of an activity. This pleasure falls under what Freud terms the "pleasurable character of sensations of movement" (Freud, 1905, p. 202) – a source of pleasure that, in his view, also includes passive movement games such as rocking, swinging and "the shaking produced by driving in carriages and later by railway-travel" (ibid., pp. 201-202). Autoerotic pleasure is pleasure found in the fluent development of an activity. That is perhaps also the kind of pleasure Freud has in mind when talking about bounded energy. However, even if autoerotism is not the same as pleasure in excitation, it can easily turn into it. Take the example of swinging, or a child being thrown up into the air and caught again. It never takes long before the urge arises to go "faster", "higher", or "again". In the pleasure of movement, sources of power are released which do not stick at all to the reassuring boundaries of satisfaction.

In all these ways, and no doubt in more, pleasure in the sense of autoerotism presents a missed opportunity for Freud to move away from his dismal image of pleasure as satisfaction.

Through Aristotle to Lacan?

Clinicians know that pleasure and satisfaction are by no means identical, which is precisely why pleasure has something disturbing about it. Take bulimia and anorexia: the craving to over-eat and the craving to starve. Both involve pleasure. Religious fasting, sanctified anorexia, is also not without pleasure. But the pleasure involved here is a pleasure that is not determined or limited by satisfaction. This pleasure is by no means reassuring but, rather, destructive, as it does not keep to the limits of well-being. In comparison, satisfaction is reassuring because it consists of reaching a point of satiety that coincides with well-being. Pleasure falling together with satisfaction is a sad, meagre affair that dies in its own completion, but pleasure that loses its tie to satisfaction risks a limitlessness that is not necessarily a good.

Why do we say that bulimia and anorexia are not without pleasure? The reason is the *abandonment* and the *enthusiasm* with which the one eats beyond all measure, the *eagerness*, the *greediness* and the *determination* or the *drive* with which the other surrenders to a rather asexualized self-control that can no longer be mastered and that transcends the limits of physical well-being. These and similar expressions of pleasure cannot be explained in terms of satisfaction. But how then is this pleasure to be characterized? This question brings us first to Aristotle's alternative account of pleasure, and then to Lacan, whose approach at first sight develops that of Aristotle, but places such a different emphasis that the question must arise whether the similarities between Lacan and Aristotle are more than just coincidental. We shall see that, unlike Freud, Lacan differentiates between two forms of pleasure – *plaisir* and *jouissance* – and that the criterion to distinguish between them is to be found in the question that Freud neglected: namely, the relation between pleasure and what can be called "good". Do they spontaneously converge, as Freud's definition (of pleasure as the release of tension) implicitly suggests?

Pleasure: A Perfection of Nature? – Enjoyment, according to Aristotle in *The Nicomachean Ethics* (Aristotle, 1968, VII, xii, 3; X, iv), is a property of an activity and not a question of satisfaction. Pleasure, then, is a question neither of satisfaction nor of restoration, but of vitality. It is a vital expression of the perfection of an action. Pleasure is the expression of an action that can develop its own *energeia* without being hindered. To be absorbed in your activity is to enjoy what you are doing. Aristotle's radical shift in perspective is decisive. But if we now return to our two clinical examples, it will at once become clear that we need a more complex vocabulary if we are to be able to describe the pleasure found in bulimia or anorexia. Aristotle suggests that enjoyment is the self-expression of an unhindered activity, while the examples show that pleasure is also connected to a tension that can be released by the enjoyment of the activity itself and disrupt the activity from within. Reserves of energy can be released that take the activity well beyond its intended goal. The action is not brought to perfection by this surplus energy, but derails.

The risk of such excess is central to Lacan's view of *jouissance*, but it is a risk foreign to Aristotle's conception of pleasure. Aristotle sees activities as oriented towards self-perfection. According to Lacan, pleasure always risks excess. And this is a risk run not only by sensual pleasures, but even – or perhaps especially – by more spiritual pleasures. No joy is more likely to go astray than that of a magnanimous search for truth. A person in thrall to the truth loses sight of the golden mean. This is not unrelated to the fact that joy often has something to do with loss of control. That is precisely what surrender or self-abandonment is. In surrendering, one is in touch with something stronger than oneself. In the finite action, something of the infinite can be felt. Further research is needed to investigate if the vocabulary roughly evoked here is still in line with Aristotle's ontological vocabulary. In any case, the new frame of reference brings us closer to Lacan.

Pleasure as Surrender – A person experiencing enjoyment surrenders to what he or she is doing. Enjoyment is the ability to give oneself up fully to the activity. However, "ability" might not be the best term: surrendering to an activity is not a purposeful decision. It is something that happens to your activity, as a result of which your activity no longer fully belongs to you. And yet, at the same time, it is not an entirely passive event. Surrender is not something you can bring about, but nor is it something that can happen to you without your participation. This is why one never quite knows what to do to make surrender take place.

In surrender, the activity takes over from you and takes possession of you. Your self is subsumed into the activity so that the action is no longer entirely your action. In a sense, the activity becomes *impersonal.* It draws on sources of power that are not entirely under your control. It is driven from within by a dynamism which surpasses, as it were, the action as it was planned, and which no longer fully adheres to the rhythm and articulated development of the activity itself. Within the action there is a tension with a force that exceeds the actual action.

This line of thought might not be entirely compatible with the ontological vocabulary of Aristotle, but, importantly, it shows that we have come a long way from pleasure as a perception of a physiological change in the body. Moreover, the perception of physiological changes is something that rather spoils pleasure in the sense of surrender. For this very reason we may say that there is pleasure even if the individual is unaware of it. In pleasure, as reconceived here, one is related to oneself in a non-reflexive manner. Take an exciting film or an engrossing book. If the film or the book carries you along, then there is pleasure. But the pleasure we describe here loses its sense of limitation. It is not inclined to bring itself to an end. If limits are reached, they are experienced as something imposed from without. Take complaining, for example. The way some people give themselves up to complaining shows that complaining, just like other autoerotic activities, is not without pleasure. The aim of complaining is, in part, simply to complain, even though discomforts or setbacks are necessary as a pretext for complaint. But here, too, we have to be attentive to the creativity of autoeroticism. A person who is in the mood for complaining will always find something to complain about, and a point is reached at which complaining becomes a self-sustaining activity. Drives create the objects that they need to feed themselves. Hence, a strong, vital hypochondriac complaint transforms the world into an expression of the complaining body. Pleasure has to do with the reversal of the usual end/means relationship. The action is no longer a means to achieve an end beyond the activity itself; what was originally the end to be attained (i.e. the relief of complaint) is transformed into a pretext for the activity.

What is Frightening about Sexual Pleasure? – The following aspects are now relevant. There can be no sexual pleasure without surrender, and that implies that one does not exactly know where the surrender will end. Enjoyment pays no heed to economic calculation. Calculation gives way to generosity. And giving yourself over to something, to your body and to the body of the other, has to do with *self-loss*, with the disappearance of the self as a separate individual. Seen in this light, pleasure has something ecstatic and, at the same time, something symbiotic about it: boundaries are erased. This self-loss is coupled with a *loss of anal self-control*, with a loss of domination of the other, and with a passage from active to passive. However, the one does not displace the other: activity does not become passivity, nor does self-control become self-loss, nor self-concern ecstatic openness. No, both poles fold into one another, so that you become at once man and woman. As in sexual enjoyment, one's own identity is dissolved by participation, through the bodily power of the other, in something stronger than your own life. Pleasure keeps touch with forces that are stronger than the forces expressing themselves in the activity.

Sexual pleasure gives vitality, a fact expressed in the myths that once told of the cycle of life and death. We become immersed in a play of forces in which we disappear as individuals. This dying to ourselves is the precondition for being reborn through participation in something stronger than ourselves. The surfacing of this impersonal substrate in enjoyment means that one cannot really say "I enjoy". It would be more true to say, as Rudi Visker puts it in *Truth and Singularity*, "it enjoys" (Visker, 1999, p. 272), i.e. it enjoys in me. There is something impersonal about sexual pleasure, which is tied to the blurring of the boundaries of one's own body.

In this respect, Levinas is more accurate than Freud (Levinas, 1969, pp. 122-142). To enjoy – and here Levinas uses the term *jouissance* rather than *plaisir* – is to participate in an ecstatic surrender to the elements of life: bathing in the sun, swimming in the sea, standing into the wind, and so forth. Enjoyment involves something of a return to our symbiotic relationship to the elements of nature. Surrender is only surrender when economic calculation vanishes. Whoever enjoys, surrenders without calculation. There can be no pleasure without generosity, but generosity is not necessarily good. This explains why enjoyment can be felt as threatening. The elements of nature, according to Levinas, are forces that can turn against us, and surrender to them entails the loss of protective boundaries. Levinas, agreeing here with Lacan, sees the same dynamic in sexual eroticism. This takes us very far from a notion of pleasure as orgastic satisfaction.

Lacan: Plaisir *and* Jouissance – Lacan distinguishes between *plaisir* and *jouissance*, and his most important criterion of distinction is their respective relation to the good, and in particular the good as coextensive with well-being. On the one hand, there is pleasure, which Lacan calls *plaisir*, which keeps to the limits of what is good for the self and for the other. The culture of this pleasure is prudent: it submits itself to the demands of a broader context, sacrifices the pleasure of the autoerotic organs for the interests of the organism, and requires that partial drives serve the needs of the whole body rather than impose their own partial perspective on it. On the other, there is *jouissance*, which does not necessarily keep to the limits of what is good for the self. *Jouissance* lacks the spontaneous moderation that keeps pleasure as *plaisir* within bounds. While *jouissance* is directly attuned to boundlessness, the other sort of pleasure (*plaisir*) may function as a buffer to keep it in check. *Jouissance* is not selfish or egocentric, at least not if this is taken to mean "seeking the good for oneself". It is an ecstatic state of surrender, without calculation and without considering the consequences for oneself or for others.

Jouissance transgresses limits, although transgression should be seen not as the goal but as the consequence of surrender. The characteristics of pleasure that we referenced earlier can easily be recognized in Lacan's *jouissance.*

Jouissance is responsible for aspects of enjoyment that could be frightening. What is frightening is that in pleasure an impersonal force – *jouissance* – takes over, a force that is insensitive to the limits of the good and expresses itself in self-loss. What is frightening is not satisfaction, but a pleasure that satisfaction cannot quench. The fantasies of obsessive neurotics and hysterics illustrate this. The pleasure of the obsessional neurotic is continually spoiled by the fear of his or her own *jouissance*, which is to say of his or her own self-loss and surrender. They have to hold themselves in, for what might not happen if they really let themselves go? From fear of unforeseen consequences, for himself and others, the neurotic never says "yes". The hysteric, on the other hand, is obsessed by fear of the *jouissance* that she provokes in the other. What will happen to me if the other really desires me and surrenders himself to a desire he cannot master? What will happen to me when I am taken up into his desiring pleasure? There is a link between *jouissance* and the transgression of boundaries. But, as has been said, transgression should not be seen as its purpose. *Jouissance* is not attracted to evil. Taking delight in evil can be an expression of *jouissance*, but does not explain its nature. The combination of *jouissance* and evil is accidental. And what of sexual perversions? In a Lacanian perspective, perversions are not an expression of *jouissance.* On the contrary, perverse scenarios exercise control over the transgression that might result from *jouissance.* Perverse scenarios dramatize the transgression in order to control it. Perversions are the opposite of surrender to pleasure. The four most significant perversions – sadism, masochism, voyeurism and exhibitionism – all show the same thing. In these perversions, distance is central: all involve the objectification of the other, control and the protection against any self-loss. In *all* perversions, the gaze plays a central role. And what does the gaze do if not create distance – a distance that, if necessary, will be maintained by pulling on gloves. Perversions avoid skin-to-skin contact because physical touch dissolves distance and the limits of the self. Perversions are everything except self-loss. The very point of perversion is that the personhood of the other is not allowed to vanish into the anonymity of the flesh: he or she may not yield to a stronger force, he or she must retain consciousness and may not surrender to the impersonal machinery of pleasure in the sense of *jouissance.* Because perversions are directed towards maintaining distance, they are mostly a fairly prudish affair.

To Conclude – Let us finally return to the initial clinical examples of bulimia and anorexia. The frightening thing about taking joy in compulsive eating and self-starvation is that ordinary satisfaction has no hold upon it. The same is true for compulsive gambling. The enjoyment is not even temporarily stilled by satiety. In these examples, satisfaction is not the natural end of the drives and has too little power or too little attraction to allay such pleasure. Enjoyment in the sense of *jouissance* is so powerful that the interest in a calming satisfaction is lost. Such enjoyment is not good and has nothing in common with the pleasure that remains within the natural boundaries of an activity. Plato mistrusts enjoyment and warns against the idea that pleasure is intrinsically good. The preceding examples illustrate and actualize Plato's view. How is that possible? Was it not Plato who had asserted that pleasure was the process of satisfaction? And have I not done my very best to argue that pleasure, in the sense of satisfaction, is a poor but reassuring reality? While this is true, I claim, nevertheless, that Plato sees pleasure from the perspective of the organism that *absolutizes* the transition, and this explains why, in the last analysis, he is closer to certain aspects of *jouissance*. His negative valuation is highly applicable to cravings, and cravings are related to *jouissance*. But there are also differences between Plato and Lacan. In Plato, derailment is related to the absolutization of the transition from empty to full. In Lacan, however, *jouissance* can be frightening because this pleasure goes together with losing the sense of what is right and wrong – that is, the sense of limits.

References

Aristotle (1968). *The Nicomachean ethics.* (H. Rackham, Trans.). The Loeb Classical Library. London: Heinemann.

Freud, S. (1900). The interpretation of dreams. *Standard Edition 5*, pp. 339-627.

———. (1905). Three essays on the theory of sexuality. *Standard Edition 7*, pp. 125-245.

———. (1930). Civilization and its discontents. *Standard Edition 21*, pp. 57-145.

Lacan, J. (1992). *The ethics of psychoanalysis. The seminar of Jacques Lacan. Book VII: 1959-1960.* (D. Porter, Trans.). London: Tavistock/Routledge.

Levinas, E. (1969). *Totality and infinity.* Duquesne Studies. Philosophical Series 24. Pittsburgh: Duquesne University Press.

Van Riel, G. (2000). *Pleasure and the good life: Plato, Aristotle and the Neoplatonists.* Philosophia Antiqua 85. Leiden: Brill.

Visker, R. (1999). *Truth and singularity.* Phaenomenologica 155. Dordrecht/London/Boston, MA: Kluwer.

Sextimacy – Freud, Mortality, and a Reconsideration of the Role of Sexuality in Psychoanalysis[1]

Adrian Johnston

Introduction

In many fields, often the most naïve and straightforward of questions pertaining to basic concepts is capable of causing a great deal of upset. Ask a roomful of theoretical physicists to agree upon a definition of so central an idea as "matter", or confront philosophers with such topics as "knowledge", "reality" or "truth", and problems are bound to arise. This, too, is the case with psychoanalysis. Despite Freud's numerous extensive discussions of the role of sexuality in mental life, there is no immediately apparent Freudian response to the query, "Why is sexuality inherently traumatic?" Of course, Freud repeatedly insists that sexual conflicts lie at the root of the various pathological formations revealed by the discovery of the unconscious (Freud, 1913a: p. 210). He also comes up with a plethora of hypotheses potentially explaining the centrality of such conflicts within the psyche; but, he fails to settle on one or several of these numerous hypotheses as providing a final, decisive explanatory account. Perhaps the problem here is that Freud suspiciously enumerates too many reasons for why sexuality provides the fundamental matrix of meanings for the mind. He never successfully articulates, in the form of a succinct thesis, exactly why "sexuality", construed either in its quotidian sense or in the broader significance assigned to it by analytic theory, is intrinsically so troublesome an issue for humanity (and not just troublesome due to temporary, shifting socio-historical circumstances). Although Freud himself notes that fledgling "scientific" discourses require flexibility in their definitions of core notions (Freud, 1915a, p. 117), this nonetheless should not exempt Freudian analysis from supplying a more thorough justification for an assumption underlying both its etiology of the neuroses and the psychoses as well as its general portrayal of human nature.

[1] An earlier version of this text originally appeared as "Intimations of Freudian Mortality: The Enigma of Sexuality and the Constitutive Blind Spots of Freud's Self-Analysis", *Journal for Lacanian Studies*, 3(2) (2005), 222-246. I would like to thank Dany Nobus, the editor of the *Journal for Lacanian Studies*, for allowing this material to appear here.

Why does Freud invariably uncover a limited range of sexual themes beneath the multitude of psychical phenomena presented to him in the course of his analytic investigations? Should one simply accept as an explanatory first principle, itself beyond any further explanation, that sexuality is the ultimate psychical problem for all individuals? Or, should one dismiss Freud's stress on sexual matters as an idiosyncratic bias meriting dismissal? The either/or choice between accepting the traumatic nature of sexuality as a ground-zero axiom of metapsychological dogma or rejecting the emphasis on sexuality as a misguided psychoanalytical essentialization of contingent, constructed factors is a false dilemma. An important question deserves to be asked prior to rushing into this decision: Is there an underlying reason why sexual contents generally tend to be the privileged nodal points for unconscious fixations? Perhaps there is something (to paraphrase Lacan) "in sexuality more than sexuality itself", an "x" that pre-determines the psychical prominence of sexual motifs. If such an "x" exists, then uncovering and identifying it might illuminate why it is that Freud continually encounters these motifs in patient after patient (and, hence, why he insists that the unconscious is always concerned with sexuality).

In the introduction to the fourth edition (1920) of the *Three Essays on the Theory of Sexuality*, Freud asserts that the cause of public resistance to psychoanalysis is that it confronts humanity with the ugly, repressed truth that a "coarse", "unrefined" and "distasteful" realm of brute corporeality underlies the higher spheres of mental life (Freud, 1905, p. 134). Although this explanation for the widespread resistance to psychoanalysis might superficially have sufficed in the context of late nineteenth-century Europe, it hardly sounds convincing as an account for why contemporary Western cultures continue to dismiss or reject it. Why would societies in which images and discussions of sexuality permeate almost the entire field of public life find a theory highlighting the importance of sexual matters so repugnant? Moreover, is Freud's focus on sexuality, as well as contemporary culture's fixation upon it, not merely a temporary historical by-product resulting from a transitory confluence of multiple processes, as, for instance, Michel Foucault alleges in his *History of Sexuality* (Foucault, 1978, pp. 158-159)? Why should one view this psychoanalytically-asserted centrality as anything more than a transitory manifestation of unstable socio-historical trends? If something can be located and delineated within sexuality that destines it to a preeminent position in the psychical lives of subjects – what is at issue here is whether there is some "excess element" embedded within the field of sexuality, an element invariably attracting the unconscious to it – then the enigma as to why clinicians and investigators of various stripes continue today to encounter a preponderance of sexual meanings and problems in human life might receive an answer.

The evolution of Freud's own thought betrays a series of encounters with excess elements in sexuality, features of sexuality that speak of its multifarious interconnections with various other areas of human experience. Most importantly, Freud's self-analysis is riddled with instances in which the ostensible explanatory powers assigned to facets of sexuality by psychoanalysis become questionable. In the examples culled from his own mental life, Freud consistently contends that the sexual meanings pinpointed by his interpretations are the genuine catalysts behind the phenomena under consideration. He uses his self-analysis to emphasize both the all-pervasive nature of the influential mechanisms of the psychically hegemonic pleasure principle as well as the predominance of childhood "family romances" in the repressed regions of the mental apparatus. Ironically, his biographers frequently point out that, in his private correspondence, Freud admittedly expressed little interest in sex (Gay, 1988, p. 162). What's more, Freud's biographies all reveal a man utterly obsessed with death – "Anxiety about death loomed large in Freud's self-analysis" (Anzieu, 1986, p. 388). Freud claimed that he pondered his own mortality every day. Although he rejected Fliess' numerological speculations about masculine and feminine cycles, he stubbornly maintained superstitious beliefs that he would die on specific dates (needless to say, his numerological predictions were each successively falsified by the uneventful passing of the given dates). Then, there are also the stories of his fainting episodes in front of Jung, brought on by Freud's conviction that he detected implicit death wishes against himself harboured by the latter. And, when the much-disputed theory of the "death drive" emerged in the 1920 text *Beyond the Pleasure Principle*, speculations abounded about the personal, circumstantial factors precipitating Freud's sweeping revision of his drive theory: everything from the recent death of his daughter Sophie to the First World War's mass-scale display of human destructiveness has been cited as responsible for prompting the second topography's "morbid" features (Freud shows particular concern with falsifying these speculations [Gay, 1988, p. 396]). Of course, to rely on the personal features of a thinker as the primary tools for evaluating his/her theories is to indulge oneself in a specious *ad hominem* approach. But, because Freud grounds many of the foundational precepts of psychoanalysis upon examples from his own self-analysis, one can procure legitimate insights into his thought through a consideration of these publicly divulged examples (assuming that this biographical level of consideration is integrated into a larger argumentative whole).

Two famous pieces of his self-analysis are particularly useful in exhibiting an intermingling of Freud's overt advancement of his hypotheses concerning the sexual unconscious with his theoretically under-emphasized private obsession about his mortality (although several other instances in Freud's *oeuvre* also illustrate this intermingling): one, the forgetting of the name Signorelli (first presented in the 1898 paper *The Psychical Mechanism of Forgetfulness* and later discussed in the 1901 text *The Psychopathology of Everyday Life*), and, two, the dream of Irma's injection (from the canonical 1900 book *The Interpretation of Dreams*). What both of these self-analytic specimens reveal is Freud's underlying preoccupation with his position as an analyst – more specifically, his desire to assume the title of "*Herr Doktor*". The assumption of this title involves an engagement in a struggle against disease, decline and, in the end, death. When this struggle appears to be in vain apropos himself and/or his patients – as any fight against finitude is, in the last instance, futile – Freud tends either to veer away from the topic of mortality, defensively truncating his interpretations, or else to shift the weight of emphasis onto unresolved sexual conflicts related to the familial past. In his later writings, Freud speaks of death, but almost exclusively as either an abstract metapsychological theme or depersonalized constituent of the general human condition. However, Freud's subsequent displacements and deferrals (effectuated through abstraction and generalization) of an analytic subjectification of his own mortal finitude can and should be reinterpreted as delayed, unrecognized resolutions of the deadlocks internal to his self-analysis. Correlatively, reassessing in this fashion the significance and stakes of certain components from Freud's self-analysis – components originally grounding specific metapsychological axioms central to psychoanalysis – promises to contribute toward a possible transformative alteration of the vision of the subject-between-life-and-death informing the very foundation of the entire psychoanalytical edifice.

Part I: Forgetting About Death – The Elision of Details in Orvieto

During a September 1898 visit to the Adriatic coast, Freud took a carriage ride from Ragusa to a nearby town in Herzegovina. His companion on this ride was a Berlin lawyer named Freyhau. Their conversation initially concerned topics having to do with the local area (i.e. Bosnia and Herzegovina). It later veered into a discussion about Italy, during which Freud recollected a trip where he saw the frescoes of the Last Judgement at Orvieto. However, Freud found himself bothered by the fact that he could not manage to recall the name of the artist who painted the frescoes. Instead of remembering the actual name, Freud produced two erroneous substitutes: Botticelli and Boltraffio. Several days after the carriage ride, an Italian man cleared things up by informing Freud that the artist's name was Signorelli.

Operating under the analytic assumption that no deficiency or failure of conscious mental activity is entirely innocent or accidental, Freud asks himself why it is that the name Signorelli happened to escape him during his journey. Matters become clearer when he mentions that one of the topics called to his mind during his discussion with his companion was a colleague's story about the attitude toward sexuality displayed by the Bosnian Turks, as well as their high regard for doctors. Freud recounts that these Turks always address doctors respectfully ("*Herr Doktor, ...*") and that, as patients, they are surprisingly accepting of the workings of fate, bearing well the news that death is near. But, remarkably, if one of these individuals is informed that disease or physical impairment will deprive him of the ability to engage in sexual activity, he proclaims that life is not worth living anymore; death is preferable to a life without sex. Although Freud uncovers multiple overdetermining factors involved in the repression of the name Signorelli and its subsequent replacement by Botticelli and Boltraffio, this story of the Bosnian Turks holds the key to explaining the inaccessibility to conscious recollection of Signorelli (the other factors mentioned by Freud explain why Botticelli and Boltraffio emerged instead of Signorelli, but not why Signorelli in particular was repressed).

Two sets of parallel connections between the story of the Turks and the name of the artist of the frescoes at Orvieto generate this instance of repression. Freud claims that, just prior to this occurrence of forgetfulness, he had been speaking a lot of Italian and was in the habit of translating statements from his native German into Italian. He thereby concludes that the Italian word "*Signor*" in Signorelli became associated with its German equivalent "*Herr*" (i.e. the fashion in which the Turks address doctors). A first associational bridge establishes itself here between the story about the Turks and the forgotten name. Moreover, the frescoes at issue portray scenes of destruction and death (namely, the coming of the Anti-Christ and the end of the world), just as losing the capacity for sexual activity is viewed by the Bosnian Turks as worse than dying itself. Freud at first assigns responsibility for this manifestation of the unconscious' powers of repression to the sexual nature of the content involved (Freud, 1898, p. 292). However, this is not an incredibly satisfying self-analytic rationalization on Freud's part. Prior to 1898, Freud had dealt frankly and extensively with sexuality in his published works as well as his personal correspondence (for example, in the same year, *Sexuality in the Aetiology of the Neuroses* appears in print). Why should the mere mention of copulation be enough to interfere with the cognitive powers of a thinker already actively concerned with the role of sexuality in human life?

Before proceeding further, it is also worth remarking upon yet another associational thread running through Freud's personal account of temporary memory loss. In his efforts to account for the specific features of the two substitutive names that surfaced instead of Signorelli, he informs readers that, just a few weeks before, he had been told of the suicide of one of his patients. The patient had killed himself because he had an "incurable sexual disorder". Freud received this bad news while staying in a small town named Trafoi (in the Tyrol). According to him, he had not consciously recalled this news while conversing with his travelling companion in the carriage ride to Herzegovina. Instead, this repressed memory returned in distorted guise as a hidden influence contributing to the emergence of Boltraffio (Freud treats the similarity between "Trafoi" and "-traffio" as a verbal bridge linking consciousness and the unconscious). Freud's unfortunate patient, in choosing death over a sexless existence, behaved exactly like the Turks that Freud consciously had in mind while conversing in the carriage with his fellow traveller. In *The Psychopathology of Everyday Life*, he says:

> I ... diverted my attention from pursuing thoughts which might have arisen in my mind from the topic of "death and sexuality". On this occasion I was still under the influence of a piece of news which had reached me a few weeks before while I was making a brief stay at *Trafoi*. A patient over whom I had taken a great deal of trouble had put an end to his life on account of an incurable sexual disorder. I know for certain that this melancholy event and everything related to it was not recalled to my conscious memory during my journey to Herzegovina. But the similarity between "Trafoi" and "Boltraffio" forces me to assume that this reminiscence, in spite of my attention being deliberately diverted from it, was brought into operation in me at the time [of the conversation]. (Freud, 1901, pp. 3-4)

When Freud refers to "this melancholy event and everything related to it", what is entailed by this "everything related to it?" Freud leaves his readers in the dark concerning this hint of larger issues emanating out from and stretching beyond the recent memory of the suicide of this one patient. Similarly, in *The Psychical Mechanism of Forgetfulness*, he confesses that the nature of the repression brought to bear against the name Signorelli touches upon matters lying at the very heart of the internal psychical struggles revealed to him by his self-analysis:

> For this topic to have been able to produce such effects it is not enough that I should have suppressed it once in conversation – an event brought about by chance motives. We must assume rather that the topic itself was also intimately bound up with trains of thought which were in a state of repression in me – that is, with trains of thought which, in spite of the intensity of the interest taken in them, were meeting with a resistance that was keeping them from being worked over by a particular psychical agency and thus from becoming conscious. That this was really true at that time of the topic of "death and sexuality" I have plenty of evidence, which I need not bring up here, derived from my own self-investigation. (Freud, 1898, pp. 293-294)

Freud deliberately defers a discussion of the intermingling of death and sexuality, insinuating that, perhaps, it will be handled later. It never really is (at least not in a sufficiently sustained manner). Throughout the subsequent writings in which further pieces of his self-analysis come to light – sometimes Freud explicitly identifies material as drawn from personal experiences and, at other times, he disguises his own psychical phenomena by attributing them to anonymous third parties – he repeatedly favours interpretations stressing the exclusively sexual nature of the content in question. His dreams, parapraxes and neurotic symptoms are always Oedipal. If death is discussed at all, it merely amounts to the imaginary, fantasized aim of infantile aggression against the father, an aggression ultimately acting at the behest of the libidinal cathexes of the mother. Throughout the early years of psychoanalysis, in which this discourse's genesis is thoroughly tied-up with Freud's own psyche in every sense possible, little is revealed about the significance of the individual's mortality within psychical life – and this despite Freud's obsession with the topic.

Regarding the thematic importance of death in Freud's 1898 case of repression, Lacan comes to the same conclusion. The crucial determinant of the conscious inaccessibility of the name Signorelli is to be found in those associations linking it to mortality (or "the absolute master", as Lacan designates death in his Hegelian parlance [Lacan, 1988a, pp. 268-269]). However, Lacan adds several crucial twists. To begin with, he implies that Freud's conscious elision of Signorelli, due to its proximity to the *Herr* of *le maître absolu*, is not simply a defensive repression of an upsetting train of thought. Death is far from being merely one psychical content among others. In the eleventh seminar, Lacan makes some strange remarks about the "disappearance" of death in this instance of Freudian forgetfulness:

> Let us turn again to an example that has never been sufficiently exploited, the first used by Freud to demonstrate his theory, namely, his forgetting, his inability to remember the word *Signorelli* after his visit to the paintings at Orvieto. ... The term *Signor*, *Herr*, passes underneath – the absolute master, I once said, which is in fact death, has disappeared there. (Lacan, 1977, p. 27)

What does it mean to say that, "the absolute master … which is in fact death, has disappeared there?" Lacan here gestures in the direction of Freud's metapsychological thesis that the unconscious is ignorant of death (Freud, 1915c, p. 296). Hence, one cannot say that death (understood in this context in a somewhat Heideggerian fashion) is repressed in the same way that a traumatic sexual memory is, since death "as such" (that is, the individual's "ownmost" death as anticipated from his/her first-person perspective) escapes the powers of mental representation. The living, conscious individual obviously cannot experience his/her own demise. Therefore, the topic of death itself cannot be repressed in the same way as other materials, since the mechanism of repression requires some minimal, concrete experiential content which it can exclude from consciousness. This is the case even for what Freud calls "primal repression" (Freud, 1915b, p. 148). As Freud defines it, primal repression (itself a speculative notion referring to something that cannot be directly observed or analytically recovered as a kind of long-lost memory of a specific episode or event) occurs at the moment when a drive is first attached to a drive-representative (that is, a *Vorstellung*), when the ideational-mnemic traces composing a distinct object are registered within a specific sector of the libidinal economy. The cathexis of this *Ur*-object creates, in a manner of speaking, a psychical black hole: a point of powerful attraction dragging everything that enters its orbit into the oblivion of repression. In more straightforward language, Freud stipulates that the original object-representative of a drive undergoes primal repression, and that all other repressions subsequent to this (that is, all "secondary repressions") are a result of other representational elements in the psyche having entered into associational connection with the mass of previously repressed materials (the accumulation of this mass being, at root, catalyzed in the first instance by primal repression). So, death, as one's ownmost mortal finitude, cannot even be "primally" repressed, since it is impossible to inscribe it within the psyche in the form of a *Vorstellung*, namely, an ideational representation capable of being acted on by the familiar regulating processes of mental life. What happens instead? How does this relate to Freud's forgetfulness?

Earlier, in the fifth seminar, Lacan speaks of the metaphoric function of the *Herr-Signor* couple. In this sense, the constellation of representations and associations linked to the *Signor* of Signorelli stands in for death, representing to the subject that which defies representational depiction:

> *Je reviens là-dessus pour vous dire qu'en cette occasion au contraire,* Signor *pour tout le contexte auquel il s'attache, c'est à savoir le peintre Signorelli, la fresque d'Orvieto, l'évocation des choses dernières, représente précisément la plus belle des élaborations qui soit de cette réalité impossible à affronter qu'est la mort. C'est précisément en nous racontant mille fictions –* fiction *est pris ici dans le sens le plus véridique – sur le sujet des fins dernières, que nous métaphorisons, apprivoisons, faisons rentrer dans le langage la confrontation à la mort. Il est donc clair que le* Signor *ici, en tant qu'il est attaché au contexte de* Signorelli, *représente bien une métaphore.* (Lacan, 1998, p. 41)

Lacan continues:

> *La mort, c'est le* Herr *absolu. Mais quand on parle du* Herr, *on ne parle pas de la mort, parce qu'on ne peut parler de la mort, parce que la mort est très précisément à la fois la limite de toute parole, et probablement aussi l'origine d'où elle part.* (ibid., p. 60)

Lacan treats death as something beyond standard forms of representation, as a limit to the cognizing powers of the subject (in the first seminar, he cites the Signorelli example while elucidating the process of *Verwerfung* [Lacan, 1988a, p. 53], a Freudian term later to be Lacanianized as "foreclosure" in the third seminar [Lacan, 1993, p. 321]; in the sixth seminar, Lacan, in the context of a discussion of Hamlet, connects the motif of a mortality-without-representation to foreclosure [Lacan, 1958-1959, session of 22 April, 1959]). However, as Freud's forgetting of the name Signorelli already indicates, elements of particular psychical representations (*Signor-Herr*, Trafoi-Boltraffio, etc.) falling into associational connections with the theme of mortality become the targets of repression. These (re)presentations are "metaphors" to the extent that they provide the psyche with determinate elements evoking death (i.e. that which is itself without presence, that which erases the living subject's experiential world). Lacan implies that, in lieu of death being definitively repressed from consciousness, secondary substitutive materials evocative of mortality are instead subjected to the vicissitudes of repression. A prior detour through representational intermediaries is necessary in order to render mortality manageable via the standard defensive strategies of the psychical apparatus.

In fact, Lacan insinuates that death (as utter and complete annihilation through physical dissolution, the evaporation of the very possibility for experiencing) can only be dealt with by the psyche *vis-à-vis* "metaphors" *qua* ideational-representational substitutes. The individual's mortal finitude – his/her ownmost death – is Real in the strict Lacanian sense insofar as it defies direct registration and inscription at the level of either the Imaginary or the Symbolic (Lacan says as much on several occasions [1988b, p. 211; 1973-1974, session of 18 December, 1973; 1974-1975, session of 8 April, 1975; 2005, p. 125]). The subject's own inevitable disappearance cannot appear to it in the form of images or words. This Real marks a "hole", an absence or blank, in the surfaces of cognizable, psychically-constituted reality; or, as Lacan phrases it in the third seminar, death is an enigmatic, mysterious "x" for subjectivity in relation to which "The signifier is incapable of providing him with the answer" (Lacan, 1993, p. 179-180). However, due to the intermingling of sex and death, sexuality (in the Freudian sense, as opposed to, for instance, Lacanian "sexuation") is a special region of the surface areas of Imaginary-Symbolic reality bordering this hole, this faceless thing around which many of the formations of the unconscious turn. Sexuality indirectly incarnates mortality insofar as it provides metaphors for that which can only be depicted indirectly in a metaphorical (rather than direct-literal) fashion; it thereby becomes an integral part of the terrain on which the subject struggles with its finitude (a struggle that can occur solely through the displacement of the Real of death onto the adjacent screens of Imaginary-Symbolic reality). Of course, Lacan engages in a series of sustained reflections on the rapport binding together mortality and sexuality in psychoanalytical thought (Lacan, 1977, p. 150); he also conceptualizes the notion of death from several different angles (especially if one takes into account his interpretations and reinterpretations of Freud's *Todestrieb*). However, examining Lacan's various and sundry musings on this topic would require several articles (or even a book) unto itself. Moreover, the author of the present article has already dealt with Lacanian understandings of death and their place in the theoretical apparatus of psychoanalytical metapsychology at length elsewhere (Johnston, 2004a; Johnston, 2004b; Johnston, 2005) – the curious reader is referred to these texts.

In the twelfth seminar, Lacan again takes up the Signorelli example. Unlike his previous handling of it in earlier seminars, no mention is made of *le maître absolu*. Instead, Lacan asserts that the *Herr* operates as a point of identification for Freud – "the disturbance that is involved here is essentially linked to identification. This *Herr* that is involved, and this *Herr* which on this occasion has kept all its weight and all its vigour ... becomes Freud for once identified with his medical personage" (Lacan, 1964-1965, session of 6 January, 1965). Is this a separate interpretive angle, one unrelated to the intermingling of death and sexuality? Quite the opposite is the case: Lacan's mention of the concept of identification makes little sense outside the discussion of death, particularly Freud's own mortality. Nonetheless, Lacan leaves it unclear as to whom exactly Freud identifies with during the Signorelli episode.

At least four interlinked levels of identification are at play for Freud here. First, in the *Herr-Signor* couple, the term *Herr* is associated with the respectful attitude of the Bosnian Turks to doctors ("*Herr Doktor*, ..."). More specifically, Freud mentions the Turks' use of this formal mode of addressing medical persons in connection with their ability to maintain a resigned attitude in the face of death ("*Herr*, what is there to be said?"). Later, in *An Autobiographical Study*, Freud recounts a walk that he took, while in Worcester, Massachusetts at Clark University to deliver his *Five Lectures on Psycho-Analysis* (1909), with the American philosopher and psychologist William James. At the time, James was suffering from heart disease, which eventually killed him a year later. Speaking of the episode, Freud states:

> I shall never forget one little scene that occurred as we were on a walk together. He stopped suddenly, handed me a bag he was carrying and asked me to walk on, saying that he would catch me up as soon as he had got through an attack of angina pectoris which was coming on. He died of that disease a year later; and I have always wished that I might be as fearless as he was in the face of approaching death. (Freud, 1925, p. 52)

Admittedly, a space of eleven years separates the Signorelli incident from the walk with James. Nonetheless, the wish that Freud so strongly expresses here (i.e. his desire to be courageous in the face of his own demise) allows a greater degree of light to be shed on a possible identificatory mechanism at work in the 1898 occurrence of temporary memory loss. In other words, perhaps Freud identifies with the Turks insofar as these individuals allegedly possess a similar acceptance of mortal fate as that exhibited by William James, an acceptance which Freud, due to the overwhelming *Todesangst* that his self-analysis never succeeded in alleviating, did not possess. Hence, one might conclude, an unconscious identification with such figures as the Turks and/or James functions as a compensation for Freud's neurotic symptoms surrounding the issue of his own mortality.

The identification with the stoic Bosnian Turks, retroactively hinted at by the recollection of the walk with William James, leads to the second and third layers of identification operative around the repression of the name Signorelli. As noted, the one instance in which the Turks do not calmly accept the contingencies of biological destiny is when they are afflicted with sexual dysfunction. In that case, they supposedly proclaim death preferable to an existence without erotic outlets. In *Letter 73* from the Fliess correspondence, dated 31 October, 1897 (a date prior to the occurrence of forgetfulness under consideration here), Freud insinuates a connection between his all-absorbing "chief interest" (i.e. his self-analysis) and his prematurely declining interest in sexual activity (Freud, 1897, p. 267). At this level, things begin to get somewhat complicated. On the one hand, Freud likely identifies with the Turks to the extent that he adamantly longs for the capacity to bear bravely the burden of his mortality. This identification is further reinforced by the associational links between the mention of an impaired sex life in his colleague's tale and Freud's own diminished libido (or, one could say, the almost total displacement of his libidinal investments in the subliminatory activity of his self-analysis).

However, this second associational thread brings Freud (unconsciously) into conflict with his obsessional fears about dying. The very means of fleeing the fear of death via identification brings him right back to a confrontation with this same fear. According to the material Freud himself divulges apropos the Signorelli episode, a Bosnian Turk undergoing the loss of sexual desire – a loss already experienced by Freud in 1898 – might very well choose to end his life (if one is to take the colleague's information too seriously or literally – which, one might surmise, Freud's unconscious irrationally did despite his conscious reasoning capacities). The wished-for attitude of resignation, evoked by the word *Herr*, sets in motion a series of identifications. However, these same identifications generate undesired conflicts with other unconscious configurations. Ironically, the individuals whom Freud wants to emulate in order to subdue his crippling death anxiety "trick" Freud's unconscious into reaching a suicidal conclusion.

This conflict at the second level of identification leads to the third identificatory layer, a layer involving the suicide of the patient learned of by Freud in Trafoi. As already remarked, this patient, given that he ended his life due to an incurable sexual problem, concretely represents an acting-out of the Bosnian Turks' suicidal stance in the face of impotence. Freud not only has heard second-hand stories of people who would go so far as to kill themselves rather than suffer a loss of sexual enjoyment, but he is intimately acquainted on a first-person basis with someone who really did this. Thus, the problematic second layer of identification is reinforced by a previous repressed experience. One might wonder either just how much of a counter-transferential bond was operative between doctor and patient during the treatment and/or if such a bond was reinforced after-the-fact of the suicide (a retroactive effect along these lines is quite likely in the context of the Signorelli example, since, as shown, Freud was led simultaneously along other lines to an inadvertent identification with a suicidal position).

Moreover, his patient's suicide brings up the painful realization for Freud that there are definite limits to his powers as a therapeutic practitioner. He refers to this analysand as someone "over whom I had taken a great deal of trouble", indicating that, especially in these early years of his work as the founder of psychoanalysis *qua* art of mental healing, a great deal was emotionally riding on this obviously unsuccessful treatment. Interconnections between Freud's evaluation of his ability to cure patients and the larger theme of human mortality resurface in subsequent pieces of his self-analysis (such as the famous dream of Irma's injection, discussed below). Apropos the Signorelli episode, Moustafa Safouan concurs that Freud's limitations as a healer and the closely linked issue of death are precisely the factors responsible for this failure of memory (Safouan, 2002, p. 18).

The fourth and final layer of identification pertains to the deceased painter whose name was temporarily forgotten. Freud's identifications triggered by the word *Herr* also, if one accepts Freud's reasoning, prompt a similar process in relation to Signorelli (via the equivalence of meaning between *Herr* and *Signor*). In a footnote to the 1901 presentation of the episode, Freud speculates that "if the repressed thoughts on the topic of death and sexual life are carefully followed up, one will be brought face to face with an idea that is by no means remote from the topic of the frescoes at Orvieto" (Freud, 1901, p. 13). Moreover, it should be noted that the paintings depicting biblical apocalypse are not all that Freud saw in Orvieto. In *The Interpretation of Dreams*, readers discover that Freud also visited an Etruscan tomb near Orvieto. The memory of seeing this tomb reappears in a dream (slightly distorted to appear as a wooden hut) dealing precisely with his self-analysis (under the influence of the dream-work's secondary revision, Freud envisions his body, instead of his psyche, being "dissected" – that is, analyzed). Additionally, in this dream, death is transformed from a feared fate into a desirable eventuality ("If you must rest in a grave, let it be the Etruscan one" – of course, Freud's fascination with ancient cultures and archaeology is common knowledge). Freud then awakes in an anxious, frightened state (Freud, 1900, pp. 454-455). Lacan accurately observes that subjects often awake from dreams in order to keep on dreaming; that is to say, they flee into waking reality so as to escape a traumatic confrontation with the Real (Žižek, 1989, p. 45). Notice that Freud wakes up exactly at the moment when the manifest dream-text's portrayal of his self-analysis terminates in a thinly veiled representation of the grave.

What about Freud's identification with Signorelli as sustained by the *Herr-Signor* association? Not only is the painter dead (an incidental and unimportant fact), but, as stated, his artistic creations at Orvieto centre on the destruction of humanity. Also, Orvieto is a place doubly associated with death given the visit to the Etruscan grave (Anzieu, 1986, p. 361). Interestingly enough, although the 1901 footnote to *The Psychopathology of Everyday Life* expresses Freud's suspicion that the theme of the frescoes plays a role in establishing intermediary mental links between both the sexual and the morbid motifs connected with Signorelli's name, he downplays the significance of the frescoes in the 1898 paper (Freud, 1898, p. 292). However, Lacan points out that Freud forgets the painter's name in a highly specific context, namely, just when he has in mind these exact paintings depicting the end of the world (Lacan, 1966, p. 447). Furthermore, another curious detail is involved concerning the artist Signorelli. Not only does Freud forget his name precisely when trying to recall who it was that painted the frescoes depicting the Last Judgement, but, at the same time that Signorelli's name escapes him, the visual image of the artist's face is vividly present in Freud's memory. Freud sees fit to comment briefly upon the strength of the visual impression haunting him during his failed attempts to recollect the name attached to this face (Freud, 1898, pp. 290-291). Lacan invokes this aspect of the episode in the session of the twelfth seminar where he claims that Freud identifies with Signorelli (Lacan, 1964-1965, session of 6 January, 1965). How should all of these loose ends be tied together interpretively?

Taking into account the fact that Freud neither forgets the visual impression of the frescoes themselves nor the image of the artist's face, his symptomatic repression clearly bears exclusively upon the name of Signorelli (Mannoni, 1971, pp. 75-76). Now, it is also known that Freud is conscious of the general theme of death on two levels during the carriage ride in which he forgets the name: one, the attitude to death displayed by the Bosnian Turks, and, two, the portrayal of the demise of humanity in the frescoes. The crucial function of the name Signorelli is its establishment of a linguistic, associative bridge between *Signor*(elli) and *Herr* (*Doktor* [Freud]). What's more, Freud later tells his readers, the event of the suicide of a patient in whom he had allegedly invested a great deal of therapeutic effort was a painful memory absent from his consciousness at the time of this instance of forgetting (a repressed that returns via the name Boltraffio). Consequently, the name Signorelli itself is repressed due to the constellation of associations and identifications branching off from its first six letters: a series of connections running from *Signor* to *Herr* (the Turks and their resignation in the face of mortality) to the position of doctor (he who protects against death and yet is often powerless to stop it—"*Herr*, what is there to be said?"), and, finally, to Freud himself (his failings as a medical therapist, concretized by his patient's suicide; his loss of sexual appetite, inadvertently identifying him with the suicidal position of both the Turks and his patient; and, at root, his own neurotic *Todesangst*). In short, Freud represses the artist's name because the threads bound up with it lead him inexorably to a personal subjectification of death, an identificatory assumption of his position as a finite, mortal individual. Further support for such an interpretation is found in his failure to report to readers another association with Orvieto, that is, the visit to the Etruscan tomb, a tomb which returns as the navel-like terminal point in a dream which represents the course of his self-analysis.

Part II: "Don't plumb the unplumbable!" – The Limitations and Prohibitions Structuring Freud's Self-Analysis

The concept of the "navel" of the dream (that is, material in the manifest dream-text that seems enigmatic and resists interpretive efforts to assign meaning to it), first appears in another famous piece of Freud's self-analysis: the dream of Irma's injection from *The Interpretation of Dreams* (1900). As with the Signorelli example, Freud brilliantly elucidates multiple features latent within this fragment of his psychical life (one feature in particular is of interest as regards the present discussion). The main theoretical purpose of the Irma dream, as evidence supporting Freud's emerging psychoanalytical perspective, is its purported validation of the thesis that all dreams function as fulfilments of wishes. Impulses normally frustrated or repressed in waking reality are discharged via the dream-work, a labour working at the behest of the pleasure principle. The wish striving for satisfaction in the Irma dream is Freud's desire to pass off responsibility for one of his patient's persisting pains, pains that his treatments had yet to alleviate. In the dream, by inventing numerous other causes for Irma's suffering (such as incurable somatic disorders beyond the powers of an analyst, or faulty treatment by other medical colleagues), Freud accomplishes the staging of a phantasmatic situation in which he is immunized from blame for his shortcomings as a healer (Freud, 1900, pp. 118-119). Already, a common motif is visible between the Signorelli episode and the Irma dream. As noted, in each case, Freud has problems accepting the limits of his therapeutic powers.

At one point within the manifest text of the dream, Freud describes a scene in which Irma is standing by a window. He must get her to open her mouth so that he, as her doctor, can examine her oral cavity. On the basis of the details of this dream scene, Freud asserts that the figure of Irma at the window is a point of condensation. She is an overdetermined composite of three other women. Irma's reluctance to open her mouth reminds Freud of a governess whose oral cavity he once examined; she had false teeth, and Freud associates a reluctance to show the insides of one's mouth with an embarrassment over a physical defect. If Irma could be shown to have similar somatic defects, then her reluctance/resistance to Freud's cure could be explained away as her own fault. The window links Irma to a second person. Freud recalls a time when he saw one of Irma's friends standing by a window after having been examined by another physician. Freud expresses his admiration and affection for this friend, and speculates that part of his dream-wish was to replace the "bad" patient Irma (an analysand who irrationally "refuses" to be cured) with her friend. Given his high estimation of this friend, Freud assumes that she would be more receptive to analytic reason. Third and finally, the "pale and puffy" appearance of the Irma figure refers to another of Irma's friends, someone who, like Irma herself, Freud believes would be stubborn and uncooperative (ibid., p. 110). He doesn't manage to explain what wish-fulfilment function this poorly regarded third figure might serve, since this friend, unlike the governess and the other well-regarded friend, represents the "bad analysand" type whom Freud wishes to replace. In a footnote, he confesses that the third woman also represents his wife, but fails to inquire further into the self-analytic repercussions of this (ibid.).

Instead, at the conclusion of the paragraph in which he alludes to his wife's presence in the fabric of the dream-text, he sees fit to add another footnote. Speaking of the overdetermined figure of Irma at the moment right before she opens her mouth for the gaze of *Herr Doktor*, Freud expresses a degree of hesitation about the course of his self-interpretation (the kind of hesitation that, if detected by an analyst in his/her analysand's verbalizations, would signal that repressed material still remains hidden):

> I had a feeling that the interpretation of this part of the dream was not carried far enough to make it possible to follow the whole of its concealed meaning. If I had pursued my comparison between the three women, it would have taken me far afield. – There is at least one spot

> in every dream at which it is unplumbable – a navel, as it were, that is its point of contact with the unknown. (ibid., p. 111)

A kind of "kettle logic" is at work here. On the one hand, a point exists in every dream that is "unplumbable", or, impossible to incorporate into a system of meaningful interpretations. On the other hand, the supposed navel of the Irma dream is not really a navel, since, as Freud admits, his unwillingness to pursue further the interpretation of the "three women" condensation phenomenon leaves behind a residue of "concealed meaning". Perhaps Freud would prefer that readers view certain inadequately elucidated portions of his self-analysis as navels, despite the obvious possibility of analyzing these "points of contact with the unknown" in much greater detail.

In the second seminar's lengthy treatment of the Irma dream, Lacan offers a potential answer to the question of why Freud truncates his examination of the triply overdetermined figure of Irma. Lacan calls attention to Freud's 1913 essay *The Theme of the Three Caskets*:

> [A]ccompanying Irma's *ego* we've found three feminine characters. Freud remarks that there is such a profusion of intercalations at this point that in the end things are knotted together and one ends up confronted with some unknown mystery. When we analyze this text, we must take into account the text in its entirety, including the notes. This is when Freud indicates that point in the associations where the dream is connected up to the unknown, which he calls its navel. We've arrived at whatever it is that lies behind the mystic trio. I say *mystic* because we now know its meaning. The three women, the three sisters, the three caskets, Freud has since shown us its meaning. The last term is death, as simple as that. (Lacan, 1988b, p. 157)

Lacan continues, substantiating this reading with reference to other concerns in Freud's personal life contemporary with the Irma dream:

> That in fact is what it is all about. We can even see it coming to the surface in the middle of the hubbub of speech in the second part. The story of the diptheric membrane is directly tied to the threat, of real significance, to the life of one of Freud's daughters two years previously. Freud had taken it to be a punishment for a therapeutic blunder he'd committed when he'd given one of his patients an excessive dose of a drug, sulphonal, unaware that its habitual usage might have harmful side-effects. He thought he was thereby paying the price for his professional mistake. (ibid.)

Whether Freud, at the time of the analysis of the Irma dream, had already formulated the ideas contained in the later piece *The Theme of the Three Caskets* is historically questionable, a matter of speculation. Lacan guesses that part of the reason for Freud's alighting upon his subsequent interpretation of the fictional "three women" motif lies in his earlier self-analysis. In other words, Freud belatedly carries out the stalled 1900 analysis of the three women in his own dream in a 1913 analysis conducted on the neutral, impersonal grounds of cultural products. Regardless, *The Theme of the Three Caskets* is worth turning to for possible insights into the supposed, so-called navel of the Irma dream.

Freud observes that various works of fiction contain a scenario in which an individual is presented with three choices. More specifically, the choice usually involves deciding between three women. Freud cites examples ranging from Shakespeare's *The Merchant of Venice* and *King Lear* to the Greek myth of the Judgement of Paris. The conclusion reached through analyzing these literary specimens is that the choice of the third woman is a wishful distortion of death as mankind's unavoidable fate. Freud arrives at this view by pointing to the inversion of the features characterizing mortality as the individual's inescapable destiny: The involuntary necessity of the subject's inevitable, unwanted demise is phantasmatically/fictionally transformed into its opposite, that is, the free choice of the most desirable and perfect of women (Freud, 1913b, pp. 298-299). Just as in the dream-work, cultural products often replace a repressed, undesirable element with its exact opposite.

At this juncture, several questions merit asking on the basis of the relationship of inversion that Freud perceives as uniting sexuality and death. If myths and works of fiction, like dreams, repress and/or reject the necessary, unavoidable fate of demise by the reversal of this into a representation of a freely chosen sexual object, does this not say something about why the unconscious has a general tendency to latch onto sexual contents? Why does Freud not extend the implicit consequences of this 1913 insight, culled from an analysis of cultural products, for the psychical functions of particular subjects? Would all this not indicate that the adult's unconscious fixation on the field of infantile sexuality is a defence mechanism bearing upon the essential mortality of the individual? Interestingly, this last possibility (namely, that the psychical investment in unconscious sexual content is a defensive reaction to something else) suggests that the core ideational constituents of the unconscious are not raw ultimate truths whose revelation through interpretation uncovers the final, self-evident nuclei of mental life normally obscured by the censoring agency of the ego. Rather, as is indicated by various Lacanian glosses on the unconscious, this system (as, for instance, Lacan's Symbolic "*automaton*" *à la* the eleventh seminar [Lacan, 1977, pp. 53-54, 67]) itself orbits around centres of psychical gravity (as, again from the eleventh seminar, Lacan's Real "*tuché*" [ibid., pp. 53-54, 54-55, 128], or, as per the seventh seminar, "*das Ding*" [Lacan, 1992, pp. 57-58, 62]) that themselves defy capture in and by the formations of the unconscious (although these centres of psychical gravity nonetheless profoundly affect and shape the said formations).

In *The Theme of the Three Caskets*, Freud mentions the maternal figure as a point of convergence for what ordinarily are viewed as mutually exclusive traits. He cites the fact that certain mother-goddesses in "oriental" religions are, all at once, creators and destroyers, simultaneously giving and taking life. The same goddess that bestows fertility is also the one that imposes annihilation (Freud, 1913b, p. 299). In the concluding paragraph of this text, Freud makes a similar observation about the possible symbolic meaning of the number three as the number of women invariably involved in the fictional scenarios of choice:

> We might argue that what is represented here are the three inevitable relations that a man has with a woman – the woman who bears him, the woman who is his mate and the woman who destroys him; or that they are the three forms taken by the figure of the mother in the course of a man's life – the mother herself, the beloved one who is chosen after her pattern, and lastly the Mother Earth who receives him once more. But it is in vain that an old man yearns for the love of woman as he had it first from his mother; the third of the Fates alone, the silent Goddess of Death, will take him into her arms. (ibid., p. 301)

If one follows Lacan's suggestion and re-reads the Irma dream in conjunction with *The Theme of the Three Caskets*, this quoted passage suddenly appears saturated with significance directly relevant to Freud's self-analysis. First, an obvious equivalence between the 1900 and 1913 texts is easily established by noting that, in each case, a feminine figure is portrayed as a singular condensation of three separate aspects or characters. Second, just as Freud's wife is included in the Irma dream in an unexplained manner, so too is the role of the wife one of the three permutations of the feminine/maternal figure in the theme of the three caskets. Third, the reference to "an old man" in the last sentence of the above quotation is almost certainly revelatory of an indirect self-reference on Freud's part. Throughout his entire career as an analyst – a career lasting over forty years – he was continually convinced that his death was extremely near, always looming on the immediate horizon (or, that he was "an old man", an aging individual with one foot in the grave). In this light, the last sentence above is Freud's lament that the intervention of time necessarily interferes with (his) libidinal life, that the ardent desire to rejoin the lost maternal figure *qua* "primary love-object" inexorably leads to the re-embracing of another of the three aspects of woman, that is, the stifling, silencing clasp of "Mother Earth". Freud's ambivalence about sexuality – he here hints at a troubling intermingling of love and mortality in the overdetermined figure of woman/mother – resurfaces in the metapsychological period of psychoanalysis as the "'ego-drives/ego-libido" versus "sexual-drives/object-libido" distinction from the 1914 paper *On Narcissism: An Introduction* (Freud, 1914, p. 78).

One of the most important connecting features between the triply overdetermined figure of Irma from *The Interpretation of Dreams* and the concluding paragraph of *The Theme of the Three Caskets* is the mention of the mother-wife relation in the latter text. In 1900, although Freud quietly confess in a footnote that his wife might be involved in his dream, he omits the obvious psychoanalytical inference that, therefore, his mother is present there as well (as early as 1897, in his *Letter 71* to Fliess of 15 October, Freud proposes the foundational, fundamental role of the Oedipus complex in the libidinal economy [Freud, 1897, p. 265]). Positing the repressed presence of a maternal figure in the Irma dream permits understanding two things: one, why the dream image of Irma is immediately succeeded, in the unfolding course of the dream, by the vision of the open mouth displaying the wounded throat, and, two, why Freud possesses the strange feeling of having confronted a navel, an enigmatic kernel, right at the moment when the overdetermined Irma figure opens her mouth. He writes: "*What I saw in her throat: a white patch and turbinal bones with scabs on them*" (Freud, 1900, p. 111). And, unsurprisingly, associations stemming from this description lead to worries about his own health, concerns about the well-being of one of his patients, the memory of the death of a "dear friend", and anxiety about an illness suffered by his eldest daughter (ibid.) – notice, too, that a similar constellation of concerns surrounds the name Signorelli.

However, more so than the Signorelli example, the Irma dream complicates the seeming straightforwardness of the meaning of mortality in the psyche (or, at least, in Freud's psyche). The opened mouth not only evokes anxieties over death. At the same time, this mouth summons an apparently opposite significance onto the stage of Freud's unconscious: the maternal vagina as the "origin of the world", the portal of entry into finite bodily existence. Just as Freud avoids drawing upon his otherwise habitual equivocation between wife and mother during his incomplete analysis of the Irma dream (the wife usually being the subliminatory substitute for the lost maternal object), so, too, does he fail to make his typical move of viewing the mouth as a dream-symbol for the woman's genitals (Freud, 1916, p. 156). Furthermore, the footnote about the navel of the dream is misplaced. The navel of this dream is not so much the figure of Irma as it is the hidden, unremarked presence of the mother whose gaping orifice fills Freud with anxiety. Lacan brings this out as follows:

> Having got the patient to open her mouth – that is precisely what's at stake in reality, that she doesn't open her mouth – what he sees in there, these turbinate bones covered with a whitish membrane, is a horrendous sight. This mouth has all the equivalences in terms of significations, all the condensations you want. Everything blends in and becomes associated in this image, from the mouth to the female sexual organ, operated on, by Fliess or by someone else. There's a horrendous discovery here, that of the flesh one never sees, the foundation of things, the other side of the head, of the face, the secretory glands *par excellence*, the flesh from which everything exudes, at the very heart of the mystery, the flesh in as much as it is suffering, is formless, in as much as its form is something which provokes anxiety. Spectre of anxiety, identification of anxiety, the final revelation of *you are this— You are this, which is so far from you, this which is the ultimate formlessness.* (Lacan, 1988b, pp. 154-155)

"*You are this*" – that is, Freud the dreamer experiences anxiety not only due to fears of an eventual demise in a future yet-to-come, but, simultaneously, by virtue of "the final revelation" of the brute fact that he emerged as living from a pre-organic state of non-existence – an emergence equally destined to disappear back into the mysterious *ex nihilo* from whence it came. The aborted analysis of this portion of the Irma dream, therefore, provides a first indication as to why sexuality, according to Freud, is both oriented around the maternal object as well as has an invariably traumatizing effect upon the subject. The mother serves as a locus wherein a dialectical "convergence of opposites" predestines her to function as a terminal node of attachment for the formations of the unconscious. Like the mother-goddesses mentioned by Freud apropos the three caskets, the mother *qua* fleshy origin of the finite, embodied world unites, in a condensed fashion, two thematic poles: creation and destruction, birth and death, vital corporeality and the inertia of decay always steadily at work within its very heart. Could these aspects be the "excess elements" that are "in sexuality more than sexuality itself", those elements responsible for the perturbing, problematic place of sexuality in the unconscious? The omissions in Freud's self-analysis (and not just its positive results) contain the germinal seeds for a more thorough theoretical (re-)grounding of psychoanalysis.

Conclusion

As evidenced by both the Signorelli and Irma examples, Freud's self-analysis and the conclusions drawn from it stand as an incomplete body of insights containing numerous inconsistencies, inconsistencies resulting from his own repressions. This should not come as a surprise. There are reasons why both analysis and self-analysis are, in principle, bound to be incomplete (or, as Freud puts it in one of his final essays, "interminable" [Freud, 1937]); also, Freud's discovery of the unconscious as an interconnected series of constitutive blind spots clouding the subject's conscious transparency to itself offers the explanation for why he (and anyone else, for that matter) could not fully understand his own neuroses. An important qualification must be made clear: Freud is not being chastised for having failed to achieve some imagined standard of impossible-to-attain self-transparency, for having timidly avoided seeing his self-analysis through "to the end" (whatever this would be) due to some sort of deplorable cognitive or affective weakness. In fact, one of the testimonies to the greatness of Freud's genius is that the conceptual and interpretive frameworks he extrapolated, in part, out of his self-analysis make possible what has been carried out here. In other words, the psychoanalytical edifice Freud constructs, an edifice whose foundations partially consist of his self-analysis, enables productive after-the-fact reassessments of its own foundations (such as the present endeavour, which employs Freudian-Lacanian tools to re-interpret key fragments of Freud's self-analysis). Psychoanalysis is, in a manner of speaking, a dynamic auto-analyzing theoretical system capable of diagnosing and dealing with its own internal limitations and shortcomings.

The Signorelli and Irma materials allude to a self-analytic significance inhering within Freud's later writings (interpreters usually treat his self-analysis as a process limited to the late 1890s and the early 1900s). Certain keys to the 1898 Signorelli episode reside in the subsequently reported dream of the Etruscan tomb as well as the description of the 1909 walk with William James; mysterious, navel-like parts of the Irma dream become remarkably decipherable after examining the 1913 *Theme of the Three Caskets* and the 1916-1917 *Introductory Lectures on Psycho-Analysis*. And, as could also be shown, the metapsychological writings of the period between 1914 and 1920 contain indirectly developed solutions to problems plaguing both the early and late periods of Freud's theorizing.

What does this mean? Succinctly stated, Freud's post-self-analytic work is, in part, a defensive, projected theoretical resolution of his internal, personal conflicts. In other words, what remains unresolved in his self-analysis (particularly the theme of mortality) receives a disguised, displaced untangling in his interpretations of others (this deflecting projection onto third parties, ranging from patients to society as a whole, is the properly defensive aspect of Freud's later work). Freud is only willing to "plumb the unplumbable" from his self-analysis within the framework of discussions dealing with either other people or cultural objects. The above reinterpretations of the Signorelli incident and the dream of Irma's injection attempt explicitly to draw the missing-yet-nascent parallels between Freud's early self-reflection and his later "externalized" analyses.

The second conclusion to be drawn here is that Freud fails to ask himself what should be a rather obvious and pressing analytic question: Why does he want to be a healer (that is, a doctor, therapist, analyst, etc.) in the first place? For Lacan, the central issue that must be clarified in order for someone to make the transition from being an analysand to being an analyst is for this person to understand what his/her desire as an analyst (i.e. to become someone occupying the position of the analyst) amounts to in terms of its unconscious significance. In the cases of both Signorelli's name and the Irma figure, issues of Freud's status and capabilities as a medical authority are at stake: his patient's suicide in the Signorelli episode, and, in the Irma dream, both the persistence of Irma's symptoms as well as the therapeutic error of endorsing the use of cocaine. Obviously, Freud is greatly troubled by those situations in which his healing powers prove ineffective. Again, the final term against which this unconscious fixation collides is the inevitability of death. The role of the healer is to combat pathologies, and the ultimate "pathology" behind all particular ailments is death itself. If Freud had asked what Lacan calls the question of "the desire of the analyst" regarding himself, would he have perceived his choice of a medical profession as influenced by a defensive projection of his own mortality? Behind the masks of all his different analysands, is the person whom he is trying to save invariably himself?

References

Anzieu, D. (1986). *Freud's self-analysis*. (P. Graham, Trans.). Madison, WI: International Universities Press.

Foucault, M. (1978). *The history of sexuality. Volume I: An introduction*. (R. Hurley, Trans.). New York, NY: Random House. (Original work published 1976).

Freud, S. (1892-1899). Extracts from the Fliess papers. *Standard Edition 1*, pp. 173-280.

———. (1898). The psychical mechanism of forgetfulness. *Standard Edition 3*, pp. 287-298.

———. (1900). The interpretation of dreams. *Standard Edition 4/5*.

———. (1901). The psychopathology of everyday life. *Standard Edition 6*.

———. (1905). Three essays on the theory of sexuality. *Standard Edition 7*, pp. 123-243.

———. (1913a). On psycho-analysis. *Standard Edition 12*, pp. 205-212.

———. (1914). On narcissism: An introduction. *Standard Edition 14*, pp. 67-102.

———. (1913b). The theme of the three caskets. *Standard Edition 12*, pp. 289-302.

———. (1915a). Instincts and their vicissitudes. *Standard Edition 14*, pp. 109-140.

———. (1915b). Repression. *Standard Edition 14*, pp. 141-148.

———. (1915c). Thoughts for the times on war and death. *Standard Edition 14*, pp. 273-300.

———. (1916). Introductory lectures on psycho-analysis. *Standard Edition 15*.

———. (1925). An autobiographical study. *Standard Edition 20*, pp. 1-74.

———. (1937). Analysis terminable and interminable. *Standard Edition 23*, pp. 209-253.

Gay, P. (1988). *Freud: A life for our time*. New York, NY: W. W. Norton and Company.

Johnston, A. (2004a). Revulsion is not without its subject: Kant, Lacan, Žižek and the symptom of subjectivity. *Pli: The Warwick Journal of Philosophy, 15*, 199-228.

———. (2004b). Against embodiment: The material ground of the immaterial subject. *Journal for Lacanian Studies, 2*(2), 230-254.

———. (2005). *Time driven: Metapsychology and the splitting of the drive*. Evanston, IL: Northwestern University Press.

Lacan, J. (1958-1959). *Le séminaire VI: Le désir et son interprétation*, unpublished.

———. (1964-1965). *Le séminaire XII: Problèmes cruciaux pour la psychanalyse*, unpublished.

———. (1966) La psychanalyse et son enseignement. In *Écrits* (pp. 437-458). Paris: Seuil.

———. (1973-1974). *Le séminaire XXI: Les non-dupes errent*, unpublished.

———. (1974-1975). *Le séminaire XXII: R.S.I.*, unpublished.

———. (1977). *The four fundamental concepts of psycho-analysis*. (A. Sheridan, Trans). New York, NY: W. W. Norton and Company.

———. (1988a). *The seminar. Book I: Freud's papers on technique. 1953-1954.* (J. Forrester, Trans). New York, NY: W. W. Norton and Company.
———. (1988b). *The seminar. Book II: The ego in Freud's theory and in the technique of psychoanalysis. 1954-1955.* (S. Tomaselli, Trans.). New York, NY: W. W. Norton and Company.
———. (1992). *The seminar. Book VII: The ethics of psychoanalysis. 1959-1960.* (D. Porter, Trans.). New York, NY: W. W. Norton and Company.
———. (1993). *The seminar. Book III: The psychoses. 1955-1956.* (R. Grigg, Trans.). New York, NY: W. W. Norton and Company.
———. (1998). *Le séminaire V: Les formations de l'inconscient. 1957-1958.* Paris: Seuil.
———. (2005). *Le séminaire XXIII: Le sinthome. 1975-1976.* Paris: Seuil.
Mannoni, O. (1971). *Freud.* (R. Bruce, Trans.). New York, NY: Random House.
Safouan, M. (2002). *The seminar of Moustafa Safouan.* (A. Shane & J. Thormann, Eds.). New York, NY: Other Press.
Žižek, S. (1989). *The sublime object of ideology*. London: Verso.

Death, Libido, and Negative Ontology in the Theory of Drives

Vladimir Safatle

Ich bin der Geist,
der stets verneint.
Goethe

"I have an ontology – why not? – just as everyone has one, naive or elaborated". This is a sentence that cannot go unnoticed, especially being stated by a psychoanalyst. Both the fact that Jacques Lacan admits to having an ontology, as everyone apparently would, and the fact that he admits it in an absolutely natural way ("why not" have one?), pose many questions. For instance: why relate considerations of an ontological character to a praxis that seems quite attached to the particularity of the clinical case, as psychoanalysis does? Why should we search for some kind of relation between ontology and the treatment's direction, which orients the analytical clinic? And, above all, what kind of ontology could provide psychoanalysis with the proper presuppositions for the direction of the treatment?

Such questions expose the consequences of a larger hypothesis concerning the Lacanian intellectual experience. At issue here is the claim that a major Lacanian contribution to psychoanalysis is the assertion that, in psychoanalysis, a complex yet decisive articulation can be found of the difference between ontology and the clinic. This is a slightly risky way of stating that the direction of the analytical clinic depends on an invariable kernel of concepts that compose what is commonly called "metapsychology".

Indeed, such an affirmation may not strike us as a given fact, especially at a time when the "clinic sovereignty" discourse is usually accepted with no further questioning – a sovereignty legitimated by the urgent reality of the suffering that brings the subject to analysis. It is as if the therapeutic efficiency that concerns an utterly normative phenomenal category such as "suffering" were enough of a condition to assure the validity of clinical devices. In this context, in which a practice measures its validity by means of its efficiency in accomplishing normative dispositions variable according to social and historical contexts, there is no room for insisting on the articulation between clinic and ontology. When a clinic is measured only according to its ability to "heal suffering", there is no room beyond the disciplinary implementation of normative devices.[1]

However, this not the standpoint one would find in the Lacanian clinical experience. It could be said that its peculiarity is due to the insistence on the relation between the direction of the treatment and the acknowledgment of the ontological dignity of certain metapsychological concepts, especially the drive (*Trieb*). On this account, Lacan states that the drive is "an absolutely central ontological notion that responds to a consciousness crisis no one has to fully apprehend, once it is lived" (Lacan, 1986, p. 152). The theory of the drive is, therefore, what invariably orients the clinic in its validity claims. We may even say that, in Lacanian theory, any changes in the theory of the drive always imply the loss of the essence of analytical practice.

In this sense, this article is part of a larger research endeavour that evaluates some major features germane to the Lacanian reconstruction of metapsychology. These features can only become clear if we abandon the traditional idea that the core of Lacanian theory lays out a simple structuralist reading of the unconscious and its formational dynamics. Lacanian theory might have been driven, instead, by the effort to provide metapsychology with an ontological status that lies beyond any structuralism. It is an ontological status that manifests itself when Lacan mentions the "being of the subject" (and why should a psychoanalyst ever mention "being"?), or when he mentions the "essence of the object" of desire, not without adding "You realized I have spoken of the essence, as did Aristotle. Then what? It means those words are absolutely usable" (Lacan, 1975, p. 55).

However, in order to properly set forth such a discussion on the Lacanian theory of the drive, we ought to return to Freud. This return may help us to identify what is crucial to the Lacanian intellectual experience beyond the long Freudian considerations on the status of the drive.

From Energetics to the Metaphysics of Death

According to Freud, a theory of drive as *Grundbegriff* adds an indelible speculative aspect to the very core of psychoanalytical thought. Even if Freud

[1] The canonical statement of Michel Foucault on the illusions of "clinic sovereignty" is valid in this quandary: "Since the XVIII century, medicine has had a tendency to tell its own history as if the death bed has always been a stable and constant place of experience, as opposed to the theories and systems that were in permanent change and masked, under this speculation, the purity of the clinical evidence". As a matter of fact, everything happens as if "In the dawn of Humanity, before any system, medicine would be in an immediate relation of suffering with that that eases it" (Foucault, 1994, pp. 59-60).

apparently stood by a certain materialist reductionism on some points – for instance, in his expecting of the day when "all of our temporary (*Vorläufigkeiten*) conceptions in psychology could be made out of organic supports (*Trägen*)" (Freud, 1999a, pp. 143-144) – one should keep in mind just how speculative the physical and chemical energetics at the basis of the scientific horizon found in Freudian theory actually were. This is what Lacan bears in mind when stating that "[E]nergetics is also metaphysics" (Lacan, 1978, p. 80). If we notice the path of the concept of drive in Freudian texts, we shall see the nature of this speculative realm of the theory of drive.

When it explicitly appeared for the first time in *Three Essays on the Theory of Sexuality*, the term "drive" sought to get a grip on the internal sources of excitement that the organism cannot escape. One of these sources of internal excitement, which was already emerging as a larger issue in Freudian concerns, was sexuality, although this was not seen as the exclusive source of internal excitement. Already in the unpublished *Project for a Scientific Psychology*, when he addressed the "urgency of life" (*Not des Lebens*) as an internal excitement that works against the inertia principle of the psychical device, Freud recalled that hunger and breathing were also sources of such excitement. In this initial treatment of drive, Freud also insists that one of its main characteristics is that it is a continuous force and not merely the force of the momentary impact of a lack felt by the organism. Hence, he defines drive as the "psychical representation (*psychische Repräsentanz*) of an endosomatic source of excitement".

So far, nothing suggests that we need to transform the concept of drive into the basis for speculative concerns. At first glance, Freud seems to be closer to a materialist explanation of psychical causal processes, or, better yet, to regard *excitement* as the primary vital fact – a view that has classically been a part of medicine ever since Broussais. However, problems concerning the definition of the status of drives appear from the moment Freud seeks to define the nature of the energy responsible for this constant internal excitement.

Freud starts with a distinction between libidinal energy proper to sexuality and "other forms of psychical energy", such as those at stake in the physiological needs of self-preservation. This distinction initiated the first drive dualism among sexual drives and self-preservation drives. Such dualism is suspended once the category of "narcissism" is born, since narcissism allows Freud to recognize that "self-preservation drives were also libidinal, were drives that had taken as objects the very self, instead of exterior objects" (Freud, 1999b, p. 231). Hence, he states: "It is enough to admit that drives are qualitatively akin and their effects are exclusively due to the excitement (*Erregungsgrössen*) value that each drive carries, or perhaps to certain functions of its quantity" (Freud, 1999a, p. 216). As we shall soon consider, this is an extremely symptomatic reduction of qualitative difference to quantitative value. After *Beyond the Pleasure Principle*, drive dualism returns in a reconfigured fashion. Upon the thorough reconfiguration of the libido idea, Freud turns to considerations on the concept of *Trieb* that take into account the German idealist tradition, especially the work of Schopenhauer (before him, the concept of *Trieb* plays an important role in Fichte and Hegel, among others).

We can see how the key idea to understanding the nature of drive energy is *libido*. Freud customarily defines it as a quantitatively variable force that allows the comparison of processes and transpositions in the realm of sexual excitement. In trying to understand the logic of sexual behaviour from the point of view of an endosomatic plastic energy quantitatively characterized, Freud updates a long rationalist tradition that seeks to define psychology as a "physics of external sense" – that is, as that which allows for the determination of "the quantitative constants of sensation and the relation between such constants" (Canguilhem, 2002, p. 370). This is how we should understand both Freud's epistemic dependence on Fechner's psychophysics – according to whom "the general principles of psychophysics involve nothing but the handling of quantitative relations" (Fechner, 1966, p. 9)[2] – and his dependence on Helmholtz and Du Bois-Raymond, for whom nothing exists but physical and chemical forces acting in the organism.[3]

Far from being merely a scientific metaphor that prevents the unveiling of the real character of psychoanalysis as a practice based on the clinical use of self-reflection processes (a theme for a long tradition of criticism of metapsychology that embraces names as distinct from one another as Politzer, Habermas and Ricoeur), however, this vocabulary of energy and force is actually the tool through which Freud manages to indicate the relationship between drive and the realm of an unreflective (and not yet structured) foundation to behaviour and thinking.

[2] Fechner's idea of kinetic energy (*lebendige Kraft*) was important to the constitution of Freud's notion of the drive and its attempt to end the dualism between the psychical and somatic. Keeping this end in mind, Fechner states, "Kinetic energy employed to chop wood and kinetic energy used in thinking are not only comparable, but each can be transformed into the other, and therefore both kinds of work are measurable on their physical side by a common yardstick" (Fechner, 1966, p. 36).

[3] In this sense, in the words of Canguilhem, "If we add that Descartes, even though he is not exactly the inventor of the term and concept of reflex, at least has affirmed the constancy of the link between excitement and reaction, we realize that a psychology understood as mathematical physics of the external sense begins with him to get to Fechner, thanks to the helping hand of physiologists such as Hermann Helmholtz" (Canguilhem, 2002, p. 370).

Here, one should recall that the characterization of libido as an energy *quantum* does not aim at some form of "measurement" of psychical processes among themselves. It is true that Freud defines the *economic* standpoint (which, along with the *topographical* and the *dynamic* standpoints, draws the apprehension perspective of meta-psychological facts) as that which "tries to follow the destinies (*Schicksale*) of the excitement (*Erregungsgrössen*) value and to obtain an estimate (*Schätzung*) at least pertinent to them" (Freud, 1999a, p. 280). However, the statement says what it means. If the estimate problem is affected by a relativism clause, it is in order to remind us that what is truly important concerns apprehending the path, the "destiny" of the libidinal energy *quanta*.[4] Actually, it demonstrates that the economic standpoint is what allows Freud to think the plasticity proper to a psychical energy characterized mainly by its ability to be transposed, inverted (in such cases, Freud uses the term *Verkehrung*), deviated, repressed – to sum up, dislocated in an apparently inexhaustible manner. Taking this constant dislocating principle into account, Freud initially characterizes libido as a freely circulating energy, a "free energy" in relation to that which could bar such movement – that is, in relation to its binding (*Bändigung*) by submission to representations (*Vorstellung*).

The fact that Freud had predominantly thought of such plasticity considering phenomena linked to sexuality is absolutely central. Indeed, he sought to show how something lies in the subject that is not reflectively determined as conscious representation, something which can only manifest itself in polymorphic, fragmented ways and necessarily finds its own privileged realm in a sexuality no longer subjected to the logic of reproduction, in a bodily impulse that knows no finalist *telos* – as reproduction does. This is why libido is at first characterized as auto-erotic,[5] inconsistent, for being subjected to primary processes, and finally, perverse, for having its targets constantly inverted, deviated and fragmented.

As we shall see later, this libido is actually dependent on a concept of *nature* conceived of as a realm that gains intelligibility when we reduce its phenomena to the general concept of "energy". However, while accounting for sexuality and determining its essentiality by means of the notion of "free energy", Freud prevents nature from emerging as the source of positive sense-

[4] On the use of the term "destiny" in such a context, David-Ménard writes: "It indicates what is at stake in a human being regarding their drives is typically human and a product of singular beings. At the same time, a drive, due to the fact that its components escape from the subject, emerges as anonymous, depersonalized, a-subjective" (David-Ménard, 2001, p. 207).

[5] Auto-erotism is a position previous to narcissism. In this sense, it indicates the polymorphy of a libido that is directed towards the pleasure of organs that are not yet subdued to a general principle of unification provided by the self as a synthetic unity.

attributions. We must say that "the image of human nature that follows from this Freudian conceptualization is that of a split (and conflictual) nature, whereby 'sexual' refers to this split" (Zupančič, 2008, p. 18). From *Beyond the Pleasure Principle* onward, such an impossibility explicitly allows for the articulation of the fundamental distinction between a theory of drive and a concept of nature as the room for a certain "negativity".

Nonetheless, some consequences are tied to this complex distinction between representation and libido conceived as free energy. One of these shall be perceptible once two canonical statements about drive are brought together. The first one is taken from the text *The Unconscious*: "[A] drive cannot be rendered into an object (*Objekt*) of consciousness; only the representation that represents it can do so (*die Vorstellung die ihn repräsentiert*)" (Freud, 1999a, pp. 275-276). The second, written around the same time, recalls how the object of drive "is that which is more variable (*variabelste*) in the drive. Originally it is not connected (*verknüpft*) to it. ... It could be replaced at will in the course of the destinies drive gets to know" (ibid., p. 215). If we define "object" as that which results from the categorization procedures of a consciousness that unifies the manifold of sensibility into synthetic representations, then we could say that the drive only manifests itself to consciousness through its binding to objects of representation. This is a feeble bind though, marked by the structural variability of that which cannot be essentially objectified; a bind operated by a representation unable to present what cannot be unified, or, what cannot be thought within structured relations.

We need to have these problems in mind if we want to understand the meaning of the concept of the "death drive" – a concept that is crucial also to Lacanian metapsychology, for, according to Lacan, "every drive is virtually a death drive" (Lacan, 1966, p. 818). As we shall see later on, this statement is fundamental for understanding the Lacanian idea of drive, because it is a reminder that the French psychoanalyst usually uses a very particular modality of *drive monism* in his clinic – and that it is not by chance that he always refers to *drive* in the singular.

Following this Lacanian trail, Jean Laplanche claims that a deep metamorphosis occurs when Freud binds the libido idea to Eros' unifying power (such as it is found in Aristophanes' myth, in Plato's *Symposium*). The definition of the libido as a unifying Eros – a power that aims at "forming, through the living thing, constantly bigger unities (*Einheiten*) and thus preserve life in its endurance taking it to more complex developments" (Freud, 1999b, p. 233) – seems to show the abandonment of the idea of libido as a free energy, an idea typical of the fragmented and polymorphic sexuality that has always been a theme in Freud's work. This abandonment is driven by Freudian thought on narcissism with its projection and introjection mechanisms that unify the destinies of the drive with the repetition of the image of the self.[6] It is as if narcissism could reveal a *pathos* of a self, understood as a synthetic unity that provides the binding principle (*Verbindung*) of the manifold of sensible experience (to a large extent, the interest of philosophers such as Theodor Adorno in psychoanalysis has its starting point here, that is, in some kind of thought on the "pathologies of transcendental schematism").

In this context, a reconstruction of the drive dualism through the pairing of Eros and the death drive would be the result of the need to find a new destiny for the un-binding power typical of the free energy that initially defined the libido. That is to say, the life and death polarity in the Freudian theory of drive actually covers the distinction between (a) energy bound to representations through the synthetic ability of the self, and (b) free energy that inaugurates the psychic dynamics.[7]

However, the reason why Freud uses the term "death" to talk about this un-binding power is not evident at first. This is a point Lacan clearly mentions: "There is a dimension beyond the homeostasis of self (*moi*), another chain, another need that ought to be distinguished in its plan. This compulsion to turning back to something that has been excluded from the subject, or that has never been absorbed by them, the *Verdrängt*, the repressed, we cannot force it onto the pleasure principle [*that is now mixed up with Eros*]. ... It is necessary then to presuppose another principle. Why did Freud name it death instinct?" (Lacan, 1978, p. 163).

This question is justified by the fact that, at first, this turn seems disproportional in relation to the dimension of the problem (to preserve the disruptive power of sexuality beyond the self-unifying force, a force whose extension was revealed mainly by narcissism). All this is so, unless the problem Freud

[6] In the words of Laplanche: "Eros is that which seeks to maintain, preserve and even enhance the cohesion and the synthetic tendency both of the living being and the psychic life. While, ever since psychoanalysis' origins, sexuality was in its essence hostile to bind, a principle of 'un-bind' or of unchaining (*Entbildung*) that would only bind through the ego intervention, that which emerges with Eros is the bound and binding form of sexuality, brought to light by the discovery of narcissism" (Laplanche, 1970, p. 187). That explains why, in Freud, "[t]he ego emerges as a defensive, inhibitory structure that functions ... to establish a restricted economics of impulses and their discharge" (Boothby, 2001, p. 285).

[7] This is what makes us come to terms with Boothby, for whom "[t]he most crucial idea, rarely stated explicitly precisely because it is so fundamental to Freud's entire outlook, is the assumption of an inevitable and irremediable disjunction between the level of somatic excitations and their psychical representation. There is always a remainder, an irrecoverable left-over, a portion of the body's energies that fail to receive adequate registration in the battery of *Triebrepräsentanzen*" (Boothby, 2001, pp. 286-287).

sensed was indeed bigger than it seemed. That is the only way we could presuppose some kind of unity between phenomena apparently so distinct as the ones Freud tries to consider by means of the death drive idea – that is, the compulsion to repeat traumatic events, the phenomenon of cure resistance and of attachment to the disease that psychoanalysis names "negative therapeutic reaction", the organization of a destiny for libido as free energy, and finally the economic problem of masochist phantasms that apparently separates desire and pleasure.

To answer the issue of the real problem, the last Freudian theory of drive strove to resolve demands to recall how the reconstruction of the theory of drive through the dichotomy life/death was something in agreement with an apparent redefinition of the very concept of drive. Drive is now a "pressure (*Drang*) inherent to the living organism towards the reestablishment of a previous [inorganic] state abandoned due to disturbing influences of exterior sources" (Freud, 1999b, p. 38), and not only the psychic representation of an endosomatic source of constant excitement. From the first to the second definition, a certain *teleological* character is added, one that orients the direction of drive-pressure to the path of an operation of return. The drive then emerges as the expression of the organic life inertia, as the demand for work towards the reestablishment of a state of tension suppression. It is a tendency that manifests itself primarily through the figure of repetition understood as returning movement towards the annihilation of an individual determined as what orients its conduct through self-conservation.

In this context, Freudian speculation flirts more clearly with a certain death metaphysics, all of it founded in a real philosophy of nature. Practically missing in the first theory of drive, this inflection towards metaphysics, especially through Schopenhauer (not to mention Plato, to illustrate the unifying power of Eros, and Empedocles), should not be seen as some kind of mere deviation. Indeed, several principles of Fechner's psychophysics that will later on appear on Helmholtz, Mach and others – an important theoretical base to the formation of the Freudian theory of drive – are familiar to Schopenhauer's philosophy and its consideration of the dynamics of force. In the same manner, such principles are not immune to metaphysical presuppositions, which is quite clear especially in Fechner. So everything goes by as if Schopenhauer provided Freud with some kind of stretched intelligibility of that which has continued to insinuate itself within the energetic.

In this context, it is worthwhile to recall how the general explanations of human and natural behaviour by means of the dynamics of force, considered as the figure of a metaphysics of the Will as being in-itself, is what provokes Schopenhauer to see in death a protocol of "return to the nature's womb" (Schopenhauer, 1998, p. 71). For the individual's death would only demonstrate the permanence of forces as opposed to the transitory nature of states and forms: "[A]lready considered a natural force, the vital force remains completely immune to the change of forms and states produced by the sequence of causes and effects" (ibid., p. 74). It could even be said that death emerges in this context as a power that suspends binding processes, a suspension of representations that produce individualizations. This is why Schopenhauer works with a dichotomy between the species' immortality as an "Idea" and the destructibility of individuals. This dichotomy emerges in a reconfigured form in the very core of Freudian drive theory; something which takes place, according to Weismann, by distinguishing between *soma* and *plasma*.

However, there are a number of fundamental differences. Schopenhauer insists on death as destruction of the individual only to remind people that "Asking for immortality in individuality really means to be willing to perpetuate an error infinitely. For, at bottom, each individuality is nothing but a special error, a misstep, something that would be better off, yes, something from which bringing us back is indeed the aim of every life" (ibid., p. 110). It could not be any different, for death is simultaneously thought of as that which is inserted in the *telos* of nature's renewing vital cycle and as a mode of access to intelligibility (access to intelligibility that is not exactly a reflective knowledge) of an unbound force dynamics that freely passes from one form to another and never perpetuates any of them. Death is the name of the process that reveals nature to be an everlasting cycle of individuation and obliteration of forces, as if we stood by a cycle of pulsation between free energy and bound energy. So, according to Schopenhauer, death, far from being a phenomenon that makes no sense, a negation with no concept, is that which guarantees nature to be a *positive pole of sense attribution*, because it unveils the mechanisms of vital force orientation.

Indeed, this is not the case when it comes to Freud. Freud believed, as well as Schopenhauer did, that death is more than the destruction of the biological organism's integrity; it is also what suspends the principle of individuation and of synthetic unity at work in the self. This is why, according to Freud, it may emerge as the source of drive dynamics responsible for processes such as the repetition of traumatic and non-symbolized events and the negative therapeutic reaction considered as resistance to the subjectivation processes at work in the analytical clinic. However, there is nothing in Freud akin to the teleological affirmation of life as an everlasting cycle of destruction and reconfiguration, a result of some kind of general principle of energy preservation. On the contrary, the death drive notion is closer to the absorption of an energetic concept such as entropy, considered as a principle of what only emerges as loss, a principle of that which cannot be configured into a state subjected to an ordination protocol.[8] In other words, Freud regards death as the presence of that which does not let itself be absorbed within a notion of nature as the positive pole of sense attribution, a presence of that which cannot be counted into vitalist economics.

However, within his theory of drive, Freud operates with a very peculiar concept of nature. The tendency to use the drive theory to explain the principles of the behaviour of organisms *in general* (which can be seen as a certain "bringing up-to-date" of the explanatory holistic principles typical of nineteenth-century psychophysics) ought to be seen as a presupposition for a non-thematized concept of nature. It is a concept of nature that cannot be thought by means of figures of a vital cycle or of some form of ordination functionalism, but one that necessarily manifests itself as a resistance to the integration of each and every principle of positive determination.[9] To base a clinic and its healing protocols on such a presupposition about the notion of nature cannot take place without difficulties.

Perhaps that explains, among other things, the symptomatic position of the death drive within the Freudian clinic. Indeed, the place the death drive occupies in the Freudian clinic is complex and hard to decipher. One need recall only that, in a later text such as *Analysis Terminable and Interminable*, Freud wonders whether there are limits to the drive's bindings (*Bändigung*) to representations – something that could be understood as a matter concerning the possibility to dominate mainly the repetition typical of the death

[8] With respect to this, Assoun states that the Freudian concept of energy "marks a 'passage' between two states that translates a mechanical expense, itself the particular expression (motion) of the general enhancement of disorder stated by the second principle of thermodynamics (Cornot-Clausius). What could be expressed from now on as: 'every drive, to the extent it is drive, is death drive'" (Assoun, 1981, pp. 182-183).

[9] Theodor Adorno has clearly understood this eminently negative definition of nature existent in Freudian considerations. Let's recall, for example, the Adornian definition of mimesis (the central operator of reconciliation between subject and nature). It is a "trend to lose oneself in the environment (*Umwelt*) instead of playing an active role in it; the tendency to let oneself go and sink back into nature. Freud called it death drive (*Todestrieb*), Caillois *le mimétisme*" (Adorno & Horkheimer, 1997, p. 227). If, according to Adorno, the death drive indicates a reconciliation with nature, then we must admit several consequences. For, the Freudian death drive exposes the libidinal economics that impulses the subject to bind to a nature understood as the realm of the inorganic, a major figure of material opacity to reflection-processes. This "tendency to get lost in the environment" that Adorno refers to, with the concept of the death drive in mind, is the result of self-recognition in that which is not symbolically unscripted (see: Safatle, 2006, pp. 9-19).

drive. The answer is programmatic: the correction *a posteriori* of the primal repression (*Urverdrängung*) may control the effective force of the quantitative factor of drive. But Freud is the first to acknowledge the infinitude of the drive force when stressing the unending character of its domain: "One may doubt dragons of the early times are actually dead to the very last" (Freud, 1999c, p. 73), as if analytical symbolization could not dissolve this repetitive forcing of the death drive.

However, the death drive's negativity will not be embodied as the engine of the healing processes by the Freudian clinic. The repetition emerges as the *boundary* of the clinic and the mechanisms of remembrance (*Erinnerung*), verbalization and reflective symbolization typical of Freudian modes of subjectivation. The only way Freud can consider the negativity of the death drive within the clinic is as a negative therapeutic reaction, as the destruction of the other in transference and as other manifestations of masochist or sadist phantasms that have to be annihilated *so as to take the subject to the end of their analysis*. The Freudian program of "binding (*bändigen*) the repetition and transforming it into a reason to remember (*Motiv fürs Erinnern*)" (Freud, 1999b, p. 134), remains valid all along even though Freud encounters a limit to its efficacy, thanks to the closure of a repetition usually mistaken for transference.

Lacan and the Clinic of the Death Drive

Given this impasse, the most common way out for Freud's psychoanalytical posterity has been to abandon this amalgam Freud made with his death drive concept. It has been widely insisted that the death drive is a social fact linked to the destructive impulse in societies that socialize subjects through repressive processes of guilt (Marcuse's work is a clear instance of such thinking) or that it is simply a metaphysical waste of time with no clinical function whatsoever, for there is no need for the clinic to appeal to abstract forces conceived of in the anteroom of the phenomena it considers.

In this sense, one of the most peculiar features in Jacques Lacan's thought has been his attempts to reorient the analytical clinic through the centrality of the death drive. Indeed, this centrality is now regarded as the engine of the progress of analysis and the direction of treatments. According to Lacan, the real clinical problem is not to limit the destructive impulse of the death drive or to allow life to constantly operate through larger processes of unification. Rather, it is about initially producing a rupture from this unity desired by

Eros, a unity that, according to Lacan, was fundamentally narcissistic and imaginary once it was connected to the projection and introjection of the self image. In this manner, Lacan has the merit of understanding the death drive beyond the repetitive compulsion of the destruction instinct. This opened up the possibility of a new path for thinking the figures of the negative in the clinic to be structured.

In this effort, Lacan initially tried to approximate the disruptive power of the death drive and the "negativity" concept inherited from French considerations on Hegel's *Begierde*, the first mode of manifestation of subjectivity's individuality. He also approximated the death drive and some moments of experience of confrontation with death that surpass the *Phenomenology of Spirit*. However, philosophical loans always bear a particularity: they are the only ones in which those who borrow take more than they realize. So, we are entitled to ask whether Lacan has not brought to the core of the psychoanalytical drive theory a concept of negation that, in Hegel, has a clearly ontological status, since it is linked to how that which is determined as essence manifests. Such a concept of negativity was used to get a grip on what was already manifesting itself when Freud sought to "naturalize" the death drive, by making it a concept that orients the intelligibility of each and every living being's behaviour.

Before we go any further on this point, we should recall that, indeed, the way Lacan has treated the psychoanalytical theory of drive can only become intelligible if it is understood as the development of his initial thoughts on the status of desire in the analytical clinic. It could even be said that the question of the status of the drive acquires centrality in Lacanian intellectual experience from the moment he finds himself in the position of dealing with some points he had left unexamined in his theory of desire.

Concerning this matter, one should remember that, according to Lacan, the main tendency of desire is to ignore any natural proceeding of objectification. Because it fundamentally lacks an object, it is a desire for "nothing to be named" (*rien de nomable*) (Lacan, 1978, p. 261). Here we perceive the careful reader of Kojève's works, the same Kojève who tried to sew the Heideggerian being-for-death to the Hegelian *Begierde* in order to allege that the truth of desire is to be the "revealing of an emptiness" (Kojève, 1992, p. 12), that is, pure negativity that transcends every natural and imaginary adherence. It is a strange desire, unable to be satisfied with empirical objects and deprived of every immediate possibility to phenomenal accomplishment.

This purely negative transcendence, connected to the intentional function of a desire that insists beyond every object relation, is given as something

Lacan cannot turn a blind eye to in his early writings and seminars. The reason that this is so comes from Lacan's development of a theory of object constitution, which is supported especially by thoughts on narcissism. In this theory, Lacan articulates the *constitutive character* of the I in connecting the manifold of sensibility with object representations and the *empirical genesis* of the function of the I by means of a logic of narcissistic identifications. It is in such a manner that, at this point of Lacanian thought, both the objects and the other empirical individuals are always narcissist projections of the I. Lacan even mentions the *egomorphic character* of the objects of the *empirical world.* What follows from this is a *fundamental narcissism* that guides every object relation, as well as the need to cross this narcissist regime of relation through a critique of the object's primacy in determining desire.

The reason for criticizing the primacy of the object emerges in Lacan's psychoanalysis, especially through the critique of relations reduced to the Imaginary realm, since most of the Lacanian Imaginary stands for the sphere of relations that compose the logic of narcissism, with its projections and introjections.[10] Roughly, it could be said that, according to Lacan, the Imaginary is some kind of *space-time categorization scheme* that works through including the manifold of sensibility in the image (in this sense, Lacan is very close to the theory of image and schematism found in Heidegger's *Kant and the Problem of Metaphysics*). This image, however, unifies the diverse by means of a binding and identity principle derived from the very I as a self-identical and synthetic unity. It is, in its turn, the real name of that which is at stake in representation – at least in Lacan's view. From here springs the Lacanian close linkage of Imaginary, narcissism and *representation.*

Here, it is necessary to emphasize an important point: the *empirical object* necessarily emerges as an *object subjected to the engineering of the Imaginary.* The possibility of libidinal fixation to an empirical non-narcissistic object is not yet given. Therefore, so as to rid the subject of fascination for objects that at bottom are narcissistic productions, psychoanalysis had to "purify the desire" for any empirical content by subjectifying the desire in its brutal point of emptiness. Indeed, the link of desire to object-representations implies the alienation of a being that is conceived of as transcendence. Hence the definition – uttered in an undeniable Sartrian accent – of desire-negativity as *manqué d'être*: "Desire is a relation of the being to the lack. This lack is lack of being (*manqué d'être*) per se. It is not lack of this or that, but lack of being through which being exists" (Lacan, 1978, p. 261). Leading the subject into

[10] "We consider narcissism to be the imaginary relation crucial to interhuman relationships" (Lacan, 1981, p. 107).

recognizing the being as lack-of-being (as Lacan will subsequently do in order to distance himself from Sartre) is his major strategy of analytical practice.

This is the scheme that animated Lacan's first few thoughts on the theory of the drive. Ever since his early seminars, Lacan had tended to understand the unity produced by the Eros as the submission of the other to the logic of narcissism, defining the binding of psychic energy as "capture by the form, apprehension by the game, absorption in life mirage" (ibid., p. 110). The Imaginary has a unifying power that consists in linking the subject to another who is essentially the ego image. As if the constantly bigger unities Freud mentions were built with the binding of the diversity of representations and affections to the *image* of the same. Thus, the disintegrating force of the death drive is from the very beginning aimed at the imaginary coherence of the I and its imaginary object relations. In several moments, the disintegrating force of this drive is presented as that which brings the subject beyond a pleasure linked to the libidinal energy submission to a principle of homeostasis guaranteed by "the transference of *Vorstellung* quantity in *Vorstellung*" (Lacan, 1986, p. 72) – that is, libidinal energy submission to the form of representations. That may explain why the emergence of drive is constantly surrounded by the theme of an enjoyment that flirts with the formless enjoyment beyond the pleasure principle, which means, at bottom, enjoyment beyond the submission to representations. At this point, Lacan finds it necessary to constantly employ reasons and examples that he obtains from Bataille.

Bataille also establishes a program that, for the most part, is close to the Lacanian imperative. "Canceling the subject and the object", he writes, "is the only way not to end in the possession of the object by the subject, that is, to avoid the absurd race of the *ipse* willing to be transformed into the whole" (Bataille, 1998, p. 67). The engine of such a cancellation emerges as well by means of a certain thematic that is connected to death, which is experienced as a way out of anthropological primacy: "[A]nyone who does not 'die' for only being a man will always be nothing but a man" (ibid., p. 47). Nevertheless, these possible filiations between Lacan and Bataille seem to cause several problems. For they could indicate that, when he transforms the death drive into a concept central to analytical progress, Lacan is actually being seduced by some kind of *clinical implementation of claims that aestheticize limit experiences, an implementation thought in accordance with themes of formlessness and heterology*.

Indeed, that is a lingering risk, but it does not concern what was truly at stake in the Lacanian intellectual experience. We should keep in mind how Lacan uses the death drive, at first, to organize a number of distinctions between the Imaginary and Symbolic realm considered from a structuralist perspective – that is, conceived as a structure of pure signifiers that organize linguistic and social differences. On the other hand, Lacan has never advocated any kind of subject cancellation, but only the cancellation of its emergence in the self-identical notion of I.

At this point we should take a moment to think about the very first sentence of *Écrits*: "Our research has led us to the point of recognizing that the repetition automatism (*Widerholungzwang*) finds its principle in what we have named the insistence of the signifier chain" (Lacan, 1966, p. 11). What Lacan says is that this repetition – which cannot fall under a logic that explains the conduct of the psychic device only in terms of of maximizing pleasure and escaping from displeasure – is actually a manifestation of the manner in which the symbolic structure works. This is something quite distinct from what Freud had in mind when he tried to think about the compulsion, of some neurotics, to repeat traumatic and unpleasant situations, or when he tried to understand the attempt to deal with processes of loss through repetition (as happens in the famous *fort-da* example).

What Lacan seeks when approximating the signifier chain and repetition automatism is, for one thing, to keep in mind that the free energy typical of the un-binding force of the death drive produces the same primary processes of condensation, dislocation and figuration that provide the ground for the dynamics of the signifier. Hence, the possibility of approximation. This is how he understands that which Freud terms the net (*Netz*) character and flow (*Flüssigkeit*) of the drive. It is a daring as well as a feeble proposition, since the articulation of the signifier chain does not know the dissemination that is recurrent in what is characterized as free energy. Rather, the signifier chain bears a coordinating and articulating power typical of every symbolic construction. That is, its task of binding is unusual in the realm of the death drive.

However, there is yet another aspect to approximation. When articulating the death drive and the signifier, Lacan seems to indicate there is no such thing as the particularity of drive and impulse in the confrontation with the social and inter-subjective linguistic universe. Instead, the drive is already somehow constitutively bound to that which allows subjects to socialize through their access to language (here there is an instructive parallel with the Hegelian concept of *Trieb*). At its utmost, it is not suppressed due to the processes of the subject's socialization. From the very start, it is this which leads subjects to the use of language – on the condition that a very peculiar regime of language is made real. For the language that Lacan has in mind is completely anti-realistic insofar as it is not composed by signs, but only by pure signifiers – that is, by terms that have no denotative force, that do not denote any object whatsoever. It is a cancellation of the factual quality of reference that Lacan describes in the following fashion: "The signifier only manifests initially the presence of the difference as such, and nothing else. The first thing implied is the relation of the sign to the thing to be erased" (Lacan, 1961-1962, session of 12 June, 1961).

On that account, Lacan could state that "the scheme of the symbol as death of the thing is found here" (Lacan, 1994, p. 377), as if the impulse to negate, which recurs in the death drive, were at work, or yet, as if it were satisfied every time the signifier appeared as a cancellation of the thing *as a reified object constituted by the Imaginary logic*. For, in its essence, the signifier is not a denotation device, but simply a device that marks the woeful inadequacy between words and things, an inadequacy between a signifier chain that is articulated in the manner of a free energy flow and the things thought of as that which is subjected to imaginary unities. Hence, Lacan seeks to fit his understanding of the centrality of the death drive into a logic of inadequacy as the surplus of the socialization processes through a language composed by signifiers. On the other hand, he links the signifier not to the issue of object denotation, but to the issue of drive satisfaction, as if all language usages were subjected to the practical interest of satisfaction.

As we said above, in its initial conception, this Lacanian strategy was ambivalent and difficult to sustain. On the one hand, the signifier chain is interdependent on a work of binding and ordaining the object world, which has nothing to do with the death drive. It is true that Lacan wants to insist that the death drive is not a sheer transgressive destruction-impulse towards a mortifying enjoyment, but that it is what seeks to handle the intelligibility of socialization processes. On the other hand, the signifier chain exactly describes the free flow of energy that denies what is bound under the form of an object, under the form of representation.

This contradiction could, however, be called creative. Clearly, Lacan seeks a formalization regime able to handle a subject's relation to a drive that cannot be thought by means of a representational language – language that, within the Lacanian cartography, is subjected to the logic of the Imaginary. However, Lacan has to explain how the subject can structure relations to what cannot be articulated according to binding principles derived from the I as synthetic unity may be properly thematized. The emphasis here is on the imperative of "structuring relations" that are not tributary to a return to some kind of immediate intuition.

An Ontological Negation for the Clinic

Before we continue, it is necessary to insist that this problem found in Lacan – a problem that could be considered as the legacy of a certain Freudian path – provides a provisory explanation to the notion of drive as an ontological concept. In linking the death drive to that which is satisfied with the negating power of language, Lacan completely reorganizes the traditional idea of symbolization as submission to the representation's organizing power, in order to find a more adequate way to deal with the modes of relation to what, to a subject, appears to be the irreducibility of the negativity typical of the death drive. Since it is based on an idea of negation as an ontological mode of access to the essence, this irreducibility has an ontological weight.

The term "ontology" may seem strange here. Nevertheless, before we legitimate this estrangement, we should wonder whether the ontology could be thought no longer as a regime of *positive discursiveness* of the being *qua* being. If this is possible, it would no longer be a regime that, as soon as it is set, tends to normalize the realms of praxis by determining *a priori* the configuration of its possibilities. When rendering problematic the relationship between positiveness and ontology, we open the doors for thinking ontology as the regime that withstands the reality of what blocks the full draining of being into a positive determination. In this sense, a *negative* ontology – that is, a thinking-regime based on the ontological reality of the negation-experiences – could guide Lacan's clinical decisions, as well as the direction he seeks to impose upon the treatment.[11]

Perhaps the difficulty in accepting such statements comes from the fact that the Lacanian path regarding the ontological character of certain metapsychological concepts can not exactly be traced in a straight line. We should recall, for instance, what he stated during his eleventh seminar, *The Four Fundamental Concepts of Psychoanalysis*, held a few days before acknowledging that he had an ontology: "[W]hen speaking of this gap (*béance*), one is dealing with an ontological function, by which I thought I had to introduce, it being the most essential, the function of the unconscious. The gap of the unconscious may be said to be *pre-ontological*. I have stressed that all too often forgotten characteristic – forgotten in a way that is not without significance – of the first emergence of the unconscious, namely, that it does not lend itself

[11] Alain Badiou points out an interesting way to conceive of ontological negation in Lacan by stating that, in Lacanian psychoanalysis, there is an access to ontology once "the unconscious is this being that subverts the metaphysical opposition between being and non-being" (Badiou, 1982, p. 152).

to ontology," (Lacan, 1997, p. 29) since that which belongs to the order of the unconscious "is neither being, nor non-being, but the unrealized" (ibid., p. 30). Indeed, this idea that what belongs to the order of the unconscious is pre-ontological takes us straight to Merleau-Ponty and his flesh *ontology*. However, it is valuable to rebuild the context of such a statement in order to realize what is at stake here.

In the previous section of this seminar, Lacan had discussed the idea of "unconscious causality" with the help of the last pages of Kant's *Attempt to Introduce the Concept of Negative Magnitudes into Philosophy*. Above all, Lacan had in mind the Kantian distinction between logical ground and real ground. Concerning logical ground, Kant states in 1763 that, given a ground, a logical consequence can be derived through obeying the identity rule. Thus: "Man is fallible, and the ground of such fallibility lies in the finitude of his nature, for when the concept of a finite spirit is decomposed the fallibility therein is revealed, that is, it coincides with that which is contained in the concept of a spirit" (Kant, 1969, p. 202). However, in the real ground, something can follow something else without obeying the rule of identity, as in when I say, for instance, that the moon phases cause the tide. Kant claims that only "simple and indecomposable concepts of real ground, whose relation to the consequence cannot be distinct at all" (ibid., p. 204) can handle the real ground. Lacan insists that this idea of an indecomposable concept that aims at formalizing the causal relation between a real ground and its consequence is adequate to determine the specificity of the causality at work in the unconscious, a causality that establishes relations of necessity between discontinuous terms. This is the very discontinuity Lacan names "*béance*". However, such *béance* does not invalidate an idea of ontology that is not at work within the position of the substance and identity ideas, but within the refusal of the essential reality of those concepts. As is evident, this topic still calls for more discussion.

At any rate, there is another problem that cannot be avoided. We could see ourselves facing a dangerous kind of *negative theology* disguised as clinical considerations, especially with the insistent repetition of the Lacanian reasons regarding the lost object, the inescapable assumption of the lack, the impossible enjoyment, and the empty place of the subject that is never completely embodied, which are all reasons that take us to an ethics of "infinite resignation" at most, as Deleuze used to say about Lacanians (Deleuze & Parnet, 1996, p. 100). Or, yet, to a "religious idealization of impossibility", as Judith Butler affirms with respect to the Lacanian relation between enjoyment and Law. Obviously, we could think all of this – but we would be wrong: wrong for not understanding what Lacan sought when transforming the confrontation with the death drive into the central axis of the analysis' progress.

This strategy of reconfiguring the death drive in the clinic becomes even clearer when we take into consideration the problem of the status of negations in Lacanian praxis. One should recall, for instance, that the modes of the subject's relation to the drive proposed by Lacan do not refer to that which Freud defined as the drive binding to object representations, even if Lacan insisted on the need to think of what could occupy the position of the drive's "object" (although the very idea of an "object" in this context forfeits its character as being that which is constituted from binding principles provided by the self as a synthetic unity).

This question directly brings us to another one, which is strictly connected to the direction of the treatment. Lacan constantly insists that subjectivation in the clinic cannot be organized based on the enlarging perspective of the reflective horizon of understanding consciousness or of reconstituting the synthetic abilities of the I. That is, subjectivation in the clinic cannot refer to the imperative of the triad of remembrance, verbalization and symbolization – a triad that guides the Freudian clinic. However, limiting the reflective processes cannot mean the complete impossibility of the subject's self-positing or even the blocking, impossible to overcome, of the subjective abilities of synthesis, regardless of how often Lacanians insist that the end of analysis is the emergence of an irreflective mute enjoyment, or, yet, the emergence of a subjective destitution that results in the abandonment of every form of synthetic aspiration of thought.

One possible way of understanding what Lacan has in mind is through taking into account the Lacanian theory of negation. Lacan is aware that the specificity of its subjectivation modes is grounded on acknowledging the eminently negative character of the "objects" to which drive connects and *in which the subject ought to recognize itself.* This demonstrates how the Lacanian clinic demands a mode of negation that is not a plain indication of a non-being, of a deprivation (*nihil privativum*), of the emptiness as sheer absence of determination, of a denial or mode of expelling from oneself that which is against the pleasure principle. It requires a negation mode that is a mode of presence of what remains outside the reflective symbolization and its identification protocols, and it does not necessarily imply some kind of return to the ineffable. For, according to Lacan – who has always linked the analytical cure to the possibilities of the self-objectivation of subjects beyond their objectivation in the Imaginary – *there is only a cure where the subject recognizes himself in a negation thought as a presence of what is the essential determination of objects no longer constituted as narcissist images of the I.* There is something deeply Hegelian about such a strategy, with the difference that, for psychoanalysis, sexuality is the field in which the experience of such negation could appear.[12] But what kind of sexuality comes from that ontology? This is a question for another article.

Translated into English by Luísa Torrano.

References

Adorno, T., & Horkheimer, M. (1997). *Dialectic of enlightenment.* London: Verso.

Assoun, P. (1981). *Introduction à l'épistémologie freudienne.* Paris: Payot.

Badiou, A. (1982). *Théorie du sujet.* Paris: Seuil.

Bataille, G. (1998). *L'expérience intérieur.* Paris: Gallimard.

Boothby, R. (2001). *Freud as philosopher: Metapsychology after Lacan.* New York, NY: Routledge.

Canguilhem, G. (2002). *Etudes d'histoire et de philosophie de la science.* Paris: Vrin.

David-Ménard, M. (2001). Les pulsions caractérisés par leurs destins: Freud s'éloigne-t-il du concept philosophique de Trieb? In M. Bienenstock (Ed.), *Tendance, désir, pulsion* (pp. 201-219). Paris: PUF.

Deleuze, G., & Parnet, C. (1996). *Dialogues.* Paris: Flammarion.

Fechner, T. (1966). *Elements of psychophysics.* New York, NY: Holt, Rinehart and Winston.

Foucault, M. (1994). *O nascimento da clínica.* (R. Machado, Trans.). Rio de Janeiro: Forense.

Freud, S. (1999a). *Gesammelte Werke: Vol. X.* Frankfurt: Fischer.

———. (1999b). *Gesammelte Werke: Vol. XIII.* Frankfurt: Fischer.

———. (1999c). *Gesammelte Werke: Vol. XVI.* Frankfurt: Fischer.

Kant, I. (1969). *Kant Werke. Bd. II.* Berlin: Walter de Gruyter.

Kojève, A. (1992). *Introduction à la lecture de Hegel.* Paris: Gallimard.

Lacan, J. (1961-1962). *Le séminaire IX: L'identification*, unpublished.

———. (1966). *Écrits.* Paris: Seuil.

———. (1975). *Le séminaire XX: Encore. 1972-1973.* Paris: Seuil.

———. (1978). *Le séminaire II: Le moi dans la théorie de Freud et dans la technique de la psychanalyse. 1954-1955.* Paris: Seuil.

———. (1981). *Le séminaire III: Les psychoses. 1955-1956.* Paris: Seuil.

———. (1986). *Le séminaire VII: L'éthique de la psychanalyse. 1959-1960.* Paris: Seuil.

———. (1994). *Le séminaire IV: La relation d'objet. 1956-1957.* Paris: Seuil.

[12] In this sense, we may agree with Alenka Zupančič when she says that we must think of "the sexual as the concept of a radical ontological gap" (Zupančič, 2008, p. 24).

———. (1997). *The four fundamental concepts of psychoanalysis.* (A. Sheridan, Trans.). London/New York, NY: W. W. Norton and Company.

Laplanche, J. (1970). *Vie et mort en psychanalyse.* Paris: Flammarion.

Safatle, V. (2006). Mirrors without images: Lacan and Adorno on mimesis and recognition. *Radical Philosophy, 139,* 2-12.

Schopenhauer, A. (1998). *Metafísica do amor, metafísica da morte.* (J. Barboza, Trans.). São Paulo: Martins Fontes.

Zupančič, A. (2008). Sexuality and ontology. In *Why Psychoanalysis?* Uppsala: NSU Press.

Love of Truth, True Love, and the Truth about Love

Ruth Ronen

"[O]nly those who have had the courage to work through Lacan's anti-philosophy without faltering deserve to be called 'contemporary philosophers'" (Badiou, 2006, p. 121). Here, Alain Badiou refers to Lacan as an anti-philosopher due to his radical interpretation of the notion of truth, the truth philosophers love.

If Lacan is an anti-philosopher, does this mean that psychoanalysis is disengaged from the philosophical commitment to truth? Does Lacan not love truth? Is it the idea that *truth* can be loved, or is it the way philosophers love their truth that Lacan objects to? As Badiou shows, it is not *truth* that is rejected by Lacan; what he counters is the philosophical love that finds its *repose* in truth, which attaches the love of truth to whatever finds its articulation in philosophical wisdom. Lacanian anti-philosophy, then, is a protestation against the philosophical wisdom which focuses too much on the *espousing* of truth to love. This espousing of truth to love is afforded to philosophy by the shelter of wisdom within which this friendship between love and truth is created and preserved. In other words, what brings about this espousing of truth to love is the philosophical indulgence in a truth bearable to thought, acceptable to philosophical wisdom, and believed to be attainable.

And yet Lacan's anti-philosophy does not amount merely to the rejection of the espousal of truth to love; it goes further than that. Lacan shows, especially in his reading of Plato's *Symposium*, how the philosophical love of truth is enacted in the tempestuous relations of love among the dialogue's participants. It is through these transferential relations that philosophy claims to love truth, while Lacan shows that, in transference, the one holding the position of the psychoanalyst (Socrates) cannot be driven by the love of truth. Psychoanalysis does not replace philosophical love of truth with an alternative notion of truth, but replaces the *love* of truth with a *desire* for truth, which is the only position from which the real power of truth can be produced as the effect of transference.

Badiou is interested in the fate of the love of truth after Lacan as he takes note of the way psychoanalysis reveals that the philosophical wisdom espousing love and truth covers up the true tumultuous relation of the philosophical subject with truth. For the contemporary philosopher to cross

Lacan's anti-philosophy, he/she would need to reconstitute the encounter between philosophical wisdom and the love of truth on different grounds.

In this paper, the philosophical love of truth as re-interpreted by Badiou's contemporary outlook, and the psychoanalytical truth about love, will be weighed against each other through the question of true love and the practice of desire presented in Plato's *Symposium*. In the *Symposium*, love of truth and the truth about love seem to coalesce in the participants' speeches (whoever succeeds to speak the truth about Eros is also the one whose love of truth was not led astray by love). In looking back at Lacan's reading of the Platonic dialogue, we may consider Badiou's restitution of the philosophical love of truth after Lacan in order to pose the following questions: In what way does the contemporary philosopher *love* truth? Can contemporary philosophical wisdom still espouse love and truth? In what way is the philosopher's love of truth different from the psychoanalyst's position vis-à-vis truth?

In order to address these questions, even if on a very limited scale, Badiou's notion of truth will first be presented to reveal the one irreducible trait that makes a philosopher: his/her love of truth. For Badiou, to restitute this philosophical passion requires getting over the psychoanalytical idea that truth, when articulated, is necessarily castrated. After Lacan, we are left with the sad insight that "truth is the mask of its own weakness … truth is the very veiling of being in its withdrawal" (Badiou, 2006, p. 122), or, to use Lacan's own phrasing in one of his later seminars: "the love of truth is the love of this weakness whose veil we have lifted, it's the love of what truth hides, which is called castration" (Lacan, 2007, p. 52 [58 in French original]). How is philosophical love affected by a truth that has been castrated, withdrawn? Here, Lacan's reading of Plato enters the philosophical considerations to demonstrate that the love of truth is constituted in the dialogue through a drama of relations, through a necessary practice of pursuing this love of truth. That is, Plato shows how the pursuit of truth, when presented in speeches, encounters serious obstacles. With respect to this psychoanalytically motivated disillusionment, Badiou concludes that, in order to restitute a place for the philosophical love of truth, the delusional foundations of such a love, and the force of truth in real situations, must first be exposed. Badiou's crossing of Lacanian anti-philosophy goes through these phases in order to rediscover, at the end of the route, the philosophical love of truth modified, yet not crippled or weakened. In the second part of this paper, Alcibiades' monologue praising Socrates will be examined after Lacan in order to suggest the precise place in which Lacan locates the delusional nature of the love of truth and to show that the delusions involved sustain rather than abolish this love.

In accordance with Lacan's idea of "the other side" (*l'envers*), the psychoanalyst's desire is the other side of the love of truth, which means that, while revealing something of its truth, analytic discourse does not resolve anything. The question that remains open after the cross-Lacanian move concerns the status of the love of truth that is restituted through this process. While Badiou points towards this love as philosophical in the deepest sense, the Platonic dialogue may imply that the one who knows something about love is also the one who cannot love. In other words, Lacan's reading of the *Symposium* may suggest that the philosopher is excluded from the place of love, as suggested by Socrates' manner of resisting the offerings of love. The third and last part of this paper will re-address the love of truth in order to question whether, in releasing love from truth (previously held together by the tight embrace of philosophical wisdom), this "wise friendship" can still be salvaged.

A. The Love of Truth

The philosophical love of truth as interpreted by Lacan, touches both the question of *what* is loved by the philosopher (is it philosophical wisdom about truth or truth *per se*?), and of *how* truth is loved by the philosopher (is it loved with what the philosopher has – that is, with knowledge – or with what the philosopher lacks – that is, with ignorance?). Hence, the love of truth is both a question about love and its risks and a question about the object this passion for truth is directed at.

As seen from a psychoanalytical perspective, the philosophical love of truth is the love of what meets our gaze on the screen, that is, the love of what philosophical wisdom can command. The philosophical love of truth, then, is based on concealment rather than on disclosure. Marrying love and truth leads philosophical wisdom to assume the immanence of truth to knowledge, to take the screen to be a way of articulating truth itself. Psychoanalytical thought, however, suggests a disengaging of love from truth, as the truth the philosopher loves turns out to be what he/she already knows to be true.

Had psychoanalysis settled merely for the imaginary status of truth, its effect would have been exhausted in the disengaging of the two through showing that truth lies elsewhere than where philosophical wisdom locates it. And yet psychoanalysis subtracts nothing from the truth which functions as the cause of philosophical desire, but, rather, transforms the foundations of coming to terms with this desire for pursuing truth. Such a transformation can already be marked in the Freudian revelation that truth cannot be fully articulated nor attained (which is the reason that analysis is immanently interminable), and is yet the aim of analysis. Psychoanalysis affects the pursuit of truth by indicating that the truth loved is castrated and its plenitude can only be subtracted from its articulation. What the philosopher's love of truth screens out is the fact that truth disappears under attempts to pursue it by way of knowledgeable articulation. The truth the philosopher loves as much as the truth the psychoanalyst desires is affected by castration, which posits an insurmountable restriction on articulating the whole truth.

Does psychoanalysis hence undermine the fundamental philosophical desire to make truth accessible to wisdom?

In answer to the psychoanalytical challenge, Badiou presents his own case as the case of the contemporary philosopher who has worked through Lacan's anti-philosophy. Badiou believes that, after Lacan, there can be no place for a primordially uncastrated truth (which is Heidegger's assumption regarding the pre-Socratic thinkers). However, he also objects to the possible consequence of psychoanalysis that philosophy should settle for a love of castrated truth. Badiou's aim is to restitute the philosopher's love of truth as a love neither weakened nor diluted by a ready-to-hand knowledge, and yet, as a love that has crossed the psychoanalytical challenge. Badiou makes a case for the philosopher's love of the truth as the love of what can be subtracted from thought yet remains powerful. In other words, his philosophical project is not only to redefine the terms of philosophy after psychoanalysis, but also to make up for the misleading impression that the psychoanalytical claim that truth is castrated empties out the notion of truth itself. The philosopher who has worked through Lacan can relate to the very truth that has disappeared under its articulation in thought, to a truth that holds to its reservoir of power and can, hence, seize the contemporary philosopher's love.

"[W]e shall have to think the powerlessness of a truth, which presupposes that we first be able to conceive its power" (Badiou, 2006, p. 130). Although truth is castrated, as psychoanalysis has forced on us, its castration is only the particular outcome of its all-powerfulness. How does the philosopher who loves truth re-gain access to the power of truth? The following statements present the direction of Badiou's solution to the problem:

(1) Truth cannot be transcendent to a *situation*. A situation, which is ontologically infinite from a subject's point of view, is given to the truth procedures conducted in each discipline (science, politics, art, etc.) (ibid., p. 156). That is, truth imposes a configuration on the infinity of a situation.

(2) In a situation, truth is yet distinguished from knowledge. While truth is produced by the multiplicity of a situation, knowledge is committed to the "regional particularity of the situation" (ibid., p. 127). To elude the equation of truth with knowledge as a result of the immanence of truth to a situation, Badiou refers to Lacan, for whom truth constitutes a hole in forms of knowledge. The immanence of truth to a situation does not turn psychoanalysis into knowledge because, had this been the case, a subject in analysis would just be the consequence of the analytic situation in which he/she is engaged (as a hysteric, a pervert or a psychotic).

(3) Hence, truth is *generic* (which for Badiou means that it is anonymous and egalitarian – that is, not-particular) (ibid.: XVI). Since truth is subtracted from the castrated language of the encyclopedia, truth is produced in a situation in "its pure multiple being" (ibid.: 127).

(4) Truth in a situation is configured incompletely and yet its force is generic. This generic power of truth is exhibited in what Badiou calls truth's "*forcing*" – that is, it creates an anticipatory dimension in knowledge "concerning not what is but *what will have been if truth attains completion*" (ibid., p. 130).

(5) While what can be articulated depends on forms of knowledge, truth brings on the anticipation of a generic truth "in the process of coming into being" (ibid., p. 132). The love of truth has to do with this anticipation of the coming into being of generic truth.

(6) However, the love of truth also has a real dimension revealed in what remains *unnameable*, what cannot be forced unto the process. It is this unnameable aspect that reveals truth as possessing "a genuinely boundless reservoir of power" (ibid., p. 134). The unnameable should not be understood in terms of available resources of knowledge and the encyclopedia, "but in the precise sense in which it remains out of reach for the veridical anticipations founded on truth ... The unnameable emerges only in the domain of truth" (ibid., p. 133).

The path of Badiou leads to recovering the place of truth and the love that attaches the philosopher to it under the strict preservation of Lacan's psychoanalytical critique. Moreover, the truth constituted by Badiou as unnameable and, yet, as forcing an anticipatory dimension on forms of knowledge, is a truth conditioned by the psychoanalytical "anti-philosophical" outlook.

B. True Love

In his seminar of 1960-61 (*Transference*), Lacan analyzes the relations between love, knowledge and truth through the enigmatic character of Alcibiades (the character erupting into the scene at the end of the line of speeches, drunk and distraught, to claim Socrates' love and to praise him). Alcibiades teaches us what it means to love when one answers the call of love neither by assuming knowledge of love nor by assuming that the truth about the cause of love can be attained. Love gains its power where one knows nothing. The role Alcibiades plays in the dialogue, as analyzed by Lacan, does not just illuminate the structure of love but also explains Socrates' insistence on declining any claim to knowledge as well as his rejection of the love he claims to know something about ("I do not see how I could myself decline, when I set up to understand nothing but love-matters") offered to him by Alcibiades (Plato, 1932, 177d-e).

In what follows, the case of Alcibiades, as analyzed by Lacan, will first reveal that love is an act. It is a particular act in the domain of the subject in which the subject turns from the status of the loved one to that of the lover. This passage to the act (*passage à l'acte*) acknowledges the place of the cause of desire in the Other, thus giving rise to a truth about love: namely, truth as "unnameable". It is at the moment where the loved one (*eronemos*) turns into a lover (*erastes*), a moment of passage to the act on the basis of a missing, yet real, unnameable, that the subject can pursue a truth essential to him/her. In this context, the unnameable is equivalent to "the lack with which one loves", a lack that replaces the question "what is there in me that makes me loveable?" This replacement isolates the moment at which an act of love is generated. Lacan describes this moment in terms of the metaphor of love; Badiou describes the moment at which the power of truth is revealed as the forcible transformation of truth into the unnameable – a truth which, for Badiou, has always been and remains generic.

To present the passage to the act on the part of Alcibiades, let us first look at the way the imaginary strongholds of love are annulled one by one through Alcibiades' discourse. It is through this undermining that the true metaphor (structure) of love, true love as conceived by Lacan through the *Symposium*, can be articulated.

The Delusions of Beauty – "[M]y dearest Alcibiades ... what a stupendous beauty you must see in me, vastly superior to your comeliness! And if on copying this you are trying for a mutual exchange of beauty for beauty, it is no slight advantage you are counting on – you are trying to get genuine in return for reputed beauties" (ibid., 218d-e). The question of the status of beauty in the drama of love is a constant issue in the dialogue. The participants in the dialogue, called on to express their praises of Eros, end up missing the subject of their speech. Speaking in praise of Eros through his qualities cannot illuminate how Eros' goodness and beauty are connected with the love attached to his figure. Eros is the love of the beautiful and consequently the love of the good and should hence manifest the way in which love is enacted by what one lacks and, hence, desires. Through the lips of Diotima, Socrates indicates that, if Eros were granted absolute beauty and goodness, he could not be a god representing love (as love requires a lack in the lover). However, Eros is also the loved one, located in the place unto which the desire of the other is directed. We need Alcibiades to grasp the place of Eros as being in between these two functions in love (the place that determines Eros as neither beautiful nor ugly): Alcibiades is beautiful, and yet, is the lover par excellence – that is, he lacks something which he locates in the Other.

In Plato's dialogue, Alcibiades is an aging man who carries but the remnants of a great former beauty and yet acknowledges that his beauty and riches of the past were of no avail when gaining the love of Socrates was at stake. Alcibiades' speech is a blatant account of his attempts to seduce Socrates which, as a result, exposes the futility of beauty. In his speech he tells of his discovery that love is blind in the sense that it knows nothing of beauty or the good: he loves Socrates who has no beauty or charm to offer and his own apparent charms do not count in his pursuit of his love.

However, as expressed in Socrates' response to Alcibiades' seductions, beauty does not exit the scene even once its delusional value has been stressed. Alcibiades was formerly beautiful but his beauty is now fading; Alcibiades loves truth and is yet presented as a compulsive manipulator, traitor and liar. Lacan states that it was well known "in the highest places" that Alcibiades was a traitor (Lacan, 1991, p. 33). He is said to have impregnated the queen of Sparta, to have betrayed the Greeks with the help of the Spartans to later betray the Spartans with the help of the Persians, and so on. Alcibiades had a "singular career", says Lacan, mainly because he could seduce, even at an advanced age, as much by his appearance as by his exceptional intelligence. Plato finds it worthwhile to report to us in full the whole extent of Alcibiades' invitations to physical intimacy with Socrates, which means that this report must contribute something important to the question of love. Alcibiades' seductions did not leave Socrates indifferent; it was well-known that Alcibiades was Socrates' greatest love (even if Socrates resisted the proposed intimacy).

The involvement of Socrates in the scene of love does not only stress that his position toward truth is immanent to a situation/practice, but also indicates that beauty, even if delusional, signals the presence of a powerful object in matters of love. Alcibiades' drunken speech is most closely related to the question of love, which stands at the centre of the dialogue (ibid., p. 37). Beauty is a mirage and, yet, it plays a crucial role in the practice of love, as Socrates' words above express. Like the symposium itself, which is the most beautiful lie, Alcibiades knows that "only liars can appropriately reply to love" (ibid., p. 39), which signals the part that beauty plays in this dialogue.

Alcibiades' attraction to Socrates would be enigmatic enough if it were not revealed that this love is motivated by Alcibiades' love of truth: "Whether anyone else has caught him in a serious moment and opened him, and seen the images inside, I know not; but I saw them one day, and thought them so divine and golden, so perfectly fair and wondrous, that I simply had to do as Socrates bade me" (Plato, 1932, 216e-217a). Both Alcibiades and Socrates are beautiful: the one's beauty is a mirage; the other's, a reflection of truth – and yet the dialogue does not downgrade the former. Alcibiades' beauty, expected to raise desire in the other, brings about an unexpected reversal: sure of his power of beauty, Alcibiades believes it to be a "rare stroke of luck … to hear all that our Socrates knew". Possessing beauty – that is, believing that he is loved – Alcibiades hopes to acquire knowledge by taking advantage of his own position of the loved one. However, as it turns out, Alcibiades' beauty has no effect on Socrates (external beauty is just a mirage), and inner beauty is nothing more than a surface. Socrates' light is not dimmed by this revelation and in Alcibiades we see *beauty transformed from a mirage to a power to an act*. Alcibiades' beauty is what enables him to change his position from that of the one loved (who is certain of his beauty) to the one who loves (who sees the desired quality in the other). While Socrates, through Diotima, refers to beauty as the main condition for procreation (as desire is annihilated by ugliness), Alcibiades' beauty does not ignite the love of the other, but ignites the love of Alcibiades himself. Beauty is essential to the subject's ability to act with what he does not have. Beauty in the lover becomes the object transferred from the subject to the object of his love, thus representing the place of Eros in the relation of love. Beauty does not lose its potency or presence but only its status, which changes from the signifier of the passivity of the loved one to the signifier of the activity of the lover. In his pursuit of Socrates' knowledge, then, it is Alcibiades who can represent with his beauty what is real in love. It is the sign of beauty which shifts positions, from that of an added asset to a mark of the object of desire lacking in the loving subject.

The Delusions of Knowledge – If the dialogue deals with the meaning of Eros, what should we expect from a speech that conveys knowledge about Eros, and what kind of knowledge do we expect to be delivered? Lacan's reading of the dialogue reveals that no such knowledge can be delivered because what we get in answer to the desire to know about love is a recounting of the way it affects discourse, which is spoken through the body's ailments and speech's impasses. However, if the truth about love cannot be articulated, how should one interpret the hazards undertaken by generations of ignorant monks and "*diversement ignorantins frères*" (Lacan, 1991, p. 35) who made the effort to deliver the dialogue in its entirety throughout the ages to be scorched into our cultural memory forever? What these "brothers" actually delivered to us, even without knowing what it was they had in their hands, has the power of truth in it, as is exhibited, among other things, in this very act of delivery.

Knowing something about love – a knowledge assigned to Socrates in the dialogue – has a somewhat deadly effect on love. While Socrates professes to know about love, Lacan points out that this is because Socrates knows that he does not love (ibid., p. 185). Socrates admits to his being loved but "it is precisely because Socrates knows, that he sets his face against having been, in any justified or justifiable way whatsoever, *eronemos*, the desirable, what is worthy of being loved" (ibid.). In this sense, knowledge of love counteracts love itself. According to Lacan, Socrates stands in the place of the object that causes desire, in the present case, the desire to know the truth about love. Paradoxically, this position excludes the possibility of Socrates himself turning into an object of satisfaction.

If not Socrates, who *can* be a lover? To be a lover requires a true passage to the act (*passage à l'acte*), defined by Lacan as the act in which the subject is dropped from the scene as an object. In this passage to the act, the subject exits the social framework that has determined his/her relation to the Other. Here, the subject does not address the Other, nor does he/she rely on the symbolic register (which is why Lacan sees the act of suicide as a passage to the act) (Lacan, 2004, p. 145). Love requires a passage to the act because in love the subject has to let go of all his/her assets (such as beauty, or other material or spiritual charms) to reveal the object *per se*, beyond understanding or meaning. The *passage à l'acte*, says Lacan, is the opening of a leaking tap without knowing what one is doing: "something happens by which a cause is liberated, by means which have nothing to do with this cause" (Lacan, 2004, p. 372).

The act of love, therefore, requires knowledge of the object, a knowledge that can explain how in being dropped from the symbolic, the subject, in his/her act of love, constitutes nothingness as something. At first in the *Symposium*, Socrates appears as knowing nothing, except about the affairs of love. This is, interprets Lacan, not knowing constituted as emptiness, as appeal of the emptiness to the centre of knowledge (Lacan, 1991, p. 186). In his very being, then, Socrates is a manifestation of the miracle of love without himself being part of it. Assuming that the position of knowledge is just momentary and gives place to the act of the lover precisely by turning the something of knowledge into nothing, Socrates resists showing signs of desire to Alcibiades, presenting himself as not worthy of his desire. Thus, when cornered by Alcibiades, Socrates declines the possession of any knowledge, claiming to know nothing. If it is at all possible to know something truthful about love – and the perseverance of the monks attests to this – this knowledge cannot be acquired in the actual practice of love (as this practice is bound to fail) nor in a prior position of knowledge. The possibility of knowing love is revealed in the empty place (Badiou's "unnameable") that constitutes knowledge itself. This hole in the form of knowledge (i.e. truth) is the place of the object that causes love, and brings about the possibility of acting in the name of love (the role taken by Alcibiades) as well as the possibility of exposing the metaphor of love as love's generic truth (which is the role assigned to Socrates).

The Delusions of Truth – What is the truth about love in the *Symposium*? Can this truth be articulated? When Alcibiades makes his dramatic entry into the scene, he first refers to Socrates' just finished speech to slander it as untrue: "[M]y gifted friend [Eryximachus], you are surely not convinced by anything that Socrates has just told you? You must know the case is quite the contrary of what he was saying" (Plato, 1932, 214d). Before beginning his own speech, Alcibiades addresses Socrates with the following question, "I shall speak the truth; now, will you permit me?" which Socrates answers saying, "Ah well, so long as it is the truth, I permit you and command you to speak" (ibid., 214e).

However, once Alcibiades terminates his talk the truth of what he has recounted is put into doubt, as the speaker's real intentions are exposed by the participants' laughter. At this point, Socrates appears to admit his own desire for Agathon while Alcibiades is blamed for delivering his speech solely to shift Agathon's attentions towards himself. Were Alcibiades' words not just destined to provoke a quarrel between Socrates and Agathon, the latter being the real object of Alcibiades' desire? Alcibiades is exposed as truly wanting to be loved by Socrates and to have Agathon as a lover, and the truthful speech he delivers to praise Socrates is suggested to be just a manipulation.

What, then, is truth in the *Symposium*? Is it the truth one articulates (Alcibiades wants to tell the whole truth)? Exposing the limitations of speech in telling the truth, the dialogue shifts the weight to another truth than the truth one aims to articulate in speech. Truth in the dialogue, claims Lacan, is the truth about love as formulated in the metaphor of love, in that miraculous structure which turns a place of emptiness into a powerful desire, which turns the loved one who thinks he has something the other desires into a desiring subject. The aim of praising love or praising the lover, claims Lacan, which, here, is substituted for an act of love as praising, is no more than a ritual (Lacan, 1991, p. 180).

C. The Truth about Love

The truth about love lies in an act of labouring for it, in the practice opened up from the place of lack. Love needs a desirer ready to engage in blind labour for what promises no part in its domain, for what promises no benefit or success. Such blind labour is illustrated in the Biblical story of Jacob who laboured for the love of Rachel for seven years, just to discover at the end of this ordeal that he has been married to her sister Leah and will have to resume his hard labour to gain the hand of the desired younger sister. To know about love requires an act of a subject, and the only one who acts for his love (by way of speech) is Alcibiades. The truth about love lies in the way love is enacted.

The truth about love is thus the truth unveiled in the structure, or, metaphor of love, which shows the signification of love to lie in the following coordinates defining love's mode of enactment (ibid., p. 53):

1. As a desirer, the subject does not know what he/she is lacking.
2. As the beloved, the subject does not know what one has that makes him/her deserve the love of the other.
3. In the lack of coincidence between the two, the beloved one desires to know what he has hidden in the other.
4. To love is to be caught in this gap, in this discord.

Given these coordinates, the place of Socrates in the structure of love is that of the one who, by declining to possess knowledge or anything else worthy of the other's desire, enables Alcibiades to desire. The one positioned in the place of being loved, or the one whose knowledge is desired by the other, can either accept the love offered or reject it. Socrates rejects it because he refuses to stand in the place of the one worthy of love – that is, the place of the one who has a privileged access to the truth about love. Socrates exhibits the position of the one true to the emptiness of knowledge about love. He absents himself from the point marked by the covetous desire of Alcibiades, a desire which locates in Socrates an *agalma*: the best object or good to be possessed (even if it will cause the lover harm). However, this object of desire as the best of objects cannot be pinned down or possessed. Alcibiades, who is loved for his beauty and his intelligence, desires to know what it is in him that makes him be desired by the Other. To know that, he directs his desire to Socrates' knowledge of love, since Socrates is the one who is supposed to love Alcibiades. What is discovered through this exchange of gestures is that the object of desire – that is, knowledge about the cause of love – cannot be known or possessed. This discovery is the truth the dialogue reveals; it is the truth that is manifested in the metaphor of love itself. As a subject, Alcibiades is not just positioned as a function in the structure of love. Indeed, Alcibiades has his own particular way of desiring to know (Lacan implicitly diagnoses him as a pervert): his position would make him chase the Other's *agalma* at any price, no matter what, as, for him, the object of desire is always the same, whether in Socrates or in Agathon (ibid., p. 181).

To know something about love is to appeal to the emptiness at the centre of knowledge, turning this centre into a cause for the desire for the Other. Socrates stands in the place of this hole in knowledge that functions as the cause of desire for Alcibiades; Alcibiades stands in the place of the lover who assumes knowledge in the Other and acts in order to gain possession over it, no matter what.

Lacan's notion of the metaphor of love presents a structure of truth about love constituted through the unfolding of the dialogue, in itself a way of practicing love. The partners in the dialogue each assume knowledge (Alcibiades in Socrates, and Socrates in himself), yet this assumption turns out to be delusional: the truth about love is that knowledge about it cannot be attained but through the emptiness at its centre. If this is the truth about love of truth, what is left for the philosopher? Badiou suggests that what is left is knowledge assumed in an anticipatory mode, so that it sets a condition of love even after the delusional nature of knowledge has been exposed. What does Lacan suggest? Lacan suggests two modes of coming to terms with the impossibility of knowing what the truth about love is. We have Alcibiades, the lover/desirer par excellence, the man of action who does not absent himself from the scene of love even when discovering that love is indifferent to its imaginary strongholds (beauty, fortune, intelligence). Socrates is the more difficult case. Lacan presents Socrates' gesture as inciting love in the Other in demonstrating to Alcibiades that the act of love transcends beauty and the good. Socrates knows something; he possesses wisdom (*Sophia*), which is the reason, claims Lacan, that he cannot love. This is Lacan's way of pointing to Socrates as the subject in the position of the analyst: he has a passion for the truth and, hence, is ready to go into the structure of love *without becoming its subject*. Socrates has desire but cannot "love back", nor can he assume a position of knowledge or of love. Socrates, in the position of the analyst, incarnates the structure of love by putting himself in the position of the cause of the desire to know about love. Yet Socrates is also the philosopher, the one whose love of wisdom puts him in the position of the subject driven to the next phase of his route, to the next dialogue in which a new terrain of wisdom will be explored.

For Lacan, Socrates is a psychoanalyst and, hence, he has a desire for truth enacted from the place empty of knowledge. From the position of the analyst, the truth desired is indifferent to the distinction between knowing something and knowing nothing. What Lacan's metaphor of love does to the love of truth is to negotiate the structure of love with its unnameable core: its truth. For Badiou, Socrates is a philosopher whose love of truth extends beyond his position in a situation towards its generic dimension. Both as an analyst and as a philosopher, for both Lacan and Badiou, Socrates' truth does not appear as a point of repose or halt, but as an anticipatory desire for truth that knows no rest.

References

Badiou, A. (2006). *Theoretical writings*. (R. Brassier & A. Toscano, Eds. & Trans.). London/New York, NY: Continuum.

Lacan, J. (1991). *Le séminaire VIII: Le transfert. 1960-1961*. Paris: Seuil.

———. (2004). *Le séminaire X: L'angoisse. 1962-1963*. Paris: Seuil.

———. (2007). *The seminar. Book XVII: The other side of psychoanalysis. 1969-1970*. (R. Grigg, Trans.). London/New York, NY: W. W. Norton and Company.

Plato. (1932). *Lysis, Symposium, Gorgias*. With an English translation by W. R. M. Lamb. The Loeb Classical Library. London: W. Heinemann.

Derrida and Lacan – An Impossible Friendship?[1]

Charles Shepherdson

The Territories of Truth

In the world today, it is difficult not to begin with a concern about allegiances, friends and enemies, discursive camps and their borders, in short, with a concern about the regimes and territories of truth. And for this context, we are concerned above all with the territories of "psychoanalysis" and "philosophy", as well as the chance, or better, the contingency (I underscore this word) of the encounter between them, and the discursive transformations that allow us to pass from one to another: from one to another, which is to say (a) respecting their borders, their differences, their disciplinary specificity (which is all too easily effaced or ignored today under the banner of "hybridity" and "interdisciplinarity"), and at the same time (b) allowing them to communicate with one another, and even to pass into one another, to find some kinship, philia, and even love for one another. A strange task – some might say an impossible task (and I underscore these words as well, for reasons that will soon be apparent).

The relation between philosophy and psychoanalysis is an especially vexed case of territorial incursion and defence, and more than ever when it comes to Jacques Lacan and Jacques Derrida. What friendship is possible when Lacan is summarily "deconstructed" in advance for a phallocentrism that is "obviously" just another metaphysics? What friendship is possible when Lacanians, from the "opposite side", have so often denounced the "infinite sliding of the signifier" that supposedly summarizes Derrida's thought, as if he claimed that no meaning or decision were possible? If we begin from the established landmarks that have guided the reception of Lacan and organized his relation to Derrida, a whole series of familiar positions would seem to confirm an irreducible opposition between these two thinkers, from the famous debate as to whether "the letter arrives at its destination" (Lacan says "always", Derrida says "never" – a simple opposition, or so we are told), to the status of the subject (psychoanalysis requires it, deconstruction eliminates it),

[1] A longer version of this paper appeared in *Differences: A Journal of Feminist Cultural Studies*, *20*(1), pp. 40-86. The paper develops issues first addressed in: Shepherdson (2003).

to the vexed question of Lacan's "stealing" all his fundamental concepts from other thinkers, especially Kojève and Hegel (whose account of the master-slave relation is said to have provided the foundation for Lacan's account of intersubjectivity and the imaginary "relation to the other"), and Lévi-Strauss and Saussure (who are said to have provided the conception of the "symbolic order"). According to this popular reception, Lacan's thought is abruptly translated into linguistics and phenomenology, explained without the slightest reference to Freud, and psychoanalysis is thereby treated as if it had no authentic conceptual foundation of its own (so much for the symptom, the drive, sexuality, the object, the body, and all the more technical vocabulary of psychoanalysis), but were merely a confused bricolage patched together from structuralism and Hegel – as if psychoanalysis itself did not exist.

In fact, Lacan came to question the supposedly transcendental status of the phallus and the very stability of the "symbolic order" more and more as his work developed, and many later Lacanian concepts – including *jouissance*, the pluralization of the "names-of-the-father", the Borromean knot, and even the "real" and the object a – were developed in response to this "incompleteness" of the law (a theme that is central in Derrida's work as well), but this does not keep Lacan's reception from putting an evil totem in place of his thinking, since it is easier to denounce his work than it is to read it. And for his part, Derrida repeatedly showed that the famous "metonymy" of the signifier always comes to rest, by a decision whose character Derrida goes on to investigate (in terms of what he even calls "desire"). But this has not kept Lacanians from concluding that the theory of "dissemination" fails to recognize the famous *point de capiton* by which even the wandering Jewish subject is inexorably captured, pinned down, and (if the phrase is not too Catholic) stigmatized. Friendship is impossible under such inflammatory conditions. Impossible, but at the same time necessary.

Derrida himself, of course, was quite interested in psychoanalysis, but it must be said that his followers – apart from the decisive contribution of Continental feminist theory – have mostly refused to read Lacan's work. After Heidegger, we all know how to recognize a transcendental discourse, and Lacanian theory is clearly "just another metaphysics". And the Lacanians are the first to agree with their adversaries: we are repeatedly told that Lacan is "not Heidegger", and certainly "not Hegel" or Merleau-Ponty, because none of these philosophers understood *jouissance*, or "the symptom", or the "objet petit a", and in any case, as the more enthusiastic Lacanians tell us, one does not have to read these philosophers at all (let us forget that Lacan himself cited them unrelentingly), because one already knows that philosophy as such is merely another "master discourse", which is, of course, quite different from the inevitably triumphant "discourse of the analyst". It seems philosophy and psychoanalysis cannot bear any contact with each other, and even love to hate each other. Bizarre indeed, when Lacan and Derrida themselves were the first to support this relationship, so that philosophy and psychoanalysis could challenge, contest, and thereby nourish each other.

I will try to develop this conversation by exploring the categories of modal logic: the necessary, the impossible, the possible and the contingent. My aim is to explore the way Derrida and Lacan both use these modal categories, and to suggest that Lacan's engagement with them not only differs from Derrida's, but also clarifies Lacan's notorious account of sexual difference in *Encore*. As I will try to show, moreover, Lacan's use of modal logic not only clarifies his treatment of sexual difference but also opens onto an account of discursive transformation that brings Lacan somewhat closer to Michel Foucault's work on the historical transformation of discourse than the popular reception of Lacan and Foucault has allowed. The issue of discursive transformation also poses a question to those aspects of Derrida's work that would seem to be captured by a certain Heideggerian legacy, in which the end of metaphysics can only be experienced as an endless repetition that no historical and discursive change can ever fundamentally displace. To put this in a very hasty and imprecise way, one might say that Derrida's use of modal logic remains rigorously philosophical – it "always comes back to the same place", as if haunted by the return of a certain philosophical traumatism – while Lacan's work, like Foucault's in fact (but supplemented by a clinical orientation, a very different theoretical apparatus, and different interests of course), pays greater attention to the cultivation of new possibilities of desire.

Structure and Temporality

Let us begin with Derrida. In the course of his work, Derrida came to rely more often, and more systematically, on a certain relationship between the "impossible" and the "necessary". In traditional philosophy, of course, these two terms are opposed to one another and logically contradict each other, since what is necessary must be and what is impossible cannot be. This opposition is not merely logical but also ontological, since it concerns what "is" and what "is not", being and nonbeing, which stand apart from one another. "For it is impossible", Aristotle tells us, "for anyone to suppose that the same thing is and is not, as some imagine that Heraclitus says" (Aristotle, 1933, pp. 23–

24). And yet, despite this traditional and well-established opposition, Derrida increasingly relied on the discovery and indeed the experience of a deeper connection between the necessary and the impossible, such that these two terms began to coincide in a curious and paradoxical conjunction.

This development eventually deepened to the point where deconstruction itself appeared to be both necessary and impossible, in defiance of traditional philosophy. In *Force of Law: 'The Mystical Foundation of Authority'*, for example, Derrida opposes the infinity of justice to the finite, written and historical instances of law, at the same time showing that no deconstruction of the law will establish, codify or institutionalize justice and put an end to the violence that inheres in the actual historical instantiation of the law. Like justice, therefore, deconstruction remains suspended in a certain way, which means that both justice and deconstruction are perpetually unfulfilled, out of reach, impossible, and, therefore, always called-for, always necessary, in an ethical sense that owes a considerable debt to Emmanuel Levinas and to what Gillian Rose once called "Walter Benjamin's Messianic political theology of divine and law-founding violence" (Rose, 1996, p. 69).

For Rose, this argument about the "infinity" of both justice and deconstruction also entails an abandonment of politics: it regards "all human law as fallen, violent and unredeemable", and "represents the most explicit emergence of the anarchic utopianism at the heart of postmodern thinking" (ibid., pp. 68–69). While I cannot agree with Rose in her assessment of Derrida's "anarchic utopianism", there is a further remark in her account that has more bearing on our concern here. Rose adds: "This is no work of mourning: it remains a baroque melancholia" (ibid., p. 69). We will not develop this criticism here, but only note that, when it comes to Lacan's engagement with the necessary and the impossible, we find a formulation that differs from Derrida's, and this difference could be related to the question of mourning ("impossible mourning" in Derrida's phrase [Derrida, 1993, p. 16]), which means our relation to the past and the loss of the metaphysical tradition. As Lacan writes in *Encore* with reference to the question of discursive transformation, every subject in analysis is confronted with certain obstacles and impasses. These are obstacles "from which we solicit an exit in analysis", Lacan says, and this involves "letting go of the other discourses (*lâchage des autres discours*)" (Lacan, 1998, p. 11). Psychoanalysis is about nothing if it is not about this discursive transformation, which Lacan goes on to develop in this seminar in terms of "love": "Love is the sign that one is changing discourses", he says, and "there is some emergence of analytic discourse with each shift from one discourse to another" (ibid., p. 16). In this sense, Lacan's work would seem to cut against the attachments and repetitions of melancholia. For the moment, however, and without pursuing this further, let us stay with our question and look more closely at the "paradox" or "aporia" that concerns us here, in which necessity and impossibility are suddenly brought together.

Deconstruction is thus both necessary and impossible. In one sense, this has a temporal significance: deconstruction is never accomplished, never completed, and must always be renewed. At the end of metaphysics, metaphysics does not simply disappear. On the contrary, it returns or repeats, which means that its deconstruction fails and must constantly begin again. One should look more closely at the temporal structure of this repetition and eternal return, however, since it is clear that repetition is not sameness: what returns, what "always comes back to the same place" (as Lacan says about the real), does not have the same status as what was there "in the beginning". Time intervenes. Indeed, deconstruction may be an "impossible" task, and the "law" as written may continue its reign, despite the arrival, or nonarrival or, rather, the "event" of infinite justice; but at the end of metaphysics, this law no longer looks the same: like Creon, perhaps, who, in contrast to Oedipus, remains the king at the end of *Antigone*, with all his enemies dead together with his wife and son – king of what remains. This kingdom is clearly no longer what it was, even if it appears to survive in the end.

A more serious elaboration of these issues is clearly needed, but for our present purposes we simply wish to note that the "structure" that links necessity and impossibility in Derrida, such that deconstruction repeats, or never arrives, and thereby remains both necessary and impossible, cannot be adequately grasped as an event that is situated "in" time, according to the linear chronology of "history". Likewise, when we speak of transformation and change in psychoanalysis (and in Foucault's work as well), this question of temporal transformation (crisis, disruption, retroaction or discursive displacement) should not be confused with historical chronology.

In another sense, however, and apart from this temporal question, we are faced with a logical or "structural" problem: if the "necessary" and the "impossible" are opposed to one another and logically contradictory, so that, by definition, they cannot coincide or be applied to the same object or event, then how exactly does Derrida understand their belonging to one another, or indeed what one might strangely call their friendship? We can understand easily enough what it means to say that deconstruction, like justice, is both necessary and impossible, but what is the "logic" or the "structure" that brings these two opposite terms together, contradicting traditional usage?

Readers of Lacan, even if they have not entered into the details of his theory, know very well that he was also interested in this problem and that he even traced the developments in calculation, mathematization and predictability or repeatability, so central to modern science, from Copernicus forward to cybernetics – following an initial interest in Alexandre Koyré and other historians of science – in order to show the irreducible rupture that Freud introduced into "science", especially with respect to temporality, intersubjective time, analytic technique, questions of memory and forgetting, and the challenge these problems present for those who would (and still do) assert that psychoanalysis should ideally aim at becoming a "science" on the model of experimental disciplines, with repeatable results, calculable effects, and the like (for the sake of insurance companies and other institutional guarantors, including "recognition" of psychoanalysis as a "properly medical science"). In fact, human time, the very "time of the subject", which is stretched across the past and the future, holding itself together by various inscriptions (anticipation, projection, retention, forgetting, stagnation, even surprises and chance encounters), and marked with a thousand signifying cuts that we call "memory" – such time is possible only if bare life has been taken up in the "law" of language. Genesis and structure, or the relation between time and language, are fundamental and mutually dependent for both thinkers.

The Aporetic Vortex

With this basic orientation in place, let us now follow Derrida's formulations more closely in order to notice a few points. Four points, to be precise.

(1) First of all, attached to the conjunction of the "necessary" and the "impossible", a problem of naming. Consider his analysis of Plato's khōra as it appears in the *Timaeus*, that quasi-maternal space, receptacle, or origin in which the "forms" are first contained. Derrida underscores Plato's remark that the khōra is neither "sensible" nor "intelligible" and that it belongs to a "third genus" that in fact engenders or makes possible the sensible/intelligible distinction and therefore cannot be grasped in terms of that opposition (Derrida, 1995, p. 89). This third genus, because it refuses our familiar philosophical categories, disrupts the language of philosophy, and Plato makes it clear – I cite from Derrida – that the thought of khōra "comes 'as in a dream'" and even from a "corrupted reasoning (*logismō nothō*)" (ibid., p. 90). Given its dream-like and mysterious character as an inscrutable origin for philosophy, one might be tempted to ascribe to the khōra a mythical status.

As a third genus, however, khōra cannot be adequately captured or named by appealing to "myth", or indeed to any distinction between logos and mythos – a distinction that already presupposes the oppositions that khōra, as a third genus, explicitly puts in question. Derrida thus writes, "Shall we gain access to the thought of the khōra by continuing to place our trust in the alternative logos/mythos?" (ibid.). The concept of the khōra cannot even be approached starting from a blending of these familiar alternatives, especially since, in Plato's account, khōra is what first allows these logical alternatives to have a place. Khōra is, therefore, the very condition for the logic of "both/and" or "neither/nor" and cannot be described by such distinctions. As Derrida says: "At times, khōra appears to be neither this nor that, at times both this and that, but this alternation ... stems perhaps only from a provisional appearance and from the constraints of rhetoric, even from *some incapacity of naming*" (ibid., p. 89, emphasis added). How, then, does one approach or claim to produce a discourse on the khōra? Speaking of this third genus, Derrida then adds – and here we come to our topic: "Is it nameable? And wouldn't it have some *impossible relation* to the *possibility of naming*? Is there something to think there, as I have just so hastily said, and to think *according to necessity*?" (ibid., p. 91, emphasis added).

(2) Second point: consider the relation that comes to operate between the terms that appear together in this formulation – a relation in which the terms are no longer "opposed" to each other in the usual way, but are involved in a kind of circle, a circle that operates, in fact, around more than two terms. Let me notice, therefore, without commenting on it much further, the conjunction of the impossible, the possible, and the necessary in this passage. What I call the "conjunction" of these terms does not mean their simple identity, as if there were no difference between the necessary and the impossible (as people sometimes say about "deconstruction"), since Derrida's formulation here would seem to proceed from an impossibility of naming, to a possibility that then, in a further step or obligation, would have to be thought, or would ask to be thought (in a sort of "obligation" or "demand") "according to necessity". And yet, circling around, this necessity in turn would never escape or eliminate the original impossibility to which it remains attached, as Derrida makes clear by speaking of an "impossible relation" that cannot be surpassed even as it moves toward some kind of necessity.

In other words, despite the urgency of this other possibility, despite the "demand" or "promise" of a naming whose "hasty" emergence (as Derrida says, stressing again the curious, anticipatory temporality of this circle or movement) would propel it beyond mere impossibility toward another possibility of thought or discourse, the persistent and undialectizable character of this impossibility would nevertheless remain, as is constantly underscored by Derrida, in numerous texts. Consider his frequent play on the word *pas*, in a formulation borrowed from Blanchot, in which the "step" (in this case a step from impossibility to necessity) is at the same time a "not". There is no step forward that is not already impossible in advance. The *pas* (step/not) of Blanchot is thus already a condensation of the aporia of the "possible/impossible/necessary". This, then, is the second point, concerning how we are to articulate the relation between the necessary and the impossible, these apparently "contradictory" terms, which are not collapsed into one another or made identical to each other, but which nevertheless remain bound together in a kind of inescapable fusion. Deconstruction neither collapses the difference between the "necessary" and the "impossible" ("as some imagine that Heraclitus says"), nor leaves them opposed to each other in a mutually exclusive form, but obliges us to think a new relationship between them, as an impasse or aporia that must be elaborated, and even as an experience that must be endured today, at the historical limit of what previous epochs would have called "contradiction".

We will come back to the question of the "relation", which may also concern the relation between friends, and perhaps even what Lacan calls the "sexual relation", which – as everyone is so quick to repeat – is "impossible" and "does not exist". But let us not be too hasty here. Does not Lacan also say, "What makes up for the sexual relationship is, quite precisely, love" (Lacan, 1998, p. 45)?

(3) For the moment, however – and keeping in mind our concern with discursive transformation – let us consider a third point: the emergence of a claim concerning the history of philosophy and a certain movement from Kant, through Hegel, to Heidegger and beyond, with respect to the question of this aporia. Derrida writes:

> Aporia, rather than antinomy: the word antinomy imposed itself up to a certain point since, in terms of the law (nomos), contradictions or antagonisms among equally imperative laws were at stake. However, the antinomy here better deserves the name of aporia insofar as it is neither an "apparent or illusory" antinomy, nor a dialectizable contradiction in the Hegelian or Marxist sense, but instead an interminable experience. (Derrida, 1993, p. 16)

This aporia marks a logical impasse but is at the same time an aporia that goes beyond logical contradiction and comes to bear on the history that moves from the antinomies of Kant ("antagonisms among mutually imperative laws") to the dialectic of Hegel and Marx (by means of which contradictions could be productively mobilized) and beyond, to a thought at the "end of metaphysics" that breaks with dialectical thinking and erupts as an "interminable experience" and, thus, as another temporal formation, beyond dialectical history. This interminable experience, of course, could be understood as a form of melancholia, an interminable state of mourning – a mourning that cannot end and cannot tolerate the loss of the object, which is, of course, the loss of the metaphysical tradition, the object that is loved and that has abandoned us, but whose loss we cannot tolerate, with the result that we keep the object alive, buried within ourselves. But we will not pursue this topic here.

Derrida thus presents us with a historical trajectory, a movement that passes from Kant to Hegel and beyond, but this trajectory is simultaneously a blockage, the encounter with something that does not change, something that always repeats and "always comes back to the same place", the same inescapable impasse. I add Heidegger's name to this list because Derrida himself notes, precisely with respect to the question of time, that this nondialectical thought of impossibility, as an impossibility that persists, may affect even Heidegger's analysis in *Being and Time*, in its efforts to establish another concept of time. Is this not what we see outlined in this passage, which speaks ("with Baroque melancholia") of an "interminable experience"? Speaking of his extremely difficult and important text on Aristotle, *Ousia* and *Grammē*, Derrida continues, noting that Heidegger was right about the tradition, but perhaps more right than he knew, or right in a different way than he intended. Derrida writes:

> [I]nstead of stopping with a mere confirmation of the Heideggerian diagnosis, which indeed sees in the whole tradition, from Aristotle to Hegel, a hegemony of the vulgar concept of time ... I oriented this very confirmation towards another suggestion. ... What if there was no other concept of time than the one Heidegger calls "vulgar?" (ibid., p. 14)

This would mean that there is no escape from the tradition, that philosophy's encounter with this aporia would be unsurpassable and that this impossibility would persist, in this case not as the "impossibility" of deconstruction or justice, but rather as the impossibility of another concept of time: impossibility, therefore, at the very moment the "vulgar" concept of time was exhausted and another concept was thus necessary, called-for or demanded.

The historical point should, therefore, be clear: the experience of this impasse that links the necessary and the impossible would be absolutely unsurpassable for Derrida, and would rupture the sequence that might otherwise lead us from Kant, to Hegel, to Heidegger and beyond, which means that Derrida brings us not so much to a new concept of time as to an impasse, an irreducible "experience" that cannot be circumvented, that "must be endured", and that functions like an original traumatism that already casts its shadow over every possible future. Like Foucault, Lacan is perhaps more optimistic on this point – more optimistic, and perhaps more "vulgar" and naive. Possibly even less melancholic.

(4) Fourth point: let me now elaborate on what we have already noticed, namely, that in the quotation above concerning the khōra, we have quietly slipped from two terms to three, and, at the same time, from one opposition (the impossible and the necessary) to another (the impossible and the possible). This proliferation of terms is important, for it brings us up against a larger problem concerning the four modal categories – the necessary, possible, contingent and impossible – that are crucial for ontology. This will be the point at which a major difference emerges between Derrida and Lacan, for whom the "paradoxical" conjunction between the necessary and the impossible is opened to other possible modes of being.

For Derrida, the conjunction of "possibility" and "impossibility" concerns an aporia or impasse, beyond the usual "logic of contradiction", an impasse that is in fact not decisively different from the one we find with the "impossible" and the "necessary". This is indeed why all three terms emerge together. It is a question, in either case, of a fundamental aporia in which both formulations, both terminologies, prove to be in play. Thus, Derrida sometimes speaks of "conditions of possibility" that are at the same time "conditions of impossibility", as in the case of the khōra, the "place" that generates and makes possible the differences it produces, while at the same time remaining a third genus that puts those very distinctions in question. "Conditions of possibility as conditions of impossibility", Derrida writes in *Finis*, for example, where he indicates that this aporetic structure underlies much of his work, from the *Tympan*, "margin" and "undecidability" to "the work of impossible mourning", the "step [*pas*] and paralysis in *Parages*", and "above all, in the places where questions of juridical, ethical, or political responsibility also concern geographical, national, ethnic, or linguistic borders" (ibid., pp. 15–16). All such borders produce the same encounter, the same experience, and we thus see how the second pair of terms can emerge: conditions of possibility are simultaneously conditions of impossibility, and the thought of this aporia confronts us like a destiny, arising out of our history like an inescapable problem that demands to be thought – and to be thought, as we have already stressed, "according to necessity" (ibid., p. 91), in the sense that this encounter presses upon us from out of our own history and cannot be avoided today. One sees, then, that these three terms are all intertwined. Derrida's two formulations thus overlap and elaborate the same discovery, which concerns an aporia that is presented through two contradictions or conjunctions, sometimes as "necessary/impossible" and sometimes as "possible/impossible".

It is this fundamental duality, this singular and inevitable impasse, that Lacan will elaborate differently, deploying the four modal categories in an equally untraditional way but giving each mode a distinctive valence, even as they impinge on one another. For we can already begin to see the fundamental duality of the aporia as it functions in Derrida's account, what I would call the "aporetic vortex" which absorbs all three modal terms into the same conceptual impasse, an impasse that is at once "necessary/impossible" and "possible/impossible". The collapse of these three categories – the "possible", "impossible", and "necessary" – into a single fundamental contradiction conceals the fact that each of these terms belongs to a larger and more diversified framework of modal logic, in which four distinct terms are developed in a way that is especially important in the history of ontology. The "necessary", "possible", and "impossible" thus designate three modal categories, three modes of being, to which traditional philosophical usage adds a fourth, the "contingent". Modal logic thus offers four modes of being, but we begin to see that Derrida collapses these modal categories into a single interminable experience – the encounter with the aporia – which consumes all differences in its wake. Lacan's work will take another direction, as we shall see.

Turning with Lacan

Let us consider Lacan's use of these same modal categories. In *Encore*, his famous or notorious text on "feminine sexuality", Lacan develops the four categories of modal logic – necessity, impossibility, contingency, and possibility – in conjunction with his account of sexual difference. As I will try to show, Lacan uses the categories of modal logic in a manner that goes beyond the dominant gestures that we find in Derrida, in which the aporia of "necessity-and-impossibility" seems to govern and determine all the other modal categories in advance, without exception, one might say. In contrast, Lacan develops the categories of "contingency" and "possibility" as a way of elaborating the question of sexual difference, the sexual relation, and the Other *jouissance*.

I will, therefore, try to show that the famous sexuation graph in *Encore* can be rewritten in terms of modal logic, and, more precisely, that the first pair of terms (necessity and impossibility) corresponds to the masculine side of this graph, while the second pair (contingency and possibility) corresponds to the feminine side, the "Other *jouissance*", which Lacan hesitates to call "feminine" because, he tells us, this name and this concept are precisely what are undergoing reconfiguration in this text.

In addition, as I will also try to show, Lacan's argument entails that each of these modal categories can be shifted or transformed into another mode. This means that we can speak of a "relation" between necessity and impossibility, or between any of the four categories, and that this relation is opened under the sign of love. "I will remind you here of the four discourses", Lacan says in the second chapter (referring to the four discourses of *Seminar XVII*): "[T]here is some emergence of psychoanalytic discourse whenever there is a movement from one discourse to another", and "love is the sign that one is changing discourses" (Lacan, 1998, p. 16).

We have seen that modal categories are important for ontology and go beyond the simple opposition between being and nonbeing, holding open other possible modes of being. Medieval theology was especially rich in deploying modal categories, as Giorgio Agamben has shown in *Potentialities*, and Lacan played with these issues in his later work, particularly in his account of femininity in *Encore*, so it is perhaps no surprise that he turns to theology and a certain discourse on God in his elaboration of the Other *jouissance*. Indeed, one has only to recall the series of formulas – "The Woman does not exist", "There is no sexual relation", "The real is the impossible", etc. – to recognize immediately that, with these formulas, Lacan is not simply dismissing all question of exploring such topics, or banishing them as naive metaphysical notions. On the contrary, it is a matter of finding how to formulate in an accurate way what can be said about these phenomena or nonphenomena, these "events" or "experiences" or "encounters" that touch on femininity, the Other *jouissance*, the sexual relation, and the real, which have this peculiar status of nonexistence, or, more precisely, of "being" in a manner that goes beyond the usual alternative between "being" and "nonbeing".

In his seminar *Encore*, Lacan explicitly elaborates the four modal categories as a reconfiguration of his famous "sexuation graph". In this seminar, Lacan argues that the conjunction between "necessity" and "impossibility" (which he had earlier elaborated as formative of all subjectivity, which is "necessarily" subjected to language, and, thereby, simultaneously confronted with the sexual relation as "impossible"), now appears as a reformulation of masculinity. This means that the question of "femininity" (or, more carefully, the Other *jouissance*) will give a new role to the other two modal categories, contingency and possibility.

Lacan's most famous or notorious account of this new distinction between phallic *jouissance* and the Other *jouissance* is given in the "sexuation graph" of *Encore*:

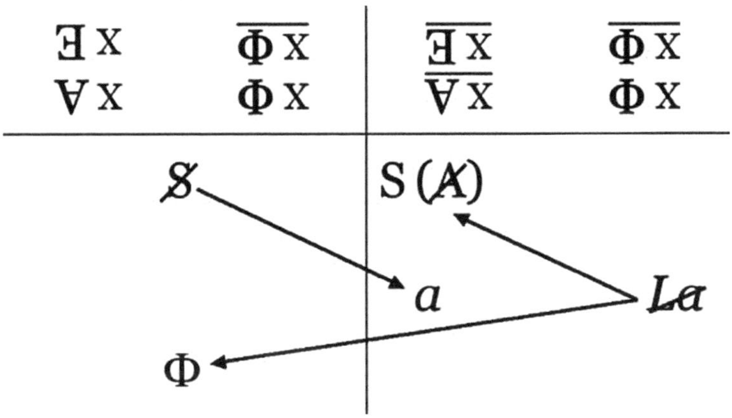

Figure one. Sexuation Graph

This graph has received extended discussion, and I will not elaborate on it any further here. It is enough to recognize that its "logic" distinguishes between the universality of the "All" (or the "whole") on the masculine side, and the "not-All" (or "not-whole") on the side of the Other *jouissance*, which counters the discourse of the universal in ways that have been important for thinkers like Alain Badiou, Jacques Rancière, and others who have sought to develop an alternative to the logic of universality. Following a few brief remarks on the symbolic logic that appears at the top of the sexuation graph, I would like to elaborate Lacan's reformulation of this logic, first in terms of modal categories (necessity, impossibility, possibility and contingency), and then in terms of ordinary language (whether there is a structural link between these two – modes of being and ordinary language – remaining open to further consideration). We will then be in a better position to grasp what I take to be his interest in discursive transformation.

As is well known, the upper part of the sexuation graph provides two pairs of formulas, two apparent "contradictions", correlated with masculinity and femininity. The first pair, on the left, commonly designated "masculine", presents a universal law stating that "All men are subject to the phallic signifier" ($\forall x \Phi x$), which is immediately "contradicted" by the exception to this law: the statement that "there is one subject who is not subjected to the phallic signifier" ($\exists x \Phi x$), namely, the primal father of Freud's *Totem and Taboo*, who escapes the law of castration, commits incest, and refuses the symbolic law of exchange. We can reformulate this logical contradiction in modal terms, such that the law governing "all men" is a "necessity" (and, in this sense, universal), while its contradiction – the exception to the law – is "impossible". Indeed, as Freud tells us, the primal father is an exception, an "outlaw" figure who must be killed and excluded from the system in order for the "law" of the community and symbolic exchange to be established (together with the exchange of women, in accordance with the principle of exogamy in Lévi-Strauss and others – a logic whose contradictions Derrida has also explored, arguing that "incest" in Lévi-Strauss is a contradictory concept, being both natural and cultural). As Lacan shows, these two "contradictory" formulas, while they are mutually exclusive, nevertheless constantly entail each other, in defiance of traditional logic. Indeed, the symbolic community of "democracy" seems to appear in a manner that is always already contaminated with its own betrayal in violence and injustice – not as a simple "failure" of democracy, but as a kind of ghost that haunts democracy with its own internal contradiction, making this community of universality at once "necessary" and "impossible". Political elaborations of Lacanian theory have developed along these lines in various forms (the "state of exception", the founding violence of democracy, the universal and the multitude, etc.), but it is enough here to see that Lacan is reformulating basic Freudian arguments about the symbolic dimension of desire (the "law") and the failures or incompleteness of symbolization that are made evident in the symptom, which the "talking cure" is intended to alleviate. Such is the logic of the law and its exception on the masculine side, now reformulated in modal terms. From this perspective, moreover, it appears that the aporia as it functions in Derrida has a close relation to "masculinity" as Lacan understands it, since masculinity is the "contradiction" in which necessity and impossibility come together.

This also means, however, that the categories of contingency and possibility will emerge on the side of the "Other *jouissance*", as an alternative to this masculine logic, opening two other modes of being, which appear under the sign of "femininity". Before exploring this point, however, it is helpful to note that Lacan's use of these modal terms contrasts with traditional formulations of the logical square as it appears in Greimas and others, where necessity is opposed to contingency:

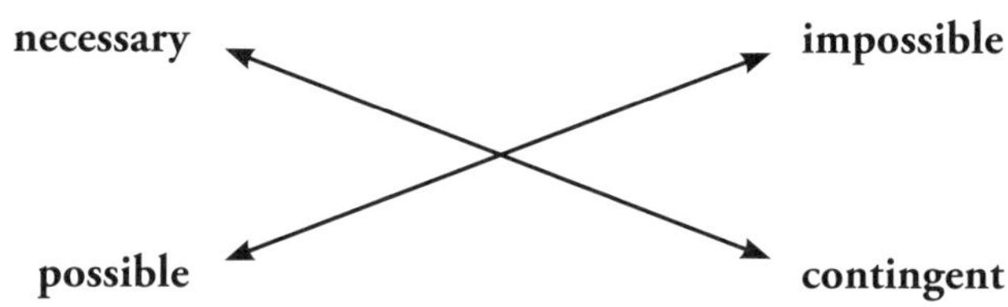

Figure two. Classical Logical Square

And Lacan is well aware of this "rupture" with respect to traditional logic: "What doesn't stop not being written" – what constantly falls outside the reach of the signifier and is thus unwritten and "impossible" – Lacan tells us, "is a modal category, and it's not the one you might have expected to be opposed to the necessary, which would have been the contingent. Can you imagine? The necessary is linked to the impossible" (ibid., p. 59). Lacan thus knows that he is deforming the classical square, and this makes all the more clear that he regards the "aporia of masculinity" as an unusual conjunction of necessity and impossibility:

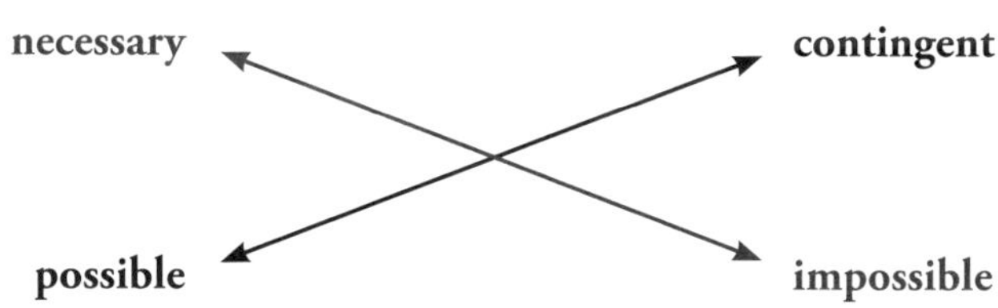

Figure three. Lacan's Revision of the Classical Square

This means the other modes of being – namely, possibility and contingency – belong to the "Other *jouissance*". This development of "possibility" and "contingency". understood as the modal categories of "femininity", however, first takes shape, not as a "logical" presentation, but by an appeal to ordinary language.

Let us now follow this development, beginning again with masculinity. As we have seen, Lacan presents masculinity as a kind of contradiction, such that the law always entails its own violation, with the primal father being a sort of "symptom" of the universality of the symbolic law (in a manner that recalls Derrida's aporetic presentation of necessity and impossibility). Lacan now presents this claim in terms of ordinary language, discovering the same "contradiction" about the "law" and its "failure" in everyday speech: "We must think about the purpose served by the old words", he says. "We know what they are used for – they are used so that there may be the *jouissance* that should be (*qu'il faut*)". One uses words to support the only kind of *jouissance* that humans have, which is not the satisfaction of natural instinct but, rather, "sexuality" as organized by the symbolic order. But Lacan continues, adding "With the caveat that, given the equivocation between faillir and falloir, the *jouissance* that should be (*qu'il faut*) must be translated as the *jouissance* that should not be/never fails (*qu'il ne faut pas*)" (ibid., pp. 58–59). Desire thus always finds itself contaminated by a resurgence of the symptomatic *jouissance* that the symbolic order was intended to eliminate (the "discontent" of civilization), and this thesis, which was previously said to cover all speaking subjects, is now provocatively ascribed to masculinity. Such is the equivocation evidenced in ordinary language, which Lacan plays on by using *il faut* ("one must"), a law which expresses its own contradiction, *il faut* being the third person singular of both *falloir* (to be necessary) and *faillir* (to fail).

If this appeal to the paradoxes or ambiguities of ordinary language reformulates what we previously saw under the sign of masculinity, what, then, of the Other *jouissance*? There is only one libido, Freud tells us, since sexuality does not divide itself into two "essentialist" forms, male and female, as is the case in the natural world. And yet, this is not the whole truth. Ordinary language allows us to speak of something else, without necessarily asserting its existence in the mode of phallic discourse (the discourse of "it is"). Conditional and subjunctive statements, for example, allow us to speak of something "contrary to fact" ("if only I were not so unhappy!"), and speaking, as we know from the performative, can be enough to bring something into being, like the Other *jouissance* perhaps, but in a mode of being that must be further elaborated, beyond mere "existence" or "non-existence". "If there were another *jouissance*..." Lacan seems to say, summoning for a moment another possibility, and all under the sign of a "condition contrary to fact", so that no assertion of existence has been made, no phallic discourse enlisted, while yet a new possibility is entertained. Indeed, throughout this seminar, he continually deploys ordinary language with just this aim in mind, for example with the term "*peut-être*" (perhaps), this "possible" being, of which we do not say that it "exists" but that nevertheless has "a little being" (*un peu d'être*), or a "strange" (*étrange*) mode of being, like the being of angels (*être-ange*) perhaps. One thus begins to see why Lacan plays with the traditions of theological discourse in this exploration of sexual difference, since those traditions were the richest, historically speaking, in their use of modal logic, and since the theology of a god who exists "necessarily" is being countered or complicated in this text, one chapter of which is appropriately titled "God and the *jouissance* of the Woman".

"Let me now return to the textual level", Lacan says, following his exposition of the masculine equivocation regarding the "law" that "always comes/never arrives". He continues, worrying over this statement that has just left his mouth: "It is the *jouissance* that shouldn't be/never fails (*qu'il ne faudrait pas*)", to which he adds: "in the conditional tense" (ibid., p. 59). Now, suddenly, he has shifted the masculine formulation (*il faut*) to another register, in which *conditional being* emerges. "That suggests to me that to use it we could employ protasis and apodosis", namely, the "if-then" structure of a conditional statement, which does not venture to assert the existence of a thing, but only to explore what that thing might be, if it were to exist.

But how or in what mode can this possibility really "appear" or "present itself" phenomenally, beyond the assertion of ontic "being", and how, moreover, can it "be said", if discourse as such is regulated by the phallic signifier? How can this other "possibility" be approached in language without falling back once again into the masculine discourse of the law and its contradiction? Lacan continues: "How are we thus going to express what shouldn't be/could never fail with respect to *jouissance*, if not by the following? Were there another *jouissance* than phallic *jouissance*, it shouldn't be/could never fail to be that one". And Lacan is very pleased with himself, adding, "That's very nice. One must really use things like that, old words, as stupid as anything, but really use them, work them to the bone" (ibid., pp. 59–60). What does he mean? He began with the momentary emergence of another possibility, the possibility of an Other *jouissance*, of which he would not predicate the existence, but which nevertheless could be approached in language under the sign of "conditional" being, further developed in the form of an "if-then" proposition ("If there were another *jouissance*..."). And when it came to the question of asserting or "expressing" the "being" of this *jouissance* ("then it would be..."), he stumbled across an obstacle – namely, that the very sentence that asserted its existence entailed a collapse into "phallic *jouissance*". "Were there another *jouissance*" (condition contrary to fact), "it shouldn't be/could never fail to be that one". Lacan continues: "What does 'that one' designate? Does it designate the other [namely, the Other *jouissance*] or the one on the basis of which we designated the other as other", namely, phallic *jouissance*? (ibid., p. 60) Lacan's sentence, then, holds open for a time – the very time of the conditional utterance, in which a new possibility is opened – the possibility of an Other *jouissance*, which is spoken without any assertion of existence, but as soon as his discourse tries to return to its familiar routine, to capture and designate that being in its "existence", the very being of this object disappears, having suddenly been reabsorbed by the phallic discourse of "being" as the sentence comes to a close ("it couldn't fail to be that one" – namely, phallic *jouissance*). "This opens up for us", Lacan says, "a little glimpse that has considerable weight in metaphysics. There may be cases in which, instead of it being us who go in search of something to reassure ourselves in the manger of metaphysics, we can even give something back to metaphysics" (ibid., p. 61). Psychoanalysis need not continually resort to philosophy to buttress its credentials, since, on the contrary, psychoanalysis may occasionally give something back to philosophy. Such is the link between femininity, language and ontology in Lacan.

Having sketched Lacan's deployment of ordinary language, let us now return to Lacan's reformulation of the logical square in order to see more clearly how these adventures in ordinary language are in turn linked to the modal categories that organize his remarks. This will bring us to our final point concerning discursive transformation.

If possibility and contingency mark a path for the Other *jouissance*, while necessity and impossibility belong to the "aporia" of masculinity, then we have just seen a curious twist whereby "possibility" – the very possibility of an Other *jouissance* – collapses back into the discourse of necessity. We can therefore map Lacan's sentence as follows:

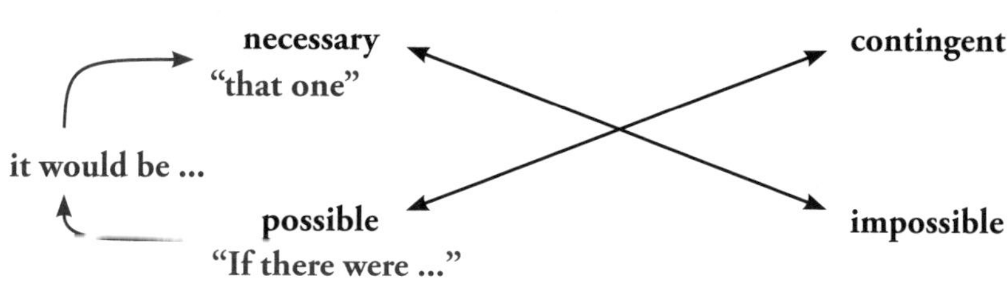

Figure four. Discursive Transformation: From the Possible to the Necessary

On this account, the possibility of another *jouissance* would appear to remain open for a time, only to fall back into the "masculine" logic of "being" and "nonbeing" as Lacan's statement proceeds. The discourse of possibility is thus lost as soon as phallic propositional discourse seeks to capture it, having been transformed into the discourse of necessity/impossibility.

But perhaps this is not the only possible transformation. How, then, might this momentary opening, this emergence of mere possibility, be transformed into the contingent emergence of an Other *jouissance*? What could be said about it, and in what new discursive mode? Given this momentary opening in which the "masculine" law is no longer the whole truth, how might that opening be cultivated so that it does not disappear again into the discourse of necessity/impossibility? These are the questions Lacan appears to be asking, and it should be noted that the initial formulation of the sexuation graph, which seems to present us with two strictly separate and distinct categories (the masculine and the feminine, the one and the Other), in fact becomes a more complex relation as he elaborates that graph, reformulating it in terms of ordinary language, and then in terms of modal logic. In other words, what the famous sexuation graph presents as two fixed and "essentialist" categories in fact appear to be capable of mobility and intertwining as Lacan's exposition proceeds. And I am suggesting that this very mobility is discovered as Lacan's means of exposition shifts from symbolic logic to ordinary language and, thence, to modal categories. Each reformation, far from repeating a "doctrine" that came before (the famous repeatable Lacanian aphorisms), actually opens new possibilities. Lacan thinks in this way, each formulation reaching for a new chance, finding a limit in previous formulations, and refining or altering what was previously thought, displacing the truisms that seemed once to be adequate. To reduce all this conceptual work to the same tired repetition of familiar Lacanian slogans does not appear to do justice to his work, nor does it allow us to recognize that this form of thinking, in its continual movement, is itself quite close to what happens in psychoanalytical practice, where the subject's "received opinions" are reviewed and reworked like "old words" until they are no longer the whole truth.

For there are indeed still other transformations in Lacan's presentation, which should be marked in conclusion. If we can entertain for a moment the possibility of another *jouissance*, simply in the mode of mere possibility, without asserting its existence, this would already mean that the phallic law on the "masculine" side is not the whole truth, which is to say that it does not have the universality that it claims for itself. Lacan is explicit: later in the seminar, following his remarks on the possibility of another *jouissance*, he takes another turn. "Because of this, the apparent necessity of the phallic function turns out to be mere contingency" (ibid., p. 94).

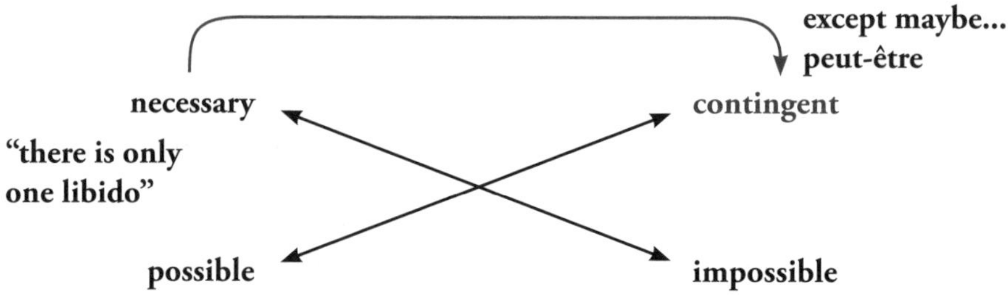

Figure five. From Necessity to Contingency

Further consequences seem to follow from this turning of Lacan's thought, since the "impossible" – that which was opposed to necessity, which never enters language, and which "doesn't stop not being written" (ibid.) – would also be set in motion. We have heard that "the real is the impossible" and indeed that the sexual relation is "impossible" outside language, as if it were never capable of being in any mode whatsoever, exiled from all language. But perhaps the story does not end there. "There is no such thing as a sexual relationship", Lacan says, and yet, "Isn't it on the basis of the confrontation with this impasse, with this impossibility by which a real is defined, that love is put to the test?" Love would, thus, be the movement in which this impasse or impossibility (perhaps the aporia which always returns to the same place) is confronted and displaced, in such a way that another contingent modality emerges and "stops not being written":

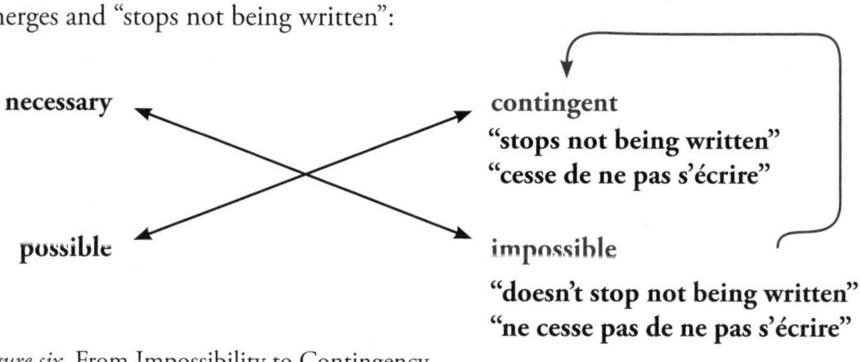

Figure six. From Impossibility to Contingency

If this kind of discursive transformation is indeed possible in Lacan, and if the "impossibility" of the sexual relation has the chance of another emergence, in some contingent form that is distinct from the logic of the "masculine" law, this would open another relation to language, in which the impossible "stops not being written". This is what Lacan calls "contingency", and he goes on to say that it would mean another mode of "recognition", "friendship" and even "love": "it is in their courage in bearing the intolerable relationship to the supreme being that friends, *philoi*, recognize and choose each other" (ibid., p. 85). Impossibility, and the hatred that goes with it, is transfigured here by the contingent event in which a new relation to the other begins to emerge, and Lacan even calls it "friendship", "recognition", and "love" – terms that no longer denote the kind of imaginary rivalry that Lacan had so strongly criticized in his early work. Indeed, these terms, so fiercely dismissed in the past, now return in Lacan's thinking, beyond the famous struggle to the death of Hegelian rivalry, with new (and dare we say "transformed") potential.

There is no sexual relation, at least in the familiar mode of predication ("there is"), and yet, as Lacan puts it at the end of the seminar, it is "on the basis of the confrontation with this impasse, with this impossibility by which a real is defined, that love is put to the test". It is through this test, this confrontation with an "impasse", that another mode of recognition emerges, beyond mere impossibility: "That recognition is nothing other than the way in which the relationship said to be sexual ... has now become a subject-to-subject relationship" and "stops not being written" (ibid., p. 144). If such a movement were possible, and if this "impossible" sexual relation were indeed open to such displacement, passing from mere "possibility" into this contingent form of being; and if, further, this possibility could be sustained and articulated by "love", which would allow the impossible to "stop not being written", then one might even venture to suppose that this writing could become a task, something that we are always invited to undertake, not in the mode of "necessity", understood as the compulsion of a law, but in the mode of another discourse, another necessity, which would be the invitation of writing more, always writing still more.

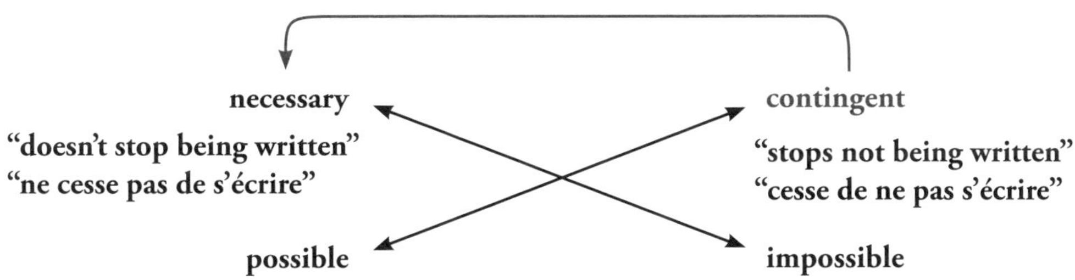

Figure seven. From Contingency to Necessity

In Lacan's words: "The displacement of the negation from 'stops not being written' to the 'doesn't stop being written', in other words, from contingency to necessity – there lies the point of suspension to which all love is attached" (ibid., p. 145).

These formulations will not satisfy all readers. Some may even hold Lacan at fault, killing the father for failing to deliver what is desired. But on writing and speech, language and being, "formalist" logic and everyday discourse, together with all the questions of sexual difference and discursive transformation – with all this, the relation between Lacan and Derrida, and, indeed, between both these thinkers and Foucault, becomes richer, more complex, and less polemically adversarial. And with this, one begins to see, perhaps, that not all discourses function according to the same logic, and that our thinking has more resources, more possibilities, more differences than this.

References

Agamben, G. (1999). *Potentialities.* (D. Heller-Roazen, Trans.). Stanford, CA: Stanford University Press.

Aristotle. (1933). *Metaphysics.* (H. Tredenick, Trans.). Cambridge, MA: Harvard University Press.

Cornell, D., Rosenfeld, M., & Carlson, D. (1992). *Deconstruction and the possibility of justice.* New York, NY: Routledge.

Derrida, J. (1993). *Aporias.* (T. Dutoit, Trans.). Stanford, CA: Stanford University Press.

———. (1995). Khōra. In T. Dutoit (Ed. and Trans.), *On the name* (pp. 89-130). Stanford, CA: Stanford University Press.

———. (2002). Force of law: "The mystical foundation of authority". In G. Anidjar (Ed.), *Acts of Religion* (pp. 228-298). New York, NY: Routledge.

Lacan, J. (1998). *The seminar. Book XX: Encore: On feminine sexuality, the limits of love and knowledge. 1972-1973.* (B. Fink, Trans.). New York, NY: W. W. Norton and Company.

Rose, G. (1996). *Mourning becomes the law: Philosophy and representation.* Cambridge: Cambridge University Press.

Shepherdson, C. (2003). Lacan and philosophy. In J. Rabaté (Ed.), *The Cambridge companion to Lacan* (pp. 116-152). Cambridge: Cambridge University Press.

Section II
Sexuality in Practice

The Sexual Animal and the Primal Scene

Elissa Marder

Although Freud's most famous and most notoriously difficult case history *From the History of an Infantile Neurosis* has received extensive commentary, there is one important question that has attracted surprisingly little attention up until now. In this case, best known by its evocative hybrid name *Wolf Man*, animals populate virtually every page, but very little has been said about the status of the animal as such.[1] Indeed, it may be almost impossible to speak about the animal "as such", precisely because the many animals and animal figures in the case operate at so many different and mutually exclusive levels of reality and psychic organization. There is, in fact, a vertiginous array of fauna, a veritable bestiary in the text. Aside from the famous wolves, there are important references to sheep, sheep dogs, flies and beetles, caterpillars, snakes, horses, a wasp, goats, a fledgling bird, a giant caterpillar, a snail, and, finally, a swallowtail butterfly that, we discover, is a second animal incarnation of the same anxiety that produced the famous wolf dream. Some of these animals are representations that come from fairy tales and picture books, some are produced as dream-images, and some are animals encountered in the world. And some are animals that stand in for humans. In short, the animals are not always, or not simply, animals. More problematically still, it seems that animals can move from one status to another with remarkable flexibility. In the pages that follow, I hope to show how animal figures operate at every level of the case and intervene in its conceptual framework in complicated ways. Indeed, I hope to demonstrate that animals occupy a critical, albeit somewhat obscure role in many, if not most, of the major theoretical issues raised by the case. These include the temporal status of the primal scene and the structure of *Nachträglichkeit*, the relationship between the primal scene and primal fantasies, the specificity of infantile sexuality, primal repression and the formation of the unconscious, castration and sexual difference, and

[1] There are several important exceptions to this claim. Most notably, Gilles Deleuze and Félix Guattari have famously taken up Freud's treatment of the number of the wolves in *Wolf Man* (Deleuze & Guattari, 1987). Also see: Genosko (1993) and Tyler (2008).

the grounds for establishing the distinction between instinct (*Instinkt*) and drive (*Trieb*).[2]

Before going any further, I want to make it clear from the outset that I am not arguing in favour of any continuity between the human and the animal realms. On the contrary, I hope to argue that, paradoxically, the animals in the text serve as strange indices to the very specificity of the human psyche. My aim in looking more closely at them is to bring the enigma of human sexuality and subjectivity more clearly into focus. Bizarrely, in what follows, it will emerge that one of the defining traits of being human is the incorporation of animal figures within the psyche; these internal animal figures are uncanny traces of our radical alterity and separation from animals.

Let me begin by returning to the famous primal scene itself. In an attempt to demonstrate the fundamental role played by infantile sexuality in individual psychic life, Freud dedicates his entire case to the derivation and discussion of the strange event known as "the primal scene". As readers of Freud well know, the term "primal scene" refers to Freud's reconstruction of an early, traumatic event: an act of coitus witnessed by the patient when he was too young to comprehend what he was seeing. On the basis of a subsequent childhood dream about wolves, analyzed as part of the treatment of the adult patient, Freud meticulously reconstitutes the existence of the traumatic event, the presumed date of its occurrence, and the precise details of the sexual content in the scene.

In order to understand why this scene is so important for Freud, one should keep in mind that the precipitating event can never be recovered by memory because it occurred before the infant had developed the capacity either to remember it or to understand it. The dream that the child produces two and

[2] In writing this paper, I have been greatly aware of the monumental contributions of Jean Laplanche concerning the primal scene and with it, fantasy, seduction, sexuality and *Nachträglichkeit*. A longer version of this paper would have to make this debt to Laplanche clearer. Also, Laplanche's work is itself divided into different periods and positions. In *Essays on Otherness*, for example, he explicitly criticizes claims about the Wolf Man made in his own earlier work (with Pontalis), *Fantasy and the Origins of Sexuality*. In thinking about the question about the specificity of human sexuality, I have also been greatly helped by Philippe Van Haute and Tomas Geyskens' recent book, *Confusion of Tongues*. In addition, I have also been influenced by André Green's recent writings on sexuality. Lacan is also unavoidable although I have done my very best to avoid him here. Although most of the following works are not addressed directly in this paper, they were all very much present in the "background" of my thinking about it: Abraham, Torok and Derrida (1986); Green (2000); Van Haute and Geyskens (2004); Laplanche (1980); Laplanche and Pontalis (1973); Laplanche and Pontalis (1999); Laplanche and Fletcher (1999).

a half years later therefore serves both as a belated recognition of the meaning of the scene and as a psychic response to it.

In thinking about the primal scene, it is important not to lose sight of the fact that the scene itself happens "twice", as it were, and involves at least two different events. In the first instance, there is the so called "real" external event witnessed by the infant. Because the precipitating event was "seen" without being assimilated, traces left by the images that were not understood from the first scene reappear, belatedly, in the dream about wolves that takes place several years later. The first traumatic event is both represented *in* the dream and reactivated *by* it. What this means is that the dream is not only a belated reproduction of the initial scene, but also that the dream itself constitutes a new event as well.

The "primal scene" must thus be understood as the relationship between these two limit events. The first, ostensibly "real" event is something that happens to the infant *before* the development of the unconscious, while the second event – the wolf dream – is not only entirely produced *by* the unconscious but is also evidence of its prior formation. Both events are traumatic in nature: the initial event overwhelms the infant and, in doing so, *activates* the psychic mechanisms from which the unconscious will be formed, whereas the dream about wolves is the psychic trace of an overpowering anxiety coming from within.

Almost all of the determining events in the case history take place during the time between these two traumas. Indeed, the "reconstructed" chronology that Freud helpfully provides in a footnote at the end of the text confirms that all of the relevant action in the case concerns events (both "real" and "psychic") that take place during this early childhood period. Put crudely, and perhaps too crudely, one might say Freud makes use of the primal scene as an attempt to make the unconscious visible, as it were. More specifically, by using the two traumatic poles of the primal scene in order to provide a temporal frame for the childhood events through which psyche and sexuality take shape, Freud is able to provide a means of representing the impact of "infantile sexuality" without relying exclusively on biological or developmental paradigms. In other words, however fantastic or fictive the image of the primal scene may appear to be, the aim of it is to document how an individual infant becomes marked as fully "human", as it were, *during* early childhood and in response to specific infantile sexual events. In this sense, the primal scene resembles something like a kind of photographic apparatus capable of capturing the impossible moment at which the psyche comes into being. It comes into being, that is, as a specifically *human* psyche – and, hence, is susceptible to perverse fixations, phobias and hysteria. Paradoxically, however, the child's dream about wolves is the sign that he has become fully "human". The very event of the wolf dream is evidence both of the fact that he is now suffering from a specifically human conflict and that his psyche is now capable of registering and processing that distress by making a dream out of it.

At this juncture (and this will become significant later on), it is interesting to note that the wolf dream does not resemble a *typical* child's dream, precisely because of the degree of distortion involved in it. As Freud explains in chapter III of *The Interpretation of Dreams*, typical children's dreams are literal and literal-minded. They are the pure, undistorted expression of a simple wish. He writes:

> The dreams of young children are frequently pure wish fulfillments and are in that case quite uninteresting compared with the dreams of adults. They raise no problems for solution; but on the other hand they are of inestimable importance in proving that, in their essential nature, dreams represent fulfillments of wishes. (Freud, 1900, p. 127)

It is not accidental that Freud concludes his discussion about typical children's dreams by invoking a speculative analogy between them and animal dreams:

> I do not myself know what animals dream of. But a proverb, to which my attention was drawn by one of my students, does claim to know. "What" asks the proverb, "do geese dream of?" And it replies: "Of maize". The whole theory that dreams are wish fulfillments is contained in these two phrases. (ibid., pp. 131-132)

Of course, as Freud knows perfectly well, and as he goes on to argue in the following chapter, dreams are not merely wishes, but manifestations of *unconscious* wishes. It is precisely because of the unbreachable divide between conscious and unconscious registers that the dream work (including condensation, displacement, distortion, etc.) becomes necessary.

The comparison between children's dreams and animal dreams is merely one instance of Freud's more general and common claim that children and animals are especially close to one another. But the precise rationale for this particular proximity is arguably more complicated than it might appear to be at first glance. On the one hand, Freud often suggests or implies (as in the passage from *The Interpretation of Dreams* cited above) that children are close to animals because they *resemble* them. According to this logic, children are similar to animals because, like animals, they are governed by instinctual or biological needs. But Freud also regularly suggests that children are close to animals not because they resemble the animals themselves, but because they resemble primitive man and hence share his predisposition for engaging in totemic practices. However, proximity to animals based on instinctual continuity and biological similarity is qualitatively different from proximity based on totemism, because where the first case presumes the existence of genuinely shared traits, the second one posits instead a representational structure (the totem) founded upon a "misrecognition" or denial of species difference. Thus, following the logic of totemism, primitive people are especially close to animals not because they are actually *like* them, but rather because of their inability to recognize the difference between them. This failed recognition of difference is apparently linked to the origin of representation itself, as identification with totem animals seemingly gives rise to the need to make use of animals as symbolic substitutes for humans. However, it should be remembered that this particular form of failure to recognize the difference between humans and animals is, after all, the very hallmark of human culture. Animals do not seem to display the same profound need or propensity for inter-species identification. In other words, in general, we do not suspect that wolves commonly dream of little boys even if little boys commonly dream of wolves.

Keeping this in mind, let us now return to the wolf dream. As we have already observed, the wolf dream is not merely a simple "representation" of the observed act of coitus but, rather, a psychic repetition and re-enactment of it. When reactivated in and by the dream, the primal scene conveys new information to the psyche about the event as well as new psychic effects. But if we look more closely at the specific meaning that Freud attributes to it in Part IV of the case history, we discover that the wolf dream combines, condenses and confuses three related questions concerning three different kinds of (sexual) differences: the difference between children and adults, the difference between men and women, and the difference between humans and animals. Through the medium of the dream, Freud explains, the child simultaneously "discovers" the existence of the vagina and develops a wolf phobia in function of that traumatic discovery:

> The activation of the primal scene in the dream now brought him back to the genital organization. He discovered the vagina and the biological significance of masculine and feminine. He understood now that active was the same as masculine, while passive was the same as feminine. His passive sexual aim should now have been transformed into a feminine one, and having expressed itself as "being copulated with by his father" instead of "being beaten by him on the genitals or on the bottom". This

> feminine aim, however, underwent repression and was obliged to let itself be replaced by fear of the wolf. (Freud, 1918, p. 47)

But the very discovery of "sexual difference" (the existence of the vagina) that is revealed *by* the dream is expressed *in* the dream through the substitution of animals in place of human figures. In the dream (re)activation of the earlier scene during which the child ostensibly witnessed *sexual* difference without understanding it, multiple wolves (who are not sexually differentiated from one another) become the tell-tale indicators of human sexual difference. In other words, the only way *human* sexual difference can be perceived or represented in the scene is through the mediation and substitution of animal figures for human ones. The subsequent emergence of the symptom of the wolf phobia (which is an effect of the dream rather than part of its explicit narrative content) indicates both that sexual difference has been recognized and that it has been repressed.

Although the questions raised by the wolf phobia are extremely important (and I will discuss them briefly later on), for the time being I would like to continue to look even more closely at how the observation of sexual difference in the primal scene is predicated upon yet another set of confusions between humans and animals. In his famous reconstruction of the act of coitus that the infant must have seen, Freud is adamant about one precise and indispensable detail: the specific postures adopted in the sexual act. He famously (and repeatedly) uses the Latin phrases "*more ferarum*" (in the manner of the animals) and "*a tergo*" (from behind), to describe these postures. As he will go on to explain, Freud's case is predicated upon the idea that only "animal-like sex" (or sex in the manner of animals) renders the genitals visible enough for the infant to perceive the evidence of sexual difference. It is this animal inspired "picture" of the revelation of the genitals that traumatizes the young child and triggers the belated production of the dream images of the wolves. Here is how Freud describes how this picture of animal-like figures gives rise to the dream of the primal scene:

> What sprang into activity that night out of the chaos of the dreamer's unconscious memory-traces was the picture of copulation between his parents, copulation in circumstances which were not entirely usual and were especially favourable for observation (ibid., p. 36). … When he woke up, he witnessed a coitus *a tergo* [from behind], three times repeated; he was able to see his mother's genitals as well as his father's organ; and he understood the process as well as its significance (ibid., pp. 37-38). … We will first proceed with the study of the relations

> between this "primal scene" and the patient's dream, his symptoms, and the history of his life; and we will trace separately the effects that followed from the essential content of the scene and from one its visual impressions. By the latter I mean the postures which he saw his parents adopt – the man upright, and the woman bent down like an animal [*die aufrechte des Mannes und die tierähnlich gebückte der Frau*]. (ibid., p. 39 [1989, p. 158])

These passages come from Part IV of the case history. At this point in his argument, Freud presents this detailed and precise visual description of the "pictures" witnessed by the infant during the primal scene in order to substantiate his claim that the event in question really "happened", and that what the child saw was an act of copulation between his two parents. But it is striking that in Freud's derivation of the scene, the child comes into contact with human sexuality and confronts sexual difference only when the humans involved do not appear to act like humans, but like animals. Once again, human sexuality becomes visible only when humans behave like animals. In the dream of wolves, therefore, the animal figures are distorted substitutes for human figures that are themselves imitating animal postures.

But there is still another detail in Freud's description that further complicates the scene. Throughout the case history, Freud not only insists that the sexual act was performed (three times) from behind, but he also places great emphasis on the difference between the posture adopted by the woman and that assumed by the man. He specifies that the man is upright, but that the woman is "bent down like an animal". Although both figures are engaged in animal-style sex, they are "animal-like" to different degrees: the man is erect and upright like a human figure, whereas the woman is explicitly compared to an animal in the language of the text. Thus it would seem that the figure of the woman is more of an animal than the figure of the man. The animal sexual act in which they are both engaged erases all traces of her "human" status, while there is some confusion concerning the species status of the upright man. It would appear that these images do not only convey information about sexual difference, but also information about species difference at the same time. In other words, the picture in the scene seems to show that to be a woman is to be more like an animal than a man.

These "postural" differences play a crucial role in Freud's interpretation of the case, as he goes on to insist that, although the wolves in the dream represent both his father and his mother, the wolf figure that gives rise to the boy's wolf phobia is a symptom of his repressed desire for his father and is related to him alone. According to Freud, the initial scene witnessed by the boy aroused his desire for his father and elicited an identification with his mother and her animal posture. In the wake of the dream, however, and in response to the "discovery" of castration and sexual difference conveyed by it, the boy's desire for the father becomes repressed and the father himself becomes transformed into a terrifying wolf. But not just any kind of scary wolf; the wolf in the phobia is an erect and human-like, upright wolf. This wolf does not live in the "real world" and, therefore, cannot be observed in it. A wolf such as this exists only in the imagination: it is a product of the mind and can only be found there or in picture books.

The "imaginary" nature of the source of this animal phobia deserves some attention as it potentially troubles some of the assumptions and claims that Freud makes more generally regarding the function and meaning of animal phobias. For Freud, the emergence of animal phobias in young boys is always a symptom of fear of castration by the father. The function of the phobia is to contain the internal conflict (fear of castration by the father) by isolating and externalizing it. Through the phobia, the fear of a seemingly omnipotent and omnipresent father is displaced onto an external animal substitute for him. In this way, the phobia insures both that the fear-inducing animal father figure can be mostly avoided, and that the real human father can be tolerated. Freud makes this general argument in several texts, but the meta-psychological stakes of the discussion of animal phobias perhaps appear most notably in *Totem and Taboo* and *Inhibitions, Symptoms and Anxiety*. In both of these texts he explicitly invokes the *Wolf Man* alongside his other famous case of infantile neurosis, *Little Hans,* in order to derive and explain the existence of castration anxiety and its essential link to the concept of death and fear of the father. Here is how he describes the mechanism in *Inhibitions, Symptoms, and Anxiety*:

> We have said that as soon as the ego recognizes the danger of castration it gives the signal of anxiety and inhibits through the pleasure-unpleasure agency (in a way which we cannot yet understand) the impending cathectic process in the id. At the same time the phobia is formed. And now the castration anxiety is directed to a different object and expressed in a distorted form, so that the patient is afraid, not of being castrated by his father, but of being bitten by a horse or devoured by a wolf. The substitute formation has two obvious advantages. In the first place it avoids a conflict due to ambivalence (for the father was a loved object, too) and in the second place it enables the ego to cease generating anxiety. For the anxiety belonging to a phobia is conditional; it only emerges when the object is perceived – and rightly

> so, since it is only then that the danger-situation is present. There is no need to be afraid of being castrated by a father who is not there. On the other hand, one cannot get rid of a father; he can appear whenever he chooses. But if he is replaced by an animal, all one has to do is to avoid the sight of it – that is – its presence – in order to be free from danger and anxiety. (Freud, 1926, pp. 125-126)

Although Freud's understanding of the *structure* of the animal phobia is fairly straightforward, its meta-psychological status is more problematic, as he seems to vacillate between two semi-tautological positions: sometimes he seems to *prove* the theory of castration anxiety based on his analysis of the clinical example, and sometimes he posits castration and then *explains* the phobia on the basis of the theory. And sometimes he seemingly does both at once by arguing that, although the specific connection between the animal phobia and castration is *innate* and thereby possesses a privileged relation to the prehistory of the psyche, this "predisposition" only produces a phobia in function of specific childhood psychic "sexual" events.

But the argument that the animal phobia is *both* a function of pre-historic knowledge of castration *and* a specific response to childhood events depends, once again, on the presumption of an ambiguous "special proximity" between boy children and large animals, and the specific psychic malleability of the figure of the animal itself. This double function is particularly evident in Freud's off-hand allusions to "totemic thought" in his presentation of the case of *Little Hans* in *Inhibitions, Symptoms and Anxiety*:

> What made it a neurosis was one thing alone: the replacement of his father by a horse. It is this displacement, then, which has a claim to be called a symptom. ... Such a displacement is made possible or facilitated at "Little Hans's" early stage because the inborn traces of totemic thought can still be easily revived. Children do not yet recognize or, at any rate, lay such an exaggerated stress upon the gulf that separates human beings from the animal world. In their eyes the grown man, the object of their fear and admiration, still belongs to the same category as the big animal who has so many enviable attributes but against whom they have been warned because he may become dangerous. (ibid., p. 103)

Freud is here suggesting that, despite the fact that the animal phobia in question is a unique psychic response to a specific early sexual conflict, the emergence of the phobia relies upon an inborn predisposition to fear of animals based upon a heightened identification with them and with their observable (and presumably genital) "enviable attributes". In this way, the animal figure has a specifically privileged relationship to the sexual dramas of childhood; it both prepares the psyche for the experience of infantile sexuality and produces visible traces of its effects. Once again, therefore, the animal figures precede and usurp human figures in the demarcation of sexual difference. In passing, it is interesting to note that Freud explicitly clarifies that everything he says about animal phobias pertains to little boys and only to little boys. And, as the explanation of the structure of the animal phobia makes clear, the drama of castration and sexual difference is now played out between the boy, his father, and his animal father substitute. When animal figures are present, the female figures apparently disappear from the scene.

In light of these remarks, if we now return to the case of the *Wolf Man*, we discover that the treatment of animal phobias in this text seem to present some special difficulties for the general theory outlined above. In the first place, the source of the wolf phobia is an imaginary animal rather than an animal observed by the boy in the world. Although Freud himself acknowledges this point, his explanation of it leaves several important questions unanswered. He writes:

> This phobia was only distinguished by other similar cases by the fact that the anxiety-animal was not an object easily accessible to observation (such as a horse or a dog), but was known to him only from stories and picture-books. (Freud, 1918, p. 32)

There are several problems with this. In the first place, the fact that the anxiety-animal is both relatively inaccessible and imaginary seems to undercut its potential ability to isolate and externalize the fear of the father inspired by it. Furthermore, according to Freud's text, the image of the dream wolves (which precipitates the phobia) is a creation of the psyche itself. The image of the dream-wolf is not merely an imaginary animal; it is the very product of the child's imagination: a composite figure composed of elements taken from fairy tale wolves and goats, real dead sheep, and real sheep dogs that the child may or may not have seen copulating. Although the wolves in the fairy tales and picture books provide some of the raw material for the wolf dream, Freud himself argues that the figure of the "erect wolf" that forms the source of the phobia does not, in fact, come from the fairy tale material, but rather from the primal "real" images of the upright father in the primal scene. In other words, the picture book wolves are merely mediating figures that provide an associative link between the traumatic primal images of the real human father and his subsequent wolf avatar. Unlike in the case of *Little Hans*, however, it is the human father himself who ostensibly provides the source images according to which the anxiety-animal is subsequently chosen rather than the other way around. As Freud points out, the critical element in the phobia is not the figure of the wolf itself, but its "erect posture":

> The wolf that he was afraid of was undoubtedly his father; but his fear of the wolf was conditioned upon the creature being in an upright position. His recollection asserted most definitely that he had not been terrified by pictures of wolves going on all fours or, as in the story of "Little Red Riding-Hood", lying in bed. The posture which, according to our construction of the primal scene, he had seen the woman assume, was of no less significance; though in this case the significance was limited to the sexual sphere. (ibid., pp. 40-41)

As it happens, these two different sexual "postures" or positions determine and correspond to two different and competing psychic positions concerning the status of sexual difference in the life of the patient. While I cannot discuss this here in detail, Freud makes it clear (and this point will be of interest later to Lacan), that, although the wolf phobia (and the erect male posture in it) is presumably a sign that the patient has "understood" sexual difference, he also continues to "deny" or "disavow" both castration and sexual difference. He maintains a life-long identification with his mother through the bowels as well as a powerful sexual fixation on women who assume a posture "bent down like an animal" proffering the buttocks. Freud will return to this patient's famous "disavowal" of sexual difference in his paper on *Fetishism* (Freud, 1927).[3] But there is also a third, hidden element in this scene that further fractures the patient's split "understanding" of sexual difference. That third element is death and, like sexual difference, it is conveyed through animal mediation in the material that arises from the primal scene and determines the dream. And, although this topic exceeds the scope of this paper, I would simply like to point out here that the child's quest for sexual knowledge coincides and crosses with evidence of the existence of death throughout in the case. Here is how Freud announces it in Part IV:

> There were several conclusions, too, to be drawn from the raw material which had been produced by the patient's first analysis of the dream,

[3] According to Abraham and Torok, Freud based his discussion in *Fetishism* of the patient whose fetish expressed itself through the multilingual pun "the shine on the nose" (*Glanz auf der Nase)* on material about the Wolf Man that he received from Ruth Mack Brunswick, in the course of her subsequent analysis of him. See: Abraham, Torok and Derrida (1986, pp. 31-32).

> and these had to be fitted into the collocation of which we were in search. Behind the mention of the sheep-breeding, evidence was to be expected of his sexual researches, his interests in which he was able to gratify during his visits with his father, but there must also have been allusions to a fear of death, since the greater part of the sheep had died of the epidemic. (Freud, 1918, p. 34)

If I mention the dead sheep at this juncture, it is in part in response to a rather astonishing assertion that appears in several of Jean Laplanche's rigorous and provocative treatments of this case history. In two of his more recent essays (most notably in *The Unfinished Copernican Revolution* and *Seduction, Persecution, Revelation*), Laplanche invokes the *Wolf Man* in order to rethink the status of seduction and the meaning of the "primal scene". For Laplanche, the importance of the primal scene lies in the inherently traumatic nature of the enigmatic sexual messages that are exchanged between adults and children. He argues that a primal scene is never something simply related to sexual content, but rather arises from the parents' active (and unconscious) communicative participation in the scene. However, in both of the essays mentioned above, he not only argues that Freud overlooks the role played by the parents, but also specifically suggests that the father actively takes the young boy to the sheep fields in order to expose him to the sight of animals copulating. In both instances in which Laplanche invokes this imagined (and arguably invented) scenario, his own rhetoric becomes strangely excessive. In *The Unfinished Copernican Revolution*, for example, he writes himself into the scene by describing it in the first person: "[W]hat is it this father wants of me by showing me, letting me see this primal scene, even if only by taking me to a field to witness animal coitus?" (Laplanche and Fletcher, 1999, p. 78), and in *Seduction, Persecution, Revelation* he produces a truly extraordinary association in the footnote that accompanies his reference to the *Wolf Man*. Laplanche writes, "When the Wolf Man's father takes the child to watch the animals copulating, are we really to imagine that nothing but an innocent stroll is intended?" (ibid., p. 170). But in the footnote to this suggestive claim about the suggestive stroll, Laplanche adds, "What could be less innocent than a stroll? I remember that, during the occupation, the few French words the German soldiers knew were '*Promenade, mademoiselle?*' a sexual invitation, coded as such" (ibid.).

Although Freud's text does clearly specify that the boy's visits to the sheep fields with his father were a particular source of pleasure for him, the text never indicates that the father explicitly or directly exposed him to the sight of animals copulating. Furthermore, and I think this is significant, Laplanche never mentions the role that is played by the animal in the transmission and production of this specific "enigmatic message" nor the fact, emphasized repeatedly by Freud, that the (beloved) sheep die from an epidemic and hence, by implication, that the father was unable to save them or somehow participated in their death. Curiously, Laplanche has not only erased the importance of the animal from the scene, but has also inserted a peculiarly over-determined personal memory from the German occupation of France into it. Laplanche's rendition of the scene transforms the encounter between a father, his son, and some animals who may or may not be copulating but some of whom are certainly dying into a sexual encounter between a man and a woman who do not speak the same language. Given his commitment to the importance of the irreducibly enigmatic nature of "primal scenes", it is understandable why Laplanche might be inclined to downplay the importance of the animal figures. However, I am suggesting here that the animals in Freud's text are not merely the brute instinctual and biological alternative to human sexuality (as Laplanche tends to imply) but, rather, that they might turn out to play a critical role in the production and transmission of "enigmatic messages" between humans. In other words, I am arguing that Laplanche's "enigmatic messages" may not be enigmatic *enough*, and that, paradoxically, the animal figure comes to stand in for something in the human sexual experience that cannot be translated, transferred, or communicated at all.

Although I must bring this discussion to a close for the time being, I have not yet come to many of the central – and, indeed, most famous – questions concerning the critical importance of the animal element in the *Wolf Man*. Thus far, I have focused almost exclusively on part IV of Freud's text, *The Dream and the Primal Scene*. This is the chapter in which Freud analyzes the wolf dream and derives the reality of the primal scene from it. However, as readers of *Wolf Man* well know, the text does not end with the derivation of the primal scene. Instead, in section V of the case history, Freud famously produces an alternative explanation for the event that gives rise to the primal scene. In this version, the traumatic images of coitus between the child's parents are the product of a retroactive fantasy projection based upon real images of an observed act of coitus performed by animals, not humans. And then, in the remaining four sections of the text, Freud simultaneously (1) argues that the fact that the coitus may have been performed by animals is not significant for his essential understanding of the structure and meaning of the primal scene and (2) presents "new" material that ostensibly substantiates his initial hypothesis that the primal scene was a real, witnessed event of coitus between his parents. Unfortunately, I cannot explore these issues in depth here.

Therefore, by way of conclusion, I would like to indicate, albeit telegraphically and suggestively, some of the points that merit further discussion.

(a) Although Freud does present two versions to explain the structure of the primal scene (real event vs. fantasy), it is interesting to note that the status of the so-called "reality" of the event also determines the status of the "reality" of the animals in question. In other words, if the primal scene is "real", then the animals (wolves) in the scene are imaginary, but if the scene itself is a fantasy, then the animals are necessarily real (child observes dogs copulating). The reality of the "event" of copulation is never put into question, merely the species status of the performers in the sexual scene. The section in which Freud introduces the two versions of the scene is section V. Section V is the precise midpoint of the text and of Freud's convoluted argument. Furthermore, the meaning of the roman numeral "V" will later be introduced as material in the case history. The arguments *in* section "V" of the text are retroactively inflected by Freud's discussion of the meaning of the roman numeral "V" in conjunction with another animal phobia, the phobia of the "swallowtail" butterfly.

(b) The central importance of the butterfly emerges in section VIII. Through an analysis of the memory of the phobia of the butterfly, Freud discovers "new material" on the basis of which he claims to have proven the reality of the primal scene. In section VIII, Freud explains that, throughout the analysis, the patient produced a recurrent childhood memory of chasing a beautiful big butterfly covered with yellow stripes. When the butterfly settled on a flower, the patient became seized with a terrible anxiety. From the evidence provided by the anxiety provoked by the movement of the butterfly's wings (that formed a "V"), along with the multi-lingual verbal associations produced by the image of the yellow stripes, Freud and the patient reconstruct the memory of an ancient and hitherto unremembered primal memory: the scene of seduction with "Grusha". According to Freud, this scene (in which the young boy, just over two years old, responds to the sight of "Grusha" scrubbing the floor on her hands and knees by urinating in excitement) provides the earliest evidence of the psychic traces produced by that primal scene. According to Freud, the movements by Grusha in the scene awaken the dormant image of the primal scene and provoke a re-enactment of it. Paradoxically, however, Freud bases his proof of the irrefutable reality of the irretrievable primal scene on the reconstructed, recovered memory of a repetition of it in the second scene. By uncovering traces (or after-images) of the primal scene in its first *repetition*, Freud claims to have finally truly "corroborated" the reality of the first one. In this sense, the primal scene "really" occurs not once, but twice; each time, it is associated with an animal phobia. In this instance, however, the animal is not an imaginary wolf, but a real butterfly. The butterfly, however, is an animal that the patiently explicitly marks as "feminine". Freud writes:

> It then appeared that his fear of the butterfly was in every respect analogous to his fear of the wolf; in both cases it was a fear of castration, which was, to begin with, referred to the person who had first uttered the threat of castration, but was then transposed on to another person to whom it was bound to become attached in accordance to phylogenetic precedence. (Freud, 1918, p. 96)

Once again, there is ambiguity concerning the nature of the link between castration and animal phobias. Here, the animal producing the phobia is marked as feminine and the person who supposedly uttered the threat of castration is feminine; nonetheless, Freud will argue that the butterfly phobia, like the wolf phobia, is both a response to the primal scene (via its repetition in the scene with Grusha) and a reincarnation of the earlier wolf phobia. The wolf and the butterfly are merely two different *animal* forms of the same "human" idea: fear of castration by the father. Furthermore, for Freud, the fact that the wolf turns into a butterfly does not deter him from arguing for the determinant "precedence" of the "phylogenetic" meaning of the animal phobia according to which the father is central to the scene and the mother is absent from it.

(c) In the final paragraphs of the *Wolf Man*, Freud's argument takes a final and enigmatic twist. After having vigorously argued for the essential role played by individual infantile sexuality throughout the entire case, and, thus, for the radical specificity of human sexuality (as opposed to animal instinct), Freud famously ends his case by invoking a form of sexual knowledge in humans that is something "like" instinctual animal knowledge about sex. Although these passages have been the object of compelling and complex commentary by Jean Laplanche, I would like to suggest that perhaps it is the very status of the "animal analogy" that needs to be further explored here. What Freud actually says, however, is that he is unable to find an adequate representative form or a conception for this deepest and most foundational stratum of human sexuality. And here, once again, when he struggles to convey the idea of that which is most foundational and "primal", he introduces an "animal figure" to stand in for what cannot be conceived otherwise:

> If one considers the behaviour of the four-year-old child towards the re-activated primal scene or even if one thinks of the far simpler reactions of the one-and-a-half-year-old child when the scene was

> actually experienced, it is hard to dismiss the view that some sort of hardly definable knowledge, something, as it were, preparatory to an understanding, was at work in the child at the time. We can form no conception of what this may have consisted in; and we have nothing at our disposal but the single analogy – and it is an excellent one – of the far-reaching *instinctive* knowledge of animals. [*Worin dies bestehen mag, entzieht sich jeder Vorstellung; wir haben nur die eine ausgezeichnete Analogie mit dem weitgehenden instinktiven Wissen des Tiere zur Verfügung*]. (ibid., p.120 [1989, p. 230])

In this final picture of *Wolf Man*'s "primal scene", via the last resort of this unique yet "excellent" animal analogy, sexual difference and human subjectivity come into being, through each other, in an absolute and obscure proximity to the very animality from which they are born.

References

Abraham, N., Torok, M., & Derrida, J. (1986). *The Wolf Man's magic word: A cryptonymy*. Theory and History of Literature: Vol. 37. Minneapolis, MN: University of Minnesota Press.

Deleuze, G., & Guattari, F. (1987). 1914: One or several wolves. In *A thousand plateaus: Capitalism and schizophrenia* (B. Massumi, Trans.) (pp. 26-38). Minneapolis, MN: University of Minnesota Press.

Freud, S. (1900). The interpretation of dreams. *Standard Edition 4*.

———. (1918). From the history of an infantile neurosis. *Standard Edition 17*, pp. 1-122. [German: (1989). *Studienausgabe: Zwei Kinderneurosen*. Frankfurt am Main: S. Fischer Verlag].

———. (1926). Inhibitions, symptoms, and anxiety. *Standard Edition 20*, pp. 77-172.

———. (1927). Fetishism. *Standard Edition 21*, pp. 47-57.

Genosko, G. (1993). Freud's bestiary: How does psychoanalysis treat animals? *Psychoanalytic Review, 80(4)*, 603-632.

Green, A. (2000). *Le temps éclaté*. Paris: Editions de Minuit.

Laplanche, J. (1980). *Castration-symbolisations: Problematiques II*. Paris: PUF.

Laplanche, J., & Pontalis, J. B. (1973). *Vocabulaire de la psychanalyse*. Paris: PUF.

———. (1999). *Fantasme originaire: Fantasmes des origines, origines du fantasme*. Paris: Hachette.

Laplanche, J., & Fletcher, J. (1999). *Essays on otherness*. London/New York, NY: Routledge.

Tyler, T. (2008). The quiescent ass and the dumbstruck wolf. *Configurations, 14(1)*, 9-28.

Van Haute, P., & Geyskens, T. (2004). *Confusion of tongues: The primacy of sexuality in Freud, Ferenczi and Laplanche*. New York, NY: Other Press.

Between Disposition, Trauma, and History – How Oedipal was Dora?

Philippe Van Haute & Tomas Geyskens

Introduction

In contradistinction to what has often been said (Kris, 1986; Anzieu, 1988; Masson, 1992; Borch-Jacobsen & Shamdasani, 2006), the abandonment of the seduction theory by Freud in 1897 ("I don't believe in my 'neurotica' anymore") did not mean that, thenceforth, he thought that the traumas his patients told him about were nothing but oedipally motivated fantasies.[1] Nor does it imply that trauma no longer played a significant role in Freud's theory of pathogenesis. It merely means that Freud gave up his belief in the *etiological* significance of trauma for pathology. From then on, this role was fulfilled, instead, by a "sexual disposition or constitution" (Freud, 1906) and by bisexuality. This disposition is systematically articulated for the first time in the first edition of Freud's famous *Three Essays on the Theory of Sexuality* (1905b). The Oedipus complex acquires increasing significance as the nuclear complex of the neuroses only subsequently, in the years following the publication of the first edition (Van Haute, 2002).

This interpretation can best be illustrated by a detailed reading of Freud's *Fragment of an Analysis of a Case of Hysteria ("Dora")* (1905a), which might be considered as a clinical complement to the *Three Essays*. Such a reading shows that the oedipal problematic only plays a marginal role in Freud's understanding of this case. It makes clear that in this text Freud develops a theory of psychopathology in general and of hysteria in particular, in which a "(hysterical, organic) disposition" is linked to trauma in an original and decisive way.

Our interpretation of the abandonment of the theory of seduction has several consequences. From an *historical* point of view, it obliges us to radically reinterpret Freud's famous dictum that he "no longer believed in his 'neurotica'". From a *therapeutic* point of view, the reference to an "organic disposition" implies that already very early on – and certainly much earlier than is commonly believed – Freud relativized the efficiency of psychoanalytical therapy while, at the same time, acknowledging the crucial importance of "or-

[1] We only know of one exception to this classical interpretation (Blass, 1992).

ganic" factors for understanding pathology. Psychoanalysis only has an effect on the symptoms that follow from the disposition and not on the disposition as such. From a *theoretical* point of view, the reference to bisexuality confronts us with the structural dissolution and uncertainty of gender-identifications as the basic problem of hysteria (and of human existence). This also means that symptoms can no longer be linked to a unique desire that can be identified as such. The belief in such a desire is probably the "metaphysical presupposition" par excellence that governs psychoanalytical thinking in many of its variants (Derrida, 1967; Borch-Jacobsen, 1982). Perhaps this is also the more fundamental reason why Freud, in the years following the publication of the *Dora* case, progressively omits any reference to bisexuality as an explanatory factor for understanding pathology.

The Dora Case

(a) Two Traumas

Freud first met Dora when she was sixteen. She was suffering from hoarseness and a nervous cough (Freud, 1905a, p. 22), but, since these symptoms disappeared spontaneously, no treatment was started. Two years later, however, after finding a suicide note and after Dora lost consciousness following a trivial argument with him, her father decided that therapy was needed after all. Freud diagnosed Dora as a case of "*petite hystérie*" (ibid., p. 23). She was suffering from a range of rather trivial bodily and psychic symptoms – aphonia, dyspnoea, nervous cough, feelings of depression, migraine attacks – for which no organic basis could be found and whose psychic meaning remained unclear.

Already at the beginning of his study on Dora, Freud states that the psychic conditions for hysteria that he and Breuer had described in their *Studies on Hysteria* – psychic trauma, conflict between the affects, and a disturbance in the sphere of sexuality (ibid., p. 24) – are also present in Dora. Regarding the trauma(s) that played a crucial role in her life, Dora's father told Freud about an incident that occurred when she was sixteen and that, according to him, explained her depressive state and suicidal thoughts (ibid., p. 23). During a walk at a lake with Herr K., a close friend of the family with whom they spent a lot of time, the latter declared his love to her. Dora reacted vehemently: she slapped Herr K. in the face and ran away. But can this incident in itself be a sufficient condition for Dora's hysteria, Freud asks. In any case, it does not explain the specific nature of Dora's symptoms. Indeed, it is difficult to establish a meaningful link between Herr K.'s declaration of love and Dora's (for instance, oral: aphonia, *tussis nervosa*) symptoms, given that a number of them already existed long before. Some of them even dated back to the time when Dora was only eight years old. Hence, the walk at the lake has no explanatory value for Dora's pathological state in itself. We have to go back further in time and look for another experience that is better suited to shed some light on Dora's symptoms.

After overcoming the first difficulties of the cure, Dora tells Freud about another incident with Herr K. that seems more likely to be the sexual trauma he was looking for. When she was fourteen years old, Herr K. managed to be alone with her in his shop, and, on that occasion, clasped the girl to him and pressed a kiss upon her lips. Freud writes that, while a healthy young woman that had never before been approached, would normally feel sexual excitement in a situation like this, Dora reacted with a violent feeling of disgust, tore herself free from the man and ran away.

Freud stresses, first of all, that Dora's behaviour on this occasion was already "completely hysterical" (ibid., p. 28). He writes: "I should without question consider a person hysterical in whom an occasion for sexual excitement elicited feelings that were preponderantly or exclusively unpleasurable" (ibid.). But this "reversal of affect" is not enough to particularize Dora's case. A displacement of affect has also occurred: instead of the pleasurable genital sensation, "Dora was overcome by the unpleasurable feeling that is proper to the tract of the mucous membrane at the entrance of the alimentary canal – that is by disgust" (ibid., p. 29). The scene also had another consequence: from time to time, a sensory hallucination occured causing her to feel the pressure of Herr K.'s embrace upon the upper part of her body. Freud links both this hallucination and Dora's unwillingness to pass a man engaged in a passionate conversation with a woman, with the fact that, during Herr K.'s embrace, she did not only experience the feeling of his kiss on her lips, but also the pressure of his erect penis against her body. According to Freud, it is this sight that she wants to avoid at all cost. This unwillingness, then, also expresses Dora's dismissive attitude towards sexuality and sexual excitement. How then can we understand Dora's affective reaction to this trauma?

(b) The Organic Foundations of Hysteria

Freud links Dora's disgust to the fact that she remained an enthusiastic thumb-sucker well into her fourth or fifth year, claiming that this predisposed her to privilege oral pleasures as an adult (ibid., p. 30). The disgust that Dora experiences leads Freud to the discovery of the erotogenic zones and to their tendency to displacement – that is, their tendency to transmit their susceptibility to stimulation to other erotogenic zones (Freud, 1905b, p. 183). These erotogenic zones are the privileged places for the experience of (sexual) pleasure *and its repression*, as in Dora's case. Dora's disgust is the symptom of this repression. Freud writes, furthermore, that the hysterical patient feels disgust for sexuality and sexual excitement because "the early Christian Father's '*inter urinas et faeces nascimur*' … cannot be detached from it in spite of every effort at idealization" (Freud, 1905a, p. 31).

We cannot understand this or similar statements without referring to the problematic of an "organic repression", which plays a more or less hidden, but structural, role in Freud's argumentation on the nature of hysteria in his text on the Dora case. In his letters to Fliess (Masson, 1985), Freud develops a phylogenetic model of the normal repression of the (infantile) oral and anal experiences of pleasure. He connects this repression with the loss of the sense of smell (olfaction) as a source of sexual excitation and with an intensification of the sexual importance of the visual due to upright walking.[2] He further specifies this idea by stating that human sexuality has to overcome its initial mixing with excremental functions (Freud, 1905a, p. 31). The separation between sexuality and the excremental functions, Freud continues, can only be realized through the introduction of the specifically human affects of disgust and shame (and guilt) and through a complex process of idealization (ibid.). Neurotic (hysterical) disgust, then, is nothing but an exaggeration of this normal disgust. More specifically, the hysterical problematic is characterized by the imminent and insurmountable threat of a contamination of the sexual by the excremental. According to Freud, this constant threat constitutes the "organic" disposition, which is the ultimate foundation of the disgust that fundamentally characterizes hysteria.[3]

Freud remarks that Dora was suffering from a genital catarrh and that she linked this condition to her father's venereal disease. She accused her father and his immoral lifestyle of being responsible for her (and her mother's) disease. For Dora, suffering from venereal disease – and are all men not like that? – meant being afflicted with a disgusting discharge: "Thus the disgust

[2] Freud writes, "[T]he notion was linked to the changed part played by sensations of smell: upright walking, nose raised from the ground, at the same time a number of formerly interesting sensations attached to the earth becoming repulsive by a process still unknown to me). (He turns up his nose = he regards himself as something particularly noble)" (Masson, 1985, p. 279).

[3] "When everything that can be got rid of by psycho-analysis has been cleared away, we are in a position to form all kinds of conjectures, which probably meet the facts, as regards the somatic basis of the symptoms – a basis which is as a rule constitutional and organic" (Freud, 1905a, p. 41)

which was transferred on to the contact of the man would be a feeling which had been projected according to the primitive mechanism … and would be related ultimately to her own leucorrhoea" (ibid., p. 84). The connection Dora makes between the leucorrhoea, venereal diseases and (male) sexuality, as the motive for her disgust, testifies to a general rejection or dismissal of the realm of sexuality as such. This connection and the rejection that follows from it are based on a spontaneous association of sexuality with disgusting bodily excretions. No specific fantasies or representations are involved at this point yet.

Freud himself is convinced that Dora's catarrh is caused by her "bad habits": "I met her half-way by assuring her that in my view the occurrence of leucorrhoea in young girls pointed primarily to masturbation" (ibid., p. 76). This is Dora's secret that she does not want to share with her doctors, nor admit to herself. Indeed, according to Freud, the reproaches against her father conceal self-reproaches with the same content (ibid., p. 35). The idea that the link between sexuality and disgusting bodily excretions finds its origin in infantile masturbation, does not contradict the concept of a hysterical "disposition". On the contrary, this link is nothing other than "the enigmatic contradiction which hysteria presents, by revealing the pair of opposites by which it is characterized – exaggerated sexual craving and excessive aversion to sexuality" (Freud, 1905b, p. 165). In other words, the link between masturbation and Dora's leucorrhoea (bodily excretions) only dramatizes, crystallizes and strengthens a pre-existing (and, in itself, universal) problematic that is at the heart of what Freud calls "organic repression".

(c) The Meaning of Dora's Symptoms

We now know that Freud is convinced of an intrinsic link between Dora's pathological condition and infantile masturbation. Freud then wonders what caused Dora to give up masturbating. He has good reason to suppose, he speculates, that, as a child, she overheard her parents while they were having intercourse. Freud adds: "The sympathetic excitement which may be supposed[4] to have occurred in Dora on such an occasion may very easily have made the child's sexuality veer round and have replaced her inclination to masturbation by an inclination to anxiety" (Freud, 1905a, p. 80). Freud does not really explain in great detail how we should understand this replacement, but we can easily imagine that overhearing her parents having intercourse confronted

[4] "Children, in such circumstances, divine something sexual in the uncanny sounds that reach their ears. Indeed, the movements expressive of sexual excitement lie within them ready at hand, as innate pieces of mechanism" (Freud, 1905a, p. 80).

Dora with something she did not understand – something "uncanny" – or, better still, something she could not link to any mental representations. Dora was unable to connect the libidinal excitement she was experiencing to specific representations. Here, Freud implicitly refers to the theory of anxiety neurosis that he developed some ten years earlier: unbound libido – i.e. libido that is not linked to specific representations – is experienced as anxiety.

Freud goes on to write that her first attack of asthma occurred a little while later: Dora wished that her absent father would come home soon and this longing reproduced the impression she had received while overhearing her parents, in the form of an attack of asthma (ibid., p. 80). This attack followed after a long and difficult walk in the mountains, which caused actual shortness of breath. Here, we find, once again, a "*somatic compliance*" without which hysteric symptoms cannot exist (ibid., p. 40). This is compounded by her belief that her father should not over-exert himself because he suffered from shortness of breath as well as by the memory of how much he had exerted himself with her mother. Dora was also afraid that she might have over-exerted herself while masturbating. This, according to Freud, is the chain of thought charged with anxiety that accompanied the first asthma attack. In this way, it becomes clear that, at first, this attack expressed a sympathetic imitation of her father. Soon, however, it also expressed Dora's self-reproach. The same group of symptoms, Freud continues, would also later represent Dora's relation with Herr K.: when he was absent she could only write to him and, consequently, lost her voice until he returned.

From all of this it becomes clear that Dora's cough and hoarseness did not appear for the first time when she was sixteen or eighteen years old. On the contrary, these symptoms already occurred when Dora was twelve (ibid., p. 22), some years prior to the first trauma. Related symptoms (chronic dyspnoea) had already appeared when she was only eight years old. This implies that the traumas are not directly at the origin of Dora's symptoms. Freud also writes that it is only after the second trauma that these symptoms can be linked to explicitly sexual representations. How can we understand this and what does it mean for the traumatic theory of hysteria that Freud seems to defend in the *Fragment of an Analysis of a Case of Hysteria*? Or, more precisely, what does this teach us about the relation between trauma, disposition and (the meaning of) the symptom?

(d) Trauma, Disposition, and Symptom

Regarding Dora's first trauma, Freud writes that the disgust did not become a permanent symptom (ibid., p. 29). Freud further remarks that this trauma did not affect Dora's relation to Herr K. and that neither of them ever mentioned the little scene. Dora merely did not want to be alone with Herr K. for some time following the incident. Hence, this first scene seems to have been of little consequence and Dora did not pay great attention to it. According to Freud, this is due to the fact that Dora – although on the verge of puberty – did not yet possess the proper sexual representations that would have allowed her to adequately understand what was happening to her. Indeed, Freud clearly states that Dora was not familiar with the physical signs of excitement in a man's body at the time of the first trauma (ibid., p. 31). Hence, Dora's reaction to the first trauma was not grounded in a specific sexual representation. Rather, Dora's reaction to the sensation of Herr K.'s erect penis – and the subsequent avoidance of men in eager conversation with a woman – reminds us of those hysterical girls who account for their disgust "by saying that the organ in question serves the function of excretion" (Freud, 1905b, p. 152). This hysterical disposition is a general, unspecific and pre-representational equation of sexuality with "dirtiness".

Herr K.'s declaration of his love during the walk at the lake reminded Dora of the first incident in his shop. Here, she reacts with disgust once again. But Dora is in puberty now, and enriched with more detailed knowledge of the "sexual facts of life". More particularly, she now realizes that other parts of the body than the genitals can be used for sexual gratification and for sexual intercourse (Freud, 1905a, p. 47). Dora was very preoccupied with the relationship between her father and Frau K. and she actively participated in it in many ways. It comes as no surprise then "that with her spasmodic cough, which, as is usual, was referred for its exciting stimulus to a tickling in her throat, she pictured to herself a scene of sexual gratification *per os* between the two people whose love-affair occupied her mind so incessantly" (ibid., p. 48). This makes clear how it is the retroactive interplay of the two traumas that makes it possible for the first time to link Dora's symptoms to explicitly sexual representations and fantasies. However, these traumas no longer have an etiological value as in the seduction theory. *They only activate and bring to completion a pre-existing "organic" disposition, which is the true foundation of hysteria*. This constitutionally determined disposition is the "basis of hysteria". Freud continues: "But if the basis of hysteria is an idiosyncrasy of the whole nervous system, the complex of ideogenic, psychically determined symptoms is erected on it as a building is on its foundations" (Freud & Breuer, 1895, p. 244). Only these psychic symptoms fall within the reach of psychoanalytical therapy (Freud, 1905a, p. 41).

(e) What about Oedipus?

In his study on *Dora*, Freud does not need the Oedipus complex to understand hysteria. The interplay between disposition, trauma and "somatic compliance", as we have described it, suffices for this. However, this failed to prevent most commentators from giving oedipal explanations of Dora's "*petite hystérie*", but also from attributing this explanation to Freud. What should we think of this?

Many readers of the *Fragment of an Analysis of a Case of Hysteria* have noticed, and, not without reason, criticized, Freud's continuous efforts to force Dora into a conventional scheme of heterosexual seduction, one that he then presses Dora to accept (Bernheim & Kahane, 1990). Indeed, a large part of Freud's analytic efforts in this cure are aimed at showing Dora how much she herself is involved in the relationship between her father, on the one hand, and Herr and Frau K., on the other. Freud agrees that there was some sort of silent deal between Dora's father and Herr K.: Dora's father could have Frau K. as long as Herr K. was not hindered in his efforts to seduce Dora (Freud, 1905a, p. 34). Freud writes that Dora accepted this situation for a very long period of time without protesting. On the contrary, she did everything she could not to disturb her father when he wanted to spend time with his mistress. It is only after the incident at the lake that Dora started to criticize her father for his unfaithfulness. The reason for this, Freud continuous, is very simple: Dora had already been in love with Herr K. for many years. According to Freud, her father's adventure gave her the opportunity to spend more time with Herr K. Therefore, her reproaches are in fact self-reproaches. We already know one of Freud's arguments supporting this interpretation: Dora's periodic aphonia. Dora lost her voice whenever Herr K. was abroad and miraculously regained her voice upon his return. Hereby she repeated Frau K.'s behaviour in a reverse form: whenever Herr K. came back he always found his wife in bad health, even if she had been quite well until the day before.

Does Freud's continuous effort to convince Dora of the essentially heterosexual character of her desire, also imply that he gives an oedipal interpretation of her dream and of her pathological state? Not necessarily. Indeed, Freud's analysis of Dora's first dream, which occurred a few days after the incident at the lake, clearly illustrates that he is not exactly thinking in oedipal terms. In this first dream, Dora is awakened by her father when the house is on fire. Her mother does not want to leave the house without saving her jewellery box. But Dora's father refuses and says: "I refuse to let myself and my two children be burnt for the sake of your jewel-case" (ibid., p. 64). When asked about this dream, Dora tells Freud about a fight between her parents about a piece of jewellery. Her mother wanted a pearl to wear in her ears and her father gave her a bracelet instead. Freud then introduces a link between the "jewel-case" (and jewellery in general) and female genitals (ibid., p. 69). He further remarks that Dora's mother is a former rival in her father's affections and that she might have wanted to "give" her father what her mother refused to give him: her jewellery. The oedipal theme is thus clearly present in this dream. On this theme Freud writes: "I have shown at length elsewhere at what an early age [in Dora's case at age six] sexual attraction makes itself felt between parents and children, and I have explained that the legend of Oedipus is probably to be regarded as a poetical rendering of what is typical in these relations" (ibid., p. 56). It follows from all this that the dream expresses, according to Freud, a revival "of germs of feeling in infancy" (ibid.) that have an oedipal character. But is revealing an oedipal theme in a dream the same thing as providing an oedipal explanation for it?

Dora also mentions to Freud that Herr K. had given her an expensive jewel-case shortly before the dream occurred. Freud then assumes that receiving an expensive gift from Herr K. also meant for Dora that she should give him something in return. Hence, Dora's mother also represents Frau K. in the dream. The meaning of the dream then becomes obvious: "So you are ready to give Herr K. what his wife withholds from him. That is the thought which has to be repressed for every one of its elements to be turned in to its opposite" (ibid., p. 70). The question then becomes how this repression is carried out.

Freud links the idea that Dora's father was trying to save her from a burning house with the fact that, as a child, she was woken up by him in the middle of the night to prevent her from wetting her bed (ibid., p. 72). He suggests that "fire" and "burning", apart from their obvious meaning ("a house is on fire"), can also have sexual connotations (e.g. "I am *burning* with desire", "I am *consumed* by love"). According to Freud, Dora's father replaces Herr K. for whom Dora is burning with desire (ibid., pp. 73-74). It is against this "fire" that Dora's father must protect her, in the same way as he protected her before against bed-wetting. Freud concludes: "My interpretation was that she had at that point summoned up an infantile affection for her father so as to be able to keep her repressed love for Herr K. in its state of repression" (ibid., p. 86).

Freud writes that the Oedipus legend expresses something that is typical in the relation between parents and children. Not only does he remain very cautious as to the sexual character of these relations.[5] He also at no point claims

[5] He writes: "At this point certain other influences, which need not be discussed here, come into play and lead to a fixation of this rudimentary feeling of love or to a reinforcement of it; so that it turns into something (either while the child is still young or not until it has reached the age of puberty) which must be put on a par with a sexual inclination and which, like the latter, has the forces of the libido at its command" (Freud, 1905a, pp. 56-57).

that these "oedipal relations" play a determinative role in Dora's pathology. Dora's oedipal (infantile) history does not help to explain the origin of her "*petite hystérie*". On the contrary, the memory of this history is only revived to help repress Dora's desire for Herr K., and, more fundamentally, for Frau K., as we will see in a moment. In his text on Dora, Freud is still far removed from the theory of an Oedipus complex that is the *nuclear* complex of all neuroses, which, in principle, allows the articulation of the fundamental dynamics of each and every one of them.

But if Freud does not give an oedipal explanation for Dora's symptoms and behaviour, what then is the fundamental dynamic at the basis of her problems? We already mentioned the problematic of "organic repression", but this is certainly not the whole story. Freud called his case study on Dora, "*Fragment* of an Analysis of a Case of Hysteria". One of the reasons that Freud spoke of a "Fragment" is that Dora broke off her analysis very soon after she started it. In a footnote that was added many years after the first publication of the text, Freud links this rupture to his inability to truly understand the importance of Dora's homosexual ties to Frau K. Because of his biased blindness, he neglected a number of essential aspects of Dora's case: Dora regularly slept in the same room as Frau K. They obviously had a very intimate relation since Dora spoke of Frau K.'s "'adorable white body' in terms more appropriate to a lover than to a defeated rival" (ibid., p. 61). Even when Frau K. disappointed Dora by not wanting to believe that her husband tried to seduce the girl, the latter remained faithful to her. And when Dora was later accused of an inappropriate interest in sexual matters, she kept silent about the fact that she got most of her insight into sexual matters from Frau K. All of this opens a new perspective on Dora's interest in the relation between her father and his mistress. This interest is not motivated by an oedipal jealousy directed towards Frau K., but by Frau K. herself:[6] the love for the father is summoned up to repress Dora's love for Herr K. and her love for the latter, more fundamentally, hides her desire for Frau K. and her "adorable white body".[7]

[6] Some have argued that Dora looks to find her mother in Frau K. This would, for instance, explain Dora's identification with her father (the cough, etc.), which would imply a negative oedipal position. However, this identification does not mean that Dora loved men from then on. Quite the contrary, as Herr K., Freud and her father experienced all too bitterly, all men disappoint her. Dora identifies with her father out of disappointment with her mother. But instead of giving up her original love for her mother, she repressed it out of consciousness and accomplished a hostile identification with her father (Lewin, 1973).

[7] "I have never yet come through a single psycho-analysis of a man or a woman without having to take into account a very considerable current of homosexuality. When in a hysterical woman or girl, the sexual libido which is directed towards men has been energetically suppressed, it will regularly be found that the libido which is directed towards women has become vicariously reinforced and even to some extent conscious" (Freud, 1905a, p. 60).

The following quotation on *Dora* from Freud's letters to Fliess no longer comes as a surprise: "'Dreams and Hysteria', if possible, should not disappoint you. The main thing in it is again psychology, the utilization of dreams, and a few peculiarities of unconscious thought processes. There are only glimpses of the organic [elements], that is, the erotogenic zones and bisexuality. ... It is a hysteria with tussis nervosa and aphonia, which can be traced back to the character of the child's sucking, and the principal issue in the conflicting thought processes is the contrast between an inclination toward men and an inclination toward women" (Masson, 1985, p. 434). In his postscript to the Dora case, Freud adds in the same line: "But, once again, in the present paper I have not gone fully into all what might be said today about 'somatic compliance', about infantile germs of perversion, about the erotogenic zones, and about our predisposition towards bisexuality. I have merely drawn attention to the points at which the analysis comes into contact with these organic bases of the symptoms" (Freud, 1905a, pp. 113-114).

(f) Bisexuality and its Consequences

Freud published his text on the Dora case in the same year as the first edition of the *Three Essays on the Theory of Sexuality*. This first edition contains several references to bisexuality as the most fundamental dynamic in human existence. For instance, Freud connects the fact that certain of the impulses to perversion occur regularly as pairs of opposites "with the opposing masculinity and femininity which are combined in bisexuality" (Freud, 1905b, p. 160). Also, in the paragraph on the differentiation between men and women he refers to bisexuality as a decisive factor (ibid., p. 220).[8] At the same time, there is no mention at all of the Oedipus complex. The text does contain one paragraph on the incest barrier, but that is obviously not the same as the Oedipus complex. References to the Oedipus complex are only introduced from 1920 onwards. Hence, for readers of Freud's texts in 1905 – and those readers were not familiar with his letters to Fliess – there could be no doubt that bisexuality was much more important for understanding pathology than the Oedipus complex (Van Haute, 2002).

At no point in the analysis of Dora does Freud make use of this explicit (but scarcely developed) theoretical position. Quite the contrary: he stubbornly tries to convince Dora that Herr K. is the true object of her desire and he

[8] "Since I have become acquainted with the notion of bisexuality I have regarded it as a decisive factor, and without taking bisexuality into account I think it would scarcely be possible to arrive at an understanding of the sexual manifestations that are actually to be observed in men and women" (Freud, 1905b, p. 220).

almost goes as far as saying that marrying Herr K. might in the end be the best possible therapy for Dora. His desperate belief that girls are made for boys and vice versa makes him blind to Dora's attachment to Frau K., and, more generally, to the possible clinical and theoretical consequences of his own (or better: Wilhelm Fliess's?) theory.[9]

Indeed, not only does Dora desire both Herr and Frau K., but she is also caught up, as Freud himself sometimes insists, in an ongoing process of shifting bisexual identifications. We will limit ourselves to some illustrations from Freud's text. Freud writes, for example, that Dora's obsessional preoccupation with the relationship between her father and Frau K. indicates that she identifies with her mother: "She felt and acted more like a jealous wife – in a way that would have been comprehensible in her mother" (Freud, 1905a, p. 56). In the scene at the lake, Dora identifies with a young governess towards whom Herr K. had made advances while his wife was away. The young girl told Dora that Herr K. implored her to yield to his entreaties, saying "that he got nothing from his wife" (ibid., p. 106). Those are the very same words Herr K. used when he tried to seduce Dora at the lake some days later (ibid., p. 98). Freud's interpretation is hardly surprising here. He says to Dora: "It was not that you were offended at his suggestion; you were actuated by jealousy and revenge", and a few lines further he continues: "'Does he dare', you said to yourself, 'to treat me like a governess, like a servant?'" (ibid., p. 106). But Dora is also in love with Frau K. Under these circumstances, it does not seem too farfetched to think that Dora is here identifying with both Frau K. and Herr K.: on the one hand, by slapping Herr K. in the face Dora rejects the contempt for Frau K. conveyed by Herr K.'s words, who, on the other hand, is by law Frau K.'s partner, who is the object of her desire (and vice versa?). From this perspective it becomes clear that not only the object of Dora's desire is uncertain, but also that the place from where she desires is far from univocal. In this context, one also remembers the following sentence from Freud's letters to Fliess: "But bisexuality! You are certainly right about it. I am accustoming myself to regarding every sexual act as a process in which four individuals are involved" (Masson, 1985, p. 364).

Freud's constant attempt to convince Dora of her hidden heterosexual desire for Herr K. undoubtedly has to do with cultural prejudices that he could not overcome despite his theoretical findings with regard to the pervert sexual constitution of all human beings and his emphasis on bisexuality. But one also wonders whether Freud's emphasis on a "natural solution" for Dora's

[9] What to make of the fact that the reference to Fliess (Freud, 1905b, p. 220) was left out, starting from the second edition (1910)?

problems is not at the same time meant to protect him from the structural dissolution of (gender) identities that would result from a general disposition towards bisexuality. Perhaps it was not so much heterosexual normality that Freud wanted to protect at all cost, but more fundamentally, the idea of an identifiable desire that is at the basis of the different symptoms Dora was suffering from.

Conclusion: An Assault on Truth?

The classical interpretation of the abandonment of the seduction theory is untenable even when Freud, in his letter of 21 September, 1897, mentions several arguments that seem to put into question the reality of the traumas that come to light in the psychoanalytical cure. In this context, Freud writes, for instance, that it is highly unlikely that there are as many perverted fathers as might be expected on the basis of what his patients tell him, or that, in the unconscious, there is no possibility to distinguish what really happened from fantasy. But these and other arguments do not express the real stakes of the debate. Indeed, it is the etiological role of trauma(s), rather than their reality as such, that Freud starts questioning from September 1897 onwards. The *Fragment of an Analysis of a Case of Hysteria* clearly shows what this means: the etiological role of trauma – whose reality is not really questioned – is taken over by an "organic disposition", which is also responsible for the sensitivity to a certain type of trauma. Traumas actualize and transform a pre-existing (and, in itself, universal) problematic that is at the heart of what Freud calls "organic repression" and which is the true foundation of hysteria. This disposition marks a limit to the power of psychoanalytical therapy. From the perspective of this interpretation, the real "assault on truth" (Masson, 1992) might well have been that both psychoanalysts and their critics – be it for different reasons – neglected or bluntly denied the fact that, up to 1905, Freud had a very consistent and coherent theory of hysteria in which disposition, trauma and history were linked in an original way and in which the Oedipus complex played no structural role at all.

Freud's early theory of hysteria limits and relativizes the efficiency of psychoanalysis as a therapeutic practice, or, at least, obliges us to rethink this practice. Indeed, this theory links biological and psychological motives in an original way. Psychoanalytical therapy aims at the psychically determined symptoms and not at the disposition on the basis of which these symptoms can arise (over and over again?).

The problematic of bisexuality confronts Freud – and all of us? – not only with a structural uncertainty with regard to the object of desire, but also with a structural uncertainty with regard to the place from where this desire is shaped and formed. Hysteria is not only characterized by a rejection of sexuality, but also by an uncertainty of gender-identifications. And just as the neurotic (hysterical) disgust of sexuality is nothing but an exaggeration of normal disgust, this uncertainty is nothing but an exaggeration of a structural and normal uncertainty that characterizes subjectivity as such. As a result, psychoanalytical practice is incapable of finding a unique desire at the basis of our symptoms that can be identified without ambiguity. This possibility, however, seems to be the "metaphysical presupposition" *par excellence* of psychoanalytical theory as such (Derrida, 1967; Borch-Jacobsen, 1982). Hence, our reading could possibly shed new light on Freud's choice for the Oedipus complex and his concomitant dismissal of bisexuality in his texts after 1905. Indeed, the unity and the unambiguously identifiable character of desire and its object had to be defended at all costs.

References

Anzieu, D. (1988). *L'auto-analyse de Freud et la découverte de la psychanalyse*. Paris: PUF.

Bernheim, C., & Kahane, C. (1990). *In Dora's case: Freud – hysteria – feminism*. New York, NY: Columbia University Press.

Borch-Jacobsen, M., & Shamdasani, S. (2006). *Le dossier Freud: Enquête sur l'histoire de la psychanalyse*. Paris: Les empêcheurs de penser en rond.

Borch-Jacobsen, M. (1982). *Le sujet freudien*. Paris: Flammarion.

Blass, R. (1992). Did Dora have an Oedipus complex? A re-examination of the theoretical context of Freud's "Fragment of an analysis". *Psychoanalytic Study of the Child*, *47*, 159-187.

Derrida, J. (1967). *De la grammatologie*. Paris: Les éditions de minuit.

Freud, S., & Breuer, J. (1895). Studies on hysteria. *Standard Edition 2*.

Freud, S. (1905a). Fragment of an analysis of a case of hysteria. *Standard Edition 7*, pp. 1-122.

———. (1905b). Three essays on the theory of sexuality. *Standard Edition 7*, pp. 123-245.

———. (1906). My views on the part played by sexuality in the aetiology of the neuroses. *Standard Edition 7*, pp. 269-279.

Kris, E. (1986). Einleitung zur Erstausgabe. In S. Freud, *Briefe an Wilhelm Fliess* (pp. 519-561). Frankfurt: Fischer. (Original work published 1952).

Lewin, K. (1973). Dora revisited. *Psychoanalytic Review*, *60*, 519-532

Masson, J. (1985). *The complete letters of Sigmund Freud to Wilhelm Fliess (1887-1904)*. Cambridge, MA: Harvard University Press.
Masson, J. (1992). *The assault on truth: Freud's suppression of the seduction theory*. New York, NY: Harper Collins.
Van Haute, P. (2002). The introduction of the Oedipus complex and the re-invention of instinct. *Radical Philosophy, 115*, 7-15.

Section III
Sexuality and Politics

Foucault versus Freud –
On Sexuality and the Unconscious

Eran Dorfman

Introduction

One of the main difficulties faced by Foucault's readers is how to understand the practical implications of his descriptions. Are we all trapped in a web of power and forces that leave us helpless? Are we doomed to passively follow paths anonymously charted for us? Can we not actively resist? And if we can, how?

A good place to start answering these questions is Foucault's first volume of *The History of Sexuality* in which he elaborates his critique of Freudian psychoanalysis. In this paper, I will follow Foucault's claim that psychoanalysis blindly pushes forth and enforces the discourse of sexuality. I will argue that the Freudian accent on sexuality is subordinated to his discovery of the unconscious, and that sexuality is only one of the instances of the unconscious. From this perspective, I will analyze the similarities and differences between Freudian descriptions of the perceptual apparatus of the mind and the Foucaultian structure of power, in order to arrive at a clearer picture of the relationship between power, the unconscious, resistance and sexuality. Thus, my aim here is not to follow the development of Foucault's attitude towards Freud, as did, to note some examples, Forrester (1990), Derrida (1994)[10] and Whitebook (1998), but, rather, to try to deepen our understanding of Freud's project through Foucault's critique of it, as well as to consider how to expand Foucault's own theory through the Freudian mechanisms of perception, filtering and resistance.

---

[10] A more relevant text by Derrida is his *Freud and the Scene of Writing* (Derrida, 1978), in which he meticulously deconstructs the Freudian notion of the unconscious. Although I analyse most of the texts commented on by Derrida, my conclusions are very different from his, partly because Derrida is not concerned with the relationship between the unconscious and sexuality.

I. Foucault's Critique of Psychoanalysis

An important passage in *The History of Sexuality* states, on the one hand, the relationship between sex, sexuality and power, and, on the other hand, Foucault's critique of psychoanalysis:

> We must not make the mistake of thinking that sex is an autonomous agency which secondarily produces manifold effects of sexuality over the entire length of its surface of contact with power. On the contrary, sex is the most speculative, most ideal, and most internal element in a deployment of sexuality organized by power in its grip on bodies and materiality, their forces, energies, sensations, and pleasures. (Foucault, 1978, p. 155)

Sexuality precedes sex; power precedes sexuality. Or, more accurately, sex cannot be conceived outside the field of sexuality, and sexuality is only one of the instances of power. Therefore, says Foucault, "we must conceptualize the deployment of sexuality on the basis of the techniques of power that are contemporary with it" (ibid., p. 150).

Foucault's criticism of Freudian psychoanalysis is thus the following: instead of relating sex to sexuality and sexuality to power, psychoanalysis conceived of sex independently, and, in this way, contributed to power's incarnation in the form of sexuality. Notably, it did so by presenting sexuality as naturally governed by the laws of kinship: "with psychoanalysis, sexuality gave body and life to the rules of alliance by saturating them with desire" (ibid., p. 113).

Moreover, not only did psychoanalysis play a crucial role in intensifying the discourse of sexuality, it also actively ignored this very role, namely, its own place in the network of power. In the name of liberation, it only helped trap Western society in the old Christian (or Stoic) rules of family and kinship institutions. Far from lending freedom to repressed desire, psychoanalysis supplied the old institutions with further force through its very use of desire. In Foucault's colourful and suggestive words:

> Parents, do not be afraid to bring your children to analysis: it will teach them that in any case it is you whom they love. Children, you really shouldn't complain that you are not orphans, that you always rediscover in your innermost selves your Object-Mother or the sovereign sign of your Father: it is through them that you gain access to desire. (ibid.)

Having posed this critique, what does Foucault suggest instead of psychoanalysis? What should we do regarding this 300-year-old state of over-spoken, garrulous sexuality culminating in the appearance of psychoanalysis? In an interview given shortly after the publication of *The History of Sexuality, Vol. I*, Foucault explains his intention regarding sex and sexuality:

> Whereas in societies with a heritage of erotic art the intensification of pleasure tends to desexualize the body, in the West this systematization of pleasure according to the "laws" of sex gave rise to the whole apparatus of sexuality. And it is this that makes us believe that we are "liberating" ourselves when we "decode" all pleasure in terms of a sex shorn at last of disguise, whereas one should aim instead at a desexualization, at a general economy of pleasure not based on sexual norms. (Foucault, 1980, p. 191)

Volumes II and III of *The History of Sexuality* realize to a large extent this goal of finding alternative forms, structures, technologies and economies of pleasure and relations to the body, which are not based on sex and sexuality, but rather on an ethical and aesthetic attitude of self-care, as practiced in Ancient Greece and Rome. However, my aim here is not to analyze the possibility of bringing such an attitude into practice in contemporary Western society, but, instead, to ask two questions: first, is it true that psychoanalysis, contrary to the explicit intention of its founder, enforces, or at least enforced existing power instead of resisting it?; and second, what kind of resistance is possible in the face of given power?

Foucault's definition of resistance in *The History of Sexuality* is quite ambiguous: "Where there is power, there is resistance, and yet, or rather consequently, this resistance is never in a position of exteriority in relation to power" (Foucault, 1978, p. 95). Now, if resistance must be effected within power, and if we suppose that Freudian psychoanalysis did want to resist, it follows that it had no other choice but to adopt one of power's main manifestations in order to transform it from within. And this manifestation, this force, was precisely sexuality.

My claim, accordingly, is the following: since no one can act in a void, the form of resistance that psychoanalysis could take up in the Victorian era had to be sexuality. But this raw material, sexuality, was then developed within a certain framework, which marks the true novelty of psychoanalysis, namely, the unconscious.

Indeed, Foucault himself argued that the significance of psychoanalysis does not lie in its discovery of sexuality, but rather in "its having opened out on to something quite different, namely the logic of the unconscious. And there sexuality is no longer what it was at the outset" (Foucault, 1980, pp. 212-213). However, the debate should not revolve around the question of whether it was Freud who stood at the point of a break in the relation of civilization to sex and sexuality,[11] but, rather, the question of how such a break is possible in the first place: how an expression of the new – i.e. the logic of the unconscious – can be achieved through the language of the old – i.e. the logic of sexuality – while transforming it. The relation between the two logics cannot be one of an either/or, an opposition between the unconscious and sexuality, as J.-A. Miller tried to argue, citing Lacan's famous axiom that "there is no sexual relation" (ibid., p. 213). It is rather a relation of mutual expression, as we are now about to see.

II. The Freudian Unconscious

There is one scheme that Freud developed and reworked throughout his career, starting as early as the 1895 *Project* (*Entwurf*), continuing in *The Interpretation of Dreams*, *Beyond the Pleasure Principle*, *The Ego and the Id*, and culminating in the 1925 *Note upon the "Mystic Writing-Pad"*. This is the scheme of the perceptual apparatus of the mind. This apparatus, Freud tells us, consists of several subordinate systems, among which we find the Perception-Consciousness system and the unconscious system.

What hierarchy governs these systems? And what force makes them function and communicate with one another? The apparatus is generally described as a receptive mechanism. In the *Project*, Freud suggests that everything starts with stimuli entering the apparatus in its external end, namely, the sense organs,[12] and, thereafter, passing through different kinds of neurons: permeable (ϕ), impermeable (ψ) and, finally, perceptual (ω).

Let us retrace the path of the stimuli. The sense organs at the external end serve both as *screens* of quantity (energy) and as *sieves* of the qualitative characteristics of the stimuli, which Freud names "periods". The modulations of periods pass through the ϕ and ψ neurons without encountering any barrier or inhibition in their way. Finally, they reach the ω neurons, which produce a conscious sensation (Freud, 1895, p. 313). However, whereas quality seems to pass smoothly from one end of the apparatus to the other, there is a serious problem with the passage of quantity or energy. This must be

[11] I refer here to the debate between Foucault and Jacques-Alain Miller. See: Foucault (1980, pp. 209-222) and Miller (1992).

[12] Freud also speaks of internal stimuli, but never provides a satisfactory account of this. Also see the "Editor's Introduction" to the *Project* (Freud, 1895, p. 291). I will return to this point later.

drastically reduced, so that almost none of it reaches the ω neurons, as they are too sensitive. In order to reduce quantity, an initial screening is performed by the sense organs; afterwards, the φ neurons deal with "the rough discharge of quantity" (ibid., p. 309); and finally come the impermeable ψ neurons, which form a system of "contact barriers" through which the stimuli must pass, and only those that succeed in doing so may arrive at consciousness and be perceived in the first place.[13] However, the barriers are not static and stable, being themselves influenced by the stimuli. As such, they serve as *memory*, registering different associations of stimuli, which then facilitate or inhibit the passage of a further quantity of the same type of stimuli (ibid., p. 300).

How can we explain the smooth passage of quality in contrast to the harsh journey of the quantitative characteristics or energy? Is the first passage conditioned by the second? Although this question remains obscure in Freud, he does affirm that only stimuli which have difficulty reaching the depth of the apparatus can leave memory traces: if the "qualitative characteristic of the stimuli ... proceeds unhindered through φ by way of ψ to ω, where it generates sensation", this sensation "does not persist for long and disappears towards the motor side; nor, since it is allowed to pass through, does it leave any memory behind it" (ibid., p. 313).

Paradoxically, what manages easily to reach the sensation-consciousness end of the apparatus does not leave any trace of memory behind it, having passed through the contact barriers unhindered. But what determines whether a stimulus meets resistance or not? And do the contact barriers of the ψ system function only when something *does not* reach consciousness?

If we turn back to Foucault, we can see that he conceives power as based upon something similar to contact barriers. He says that power is always relational, and that the existence of power relationships "depends on a multiplicity of points of resistance: these play the role of adversary, target, support, or handle in power relations. These points of resistance are present everywhere in the power network. Hence, there is no single locus of great Refusal, no soul of revolt, source of all rebellions, or pure law of the revolutionary. Instead there is a plurality of resistances" (Foucault, 1978, pp. 95-96).

We observed earlier that resistance is never in a position of exteriority in relation to power, and now we see that power is dependent upon multiple points of resistance, which serve as its vehicle rather than its obstacle. This idea is obviously very similar to the notion of the unconscious as various

[13] As Strachey emphasizes, Freud is playing here with the similarity between ω (omega) and W (*Wahrnehmung*, perception) (ibid., pp. 288-289).

filters, which serve both to resist and conduct power. In order to deepen our understanding of the Freudian apparatus, let us examine an 1896 letter from Freud to Fliess in which he presents a graphic diagram of it, anticipating the one presented in chapter VII of *The Interpretation of Dreams*. Below is the first diagram (Freud, 1896, p. 234):

			I		II		III	
Pcpt		Pcpt-s		Ucs		Pcs		Cs
	---------		-------		--------		--------	

The diagram seems to fit well the description of the apparatus given in the *Project*. The first layer, Perception, is equivalent to the φ neurons. It does not have memory and does not register anything. The first registration (I) takes place only at the second layer, called Perception-signs (*Wahrnehmungszeichen*, or *Wz*). The second registration (II) subsequently takes place in the unconscious, with Freud adding that "Ucs traces would perhaps correspond to conceptual memories" (ibid., p. 234). The third registration occurs in the preconscious, and is "attached to word presentations and corresponding to our official ego" (ibid., pp. 234-235). Only after these three registrations, each of which is more conceptual and less perceptual than the one before, can consciousness appear, which is described by Freud as "secondary thought-consciousness."

All three registrations consist of memory and, consequently, as in the *Project* and all of Freud's writings, they are not conscious themselves, since "consciousness and memory are mutually exclusive" (ibid., p. 234). But the main difference between this diagram, as well as its further elaboration in *The Interpretation of Dreams*, and the description of the apparatus given in the *Project*, does not lie in what *follows* the registrations but, rather, in what *precedes* them. For here Freud splits consciousness into two: a primary, perceptive consciousness, which appears at the very beginning, that is, the external end of the apparatus, and a secondary thought-consciousness, which is "subsequent in time, and is probably linked to the hallucinatory activation of word-presentations, so that the neurons of consciousness would once again be perceptual neurons and in themselves without memory" (ibid., p. 235).

There are thus primary perceptual neurons at the external end of the apparatus and more sophisticated, semi-linguistic neurons at the internal end of it. But by what process does the stimulus pass between these two extremes? And what kind of consciousness does primal perception possess?

Here, we should turn back to sexuality. Freud conceives of the passage from one layer or registration of the apparatus to another as *translation*. Normally, every registration leads to a further passage of the stimulus, which consists of translating the registration to the language of the next layer. However, a failure of translation frequently occurs, which Freud names *repression* (ibid.). Contrary to a normal defence, as in the case of the defence of the contact barriers, repression is characterized by Freud as *pathological*, and it "only occurs against a memory-trace from an earlier phase which has not yet been translated" (ibid.).

What does it mean for a registration to remain non-translated? It means that the registration is not perceived at the next phase as a *memory*, but rather as a fresh *event* with all its force, since the contact barriers did not manage to filter the dangerous force of the stimulus. Therefore, instead of a normal inhibition, a more drastic measure needs to be taken, namely repression, which entails blocking the stimulus and preventing it from going further into the depths of the apparatus.

What kind of stimulus or event can launch such a reaction? According to Freud, only one family of events leads to a memory "behaving as though it were some current event." These are, of course, *sexual* events, "because the magnitudes of the excitations which these release increase of themselves with time (with sexual development)" (ibid., p. 236).

In order to explain how the magnitudes of excitations can increase with time, Freud stresses that the diagram representing the apparatus applies not only to a momentary perception of a stimulus, but also to what he names "the psychical achievement of successive epochs of life" (ibid.). Thus, it is only at the age of 14 or 15 that, according to Freud, the third registration can be achieved, and that adult consciousness can take place (ibid., pp. 236-237). It is tempting to criticize and even reject this highly speculative developmental theory, but let us instead consider it as advancing a double character of perception: instantaneous and genealogical, the two mutually dependent.

Sexual events are thus first perceived normally, as any other stimulus that penetrates the apparatus, and only with time their registration or memory becomes itself an event, or, at least, is felt as such. Consequently, it must be repressed due to its inappropriate amount of energy, which threatens the apparatus.

It is now easier to understand the nature of primary perception at the external edge of the apparatus, which is supposed to be free from power, forces and points of resistance. Such a perception would be instantaneous but deprived of memory. Now, if we combine the instantaneous and genealogical or developmental models of the apparatus, we can see that repressed events always begin as primary perception, which naïvely enters the apparatus and then waits, somewhere inside, for its translation, which would give it memory, consciousness, or, in other words, objective existence. Freud characterizes such perceptions as sexual, but it is important to note that the condition for these latent perceptions' occurrence is not their sexual content *per se*, but, rather, their ability to be retained in the apparatus without translation, waiting for the day that their force bursts into consciousness, directly or indirectly through the symptom.

We should, therefore, ask, on the one hand, if there are not other kinds of perceptions that can cause such an effect, and, on the other hand, what the status of these perceptions is: are they real, mythological, or do they perhaps belong to a limit case, which can never be fully conceptualized? Among these three possibilities, Foucault would have probably chosen the third, and yet what access do we have to such perceptions?

In order to answer these questions, we should further explore the structure of the perceptual apparatus, and especially the relation between its two ends. In *The Interpretation of Dreams*, Freud reiterates his basic assumption that the apparatus works in a linear and unidirectional way: "All our psychical activity starts from stimuli (whether internal or external) and ends in innervations" (Freud, 1900, p. 537). And yet, it is already in this text that Freud start to shift consciousness from the back of the apparatus to the front of it: "We shall suppose that a system in the very front of the apparatus receives the perceptual stimuli but retains no trace of them and thus has no memory, while behind it there lies a second system which transforms the momentary excitations of the first system into permanent traces" (ibid., p. 538).

It is this picture of two main systems, and not three, that is ultimately retained by Freud: perception in the front, and unconscious memories behind. But what lies behind the unconscious? Do we find there, as we saw earlier, a more elaborated and linguistic consciousness? In *Seminar II*, Lacan and his audience tried to dispel the mystery surrounding the Freudian apparatus, but without, so it seems, much success. One of the participants in the seminar suggested that the only way to understand this diagram is to conceive of it as *circular* and not linear (Lacan, 1988, p. 139). The main problem is, indeed, to understand how memory affects perception and consciousness, and not only how perception and consciousness can affect memory.

In *The Interpretation of Dreams*, Freud claims that memory is in fact the formation of associations, and furthermore, that it has the function of conducting the stimulus: "Association would thus consist in the fact that, as a result of a diminution in resistances and of the laying down of facilitating paths, an excitation is transmitted from a given *Mnem.* element more readily to one *Mnem.* element than to another" (Freud, 1900, p. 539). According to the various memories associated with each stimulus, the system gradually takes on a certain character, determined by "the degrees of conductive resistance which it offered to the passage of excitation" (ibid.). Consequently, the character of the apparatus stems from unconscious memories: "What we describe as our 'character' is based on the memory-traces of our impressions; and, moreover, the impressions which have had the greatest impact on us – those of our earlier youth – are precisely the ones which scarcely ever become conscious" (ibid., pp. 539-540).

Our character, therefore, is hardly determined by us, but rather by unconscious impressions that never manage to arrive at consciousness. It seems that these impressions are perceived, but then get stuck somewhere in the apparatus, without receiving the translation which would enable them to become conscious again. Their increasing force, after entering the apparatus in the first place, goes together with their repression by the contact barriers, so that there is a whole series of violent dramas that remain completely interior, and yet it is these dramas that determine what we are and who we are.

So, what access do we have to these dramas? Almost thirty years after the diagram in the letter to Fliess, Freud supplies us with a highly illustrative description of the perceptual apparatus of the mind, in the 1925 *Note upon the "Mystic Writing-Pad"*. Here, Freud compares the apparatus to a self-erasing writing-pad, a popular toy among children. The writing-pad is composed of three layers: the most external one is a transparent piece of celluloid, whose only function is to protect a second layer attached below. This second, lower layer is made of thin translucent waxed paper. Finally, below these two layers stands a wax slab. When one scratches the face of the upper layer, the pressure operated by the wax paper upon the wax slab creates dark inscriptions. The inscriptions can easily be erased if one raises the two sheets from the wax slab. Then, the writing-pad becomes clear and ready to receive fresh impressions, which produce new inscriptions (Freud, 1925a, pp. 228-229).

The analogy between the mystic writing-pad and the perceptual apparatus is as follows: the most external layer, i.e. the celluloid sheet, is "a protective shield against stimuli". Secondly, the wax paper is "the layer which actually receives the stimuli" (ibid., p. 230), and is thus analogous to the system *Pcpt.-Cs.* Finally, the wax slab, which conserves permanent traces of the pressure, is analogous to memory, or, more accurately, to the unconscious. Moreover, the analogy concerns not only the structure of the two apparatuses, but also their mode of functioning, with Freud comparing "the appearance and disappearance of the writing" to "the flickering-up and passing-away of consciousness in the process of perception" (ibid., p. 231).

This model now obliges us to reconsider our view of the perceptual apparatus. Whereas, until now, Freud hesitated as to whether the unconscious was to be placed *between* perception and consciousness or *behind* the two, he now affirms that perception and consciousness form one and the same system, which is in the front.[14] But how, then, is perception filtered? And what determines whether a certain impression gains access to consciousness or not? Do all impressions now become conscious? The answer is no, since Freud no longer considers the unconscious as a device of passive filtering, but rather conceives it as an active agency, from which:

> cathectic innervations are sent out and withdrawn in rapid periodic impulses from within into the completely pervious system Pcpt.-Cs. So long as that system is cathected in this manner, it receives perceptions (which are accompanied by consciousness) and passes the excitation on to the unconscious mnemic systems; but as soon as the cathexis is withdrawn, consciousness is extinguished and the functioning of the system comes to a standstill. It is as though the unconscious stretches out feelers, through the medium of the system Pcpt.-Cs., towards the external world and hastily withdraws them as soon as they have sampled the excitations coming from it. (ibid.)

Hence, the unconscious is emancipated and, moreover, it is that which decides whether consciousness takes place or not. But what determines the shape and rhythm of the work of the feelers, of this sending out and drawing back of innervations? In other words, what agency does the unconscious have? Do we not witness here a failure already discovered and criticized by Sartre, by which the different systems are attributed a human, all knowing character? This criticism is reinforced in light of the 1925 text *Negation*, where Freud replaces the unconscious with the ego, stating that "perception is not a purely passive process. The ego periodically sends out small amounts of cathexes into the perceptual system, by means of which it samples the external stimuli, and then after every such tentative advance it draws back again" (Freud, 1925b, p. 238).

[14] Consequently, in 1919 Freud added a footnote to the description of the apparatus in *The Interpretation of Dreams*, positing that perception and consciousness form one system.

We witness here the development of the structural model where the ego becomes the central agency, although it ultimately finds itself, to use Lacan's terminology, de-centred. The first model we examined – the topographical one – is more anonymous, less subjective, so it seems to better fit the Foucaultian model of numerous points of unconscious resistance. The structural model, on the other hand, has the advantage of a double directionality. Not only from the outside to the inside, the stimulus passing an array of filters on the way to consciousness, but also from the inside outwards, sending out feelers from the unconscious towards consciousness. Now, if we combine the two models instead of opposing them to each other, if we consider the double directionality of the stimulus, the partial sovereignty of the subject, which is always subordinated to external stimuli internalized in the apparatus and affecting it from within, then we can better understand what Foucault seems to ignore: the question of the energetic source of the apparatus, and the ways in which the subject, as limited and powerless as it may be, can nonetheless influence and resist the mechanisms of power in which it is trapped.

Conclusion: The Possibility of Experience

In a 1978 interview, Foucault declared:

> I aim at having an experience myself – by passing through a determinate historical content – an experience of what we are today, of what is not only our past but also our present. And I invite others to share the experience. That is, an experience of our modernity that might permit us to emerge from it transformed. (Foucault, 1991, pp. 33-34)

How can such an experience take place, and what kind of experience is this? For Foucault, this is an experience which calls the subject into question, an experience that implies "its real destruction or dissociation, its explosion or upheaval into something radically 'other'" (ibid., p. 46).

Now, I have tried to show in this paper that Freudian psychoanalysis is one of the agencies that can help us realize such an experience, yet, in certain limits, dictated by historical context. Sexuality was one of the main fields that appeared to be transformable at the end of the nineteenth century. Psychoanalysis did not only aid in the experience of sexuality, but it also helped it to emerge from this experience transformed, not only through confession, as Foucault argued, but also through the work of translation and interpretation. And yet, modernity is in constant flux. New forces emerge, penetrating and reshaping it. Therefore, we need to continue this work of translating and transforming impressions and stimuli without limiting them to the field of sexuality.

Walter Benjamin, for instance, uses the Freudian model in order to show how the traumatic event of "the crowd" penetrates the apparatus and forces it to adapt everyday mechanisms of resistance and repetition. It is such mechanisms that we now need to analyze: not mechanisms of ego defence, or defence against specific repressive forces, but rather the mechanisms that take place in the encounter between different forces within the apparatus itself, and the ways in which this encounter makes an experience possible in the first place. We must describe, analyze and translate the encounter of subjectivity with what transcends it: sexuality, but also the crowd, the culture industry, capital, money and all the old and new institutions that are founded around them. We must understand how all these penetrate subjective experience, but also how the subject resists them, holds them back, represses or internalizes them. For it is not by turning away from modernity, but rather by experiencing it, that we may be able to transform it and ourselves together.

References

Derrida, J. (1978). Freud and the scene of writing. In *Writing and difference* (A. Bass, Trans.) (pp. 196-231). London: Routledge.

———. (1994). "To do justice to Freud": The history of madness in the age of psychoanalysis. (P. Brault et al., Trans.). *Critical Inquiry*, *20*, 227-265.

Forrester, J. (1990). Michel Foucault and the history of psychoanalysis. In J. Forrester (Ed.), *The seductions of psychoanalysis: Freud, Lacan and Derrida* (pp. 286-316). Cambridge: Cambridge University Press.

Foucault, M. (1978). *The history of sexuality. Volume I: An introduction.* (R. Hurley, Trans.). New York, NY: Random House. (Original work published 1976).

———. (1980). *Power/knowledge: Selected interviews & other writings 1972-1977.* (C. Gordon, Ed.). New York, NY: Pantheon Books.

———. (1991). *Remarks on Marx.* (J. Goldstein & J. Cascaito, Trans.). New York, NY: Semiotext(e).

Freud, S. (1895). Project for a scientific psychology. *Standard Edition 1*, pp. 295-344.

———. (1896). Extracts from the *Fliess* papers. Letter *52*, December 6. *Standard Edition 1*, pp. 233-239.

———. (1900). The interpretation of dreams. *Standard Edition 4-5*.

———. (1925a). A note upon the "mystic writing pad". *Standard Edition 19*, pp. 227-232.

———. (1925b). Negation. *Standard Edition 19*, pp. 235-239.

Lacan, J. (1988). *The seminar. Book II: The ego in Freud's theory and in the technique of psychoanalysis. 1954-1955.* (S. Tomaselli, Trans.). Cambridge: Cambridge University Press.

Miller, J. (1992). Michel Foucault and psychoanalysis. In T. J. Armstrong (Ed. and Trans.) *Michel Foucault: Philosopher* (pp. 58-64). New York, NY: Routledge.

Whitebook, J. (1998). Freud, Foucault, and the "diàlogue with unreason". *Philosophy and Social Criticism, 25*(6), 29-66.

The Psyche and the Social – Judith Butler's Politicizing of Psychoanalytical Theory

Veronica Vasterling

Since its inception, the theories and concepts of psychoanalysis have been used to analyze and clarify political phenomena and, conversely, political perspectives have been applied critically to psychoanalytical theories and practices. Feminism's interest in psychoanalytical theory is part of this long history of reciprocal engagements between psychoanalysis and politics. Ever since the publication of Juliet Mitchell's landmark book *Psychoanalysis and Feminism* in 1974, there has been a steady appropriation and politically inspired transformation of psychoanalytical theories and concepts by feminist and gender theorists. One of the most influential recent sources of this feminist appropriation and transformation of psychoanalysis is the work of Judith Butler.

From *Gender Trouble* (1990) onwards, psychoanalytical theory has played an increasingly important role in Butler's work. Psychoanalytical theory, and more in particular, anti-naturalist Lacanian theory, has become an indispensable resource for the well-known project pursued in Butler's work, i.e. the deconstruction of binary gender and heterosexuality as facts of nature. The main thrust of Butler's argument amounts to the following. Far from being a natural given, heterosexuality is a heavily policed compulsory norm enforcing the pervasive categorization of people as either male or female. Upholding the myth of a natural (hetero)sexuality that is hard-wired in our bodies – in the course of millions of years of evolutionary adaptation, according to the latest scientific version of this popular myth – requires the unwavering belief in and commitment to the existence of two kinds of people who are sexually different and yet attuned, whose bodies and psyches have evolved in different but complimentary ways under the pressures of the evolutionary law of sexual selection.

Butler develops the account of gender performativity in order to explain how binary gender and heterosexuality acquire their status of indubitable natural fact. Drawing on Foucault's concept of power, in addition to psychoanalytical theories of subject constitution and Derrida's notion of iterability, the account of gender performativity theorizes sexual identity as the precarious, unstable and open-ended result of the reiteration of norms which regulate the conditions of a socially acceptable and intelligible subject status, most importantly the interdependent conditions of binary gender and hetero-normativity. By reiterating the normative discursive practices that constitute heterosexual masculinity and femininity, the subject materializes itself as a socially intelligible and acceptable subject. Thus, gender comes down to performance, if performance is understood as the repeated citation and, over the course of time, embodiment of compelling norms. The very reiteration and embodiment of the norms causes the semblance of self-evident naturalness, which, in turn, strengthens the inveterate and largely unquestioned assumption that binary gender and heterosexuality are facts of nature. At the same time, however, reiteration is a process of continuous change. Analogous to citations, reiterations of norms, depending on context, may emphasize or play down, confirm or undermine the power and meaning of the cited norms.

The early version of the account of gender performativity, in *Gender Trouble*, appears to be mainly Foucault inspired. The later version elaborated in *Bodies That Matter* (1993) accords an important but ambiguous role to Lacanian psychoanalysis, a role which is clarified, to a certain extent, in a subsequent book, *The Psychic Life of Power* (1997). In this essay I will draw on these two books, and in particular on the latter, with the aim of sketching the outline of Butler's project of bringing Foucault (politics) and Lacan (psychoanalysis) together. The title *The Psychic Life of Power* succinctly summarizes her project of politicizing psychoanalytical theory. In addressing the psychic life of power, Butler tries to unravel the dynamic interplay of the psychic and the social with the subject as the intersection of both. I will first introduce this project and then discuss two interesting questions Butler raises in the course of this project.

The Psyche and the Social

The discussion which frames Butler's account of the interplay of the psyche and the social is the well-known debate on the question of the universality of the Oedipus complex in Freud, and of symbolic castration and the meaning of the phallus – and, thus, of sexual difference – in Lacan. To schematize a more complex debate, those who defend the universality of these key notions corroborate Freud's naturalist explanation of the Oedipus complex with evolutionary arguments (Van Haute, 2006, p. 80), while Lacan's structuralist approach is supported with (quasi-)transcendental arguments (Copjec, 1994; Žižek, 2000). The opposite camp argues that anthropological research has established cultural and historical variation in kinship structures, thereby falsifying the assumption of universal validity of the Freudian Oedipus complex (Moore, 2007) while critics of Lacan object that the key notions of his theory are invariant and, as such, a-historical. In orthodox Lacanian theory, castration and phallus appear to have the same impact and meaning everywhere and always, independent of cultural and social context.

Butler's work sides more with the critics of Lacan than with Lacanians like Žižek. While the latter appear to accord causal privilege to the psyche in relation to the social, Butler seems to reverse this state of affairs when she claims that the psyche is derived "from prior social operations" (Butler, 1997, p. 21). A crucial aspect of this reversal is her re-interpretation of the symbolic law. Disputing its invariant and quasi-transcendental status, she re-interprets the symbolic law in terms of historical and social contingency as a phenomenon of power, and, more precisely, as a variable set of prohibitions, norms, threats, idealizations and the like. The source of this re-interpretation of the symbolic in terms of the social is the work of Foucault. But while she adopts Foucault's concept of power, Butler does not follow his view of the subject as, simply and only, the product of disciplinary and normalizing power. She argues that Foucault's conception of the subject is inadequate because he reduces the psyche – or the soul, as he calls it – to the social as well. In *Discipline and Punish* (1979), Foucault describes how the disciplinary power of institutions – with the panoptic prison as exemplary instance – results in the formation of an inner agency of control and surveillance which he calls the soul. In so far as the soul can be taken as a psyche of sorts, this psyche is an effect of the social and, as such, reducible to the social. Butler points out that the reduction of the psyche deprives Foucault of the possibility to explain why and how the subject becomes passionately attached to the regulatory regimes of the social of which it is an effect. As interior organ of control and reflexivity brought into existence by disciplinary power, the soul is not only an unlikely source of passionate attachment; it is also unclear what drives the subject to passionately attach to power structures that constrain and subordinate it. The other important issue Butler draws our attention to is the question of how "psychic resistance to normalization" is possible (Butler, 1997, p. 87). She suggests that it is "the incommensurability between psyche and subject" that enables psychic resistance to the compelling power of norms, or, in general, to the normalizing power of the social (ibid.). Though she does not use the term when talking about her own conception, Butler appears to allude to the unconscious, the psychic agency or structure that is, indeed, incommensurable with the conscious ego which is here more or less equated with the Foucauldian subject.

Butler's use of the term "psyche" instead of the "unconscious" indicates that she wants to distance herself from traditional psychoanalytical notions of the unconscious. Her explicit critique of psychoanalytical theory is mostly aimed at the work of Lacan and Lacanians, with a special focus on the Lacanian notion of the unconscious and of resistance. Butler takes issue with the Lacanian notion of the real, that is, with an unconscious "which resists symbolization absolutely" (Lacan, 1988, p. 66). As that which "is impossible to imagine, impossible to integrate into the symbolic order, and impossible to attain in any way" (Evans, 1996, p. 160), the real appears to refer to an absolute outside. And that is precisely Butler's problem with the real. Whereas it constrains the symbolical and the imaginary from outside, the real itself is impossible to attain and integrate in any way. It is therefore inassimilable to the social. In Butler, by contrast, the psyche (the unconscious) is derived from the social. Butler's use of the term "derived" is meant to carve out a sort of middle position between Foucault and Lacan, between a soul that is nothing but an effect of the social, and, as such, reducible to the social, and an unconscious that constrains the social while being itself completely sealed off from the social. Derived from the social as well as incommensurable with the Foucauldian subject, the Butlerian psyche does not refer to an absolute outside – because it is derived from the social – but to a constitutive outside. That is, an outside constitutive of but not commensurable with the Foucauldian subject, and, hence, not reducible to the social.

Butler also finds fault with the Lacanian notion of resistance. Pointing out that, in Lacanian theory, resistance against the symbolic law is located in the domain of the imaginary, Butler continues with the following observation:

> The imaginary thwarts the efficacy of the symbolic law but cannot turn back upon the law, demanding or effecting its reformulation. In this sense, psychic resistance thwarts the law in its effects, but cannot redirect the law or its effects. Resistance is thus located in a domain that is virtually powerless to alter the law that it opposes. Hence, psychic resistance presumes the continuation of the law in its anterior, symbolic form and, in that sense, contributes to its status quo. In such a view, resistance appears doomed to perpetual defeat. (Butler, 1997, p. 98)

A good example of this self-defeating logic of resistance is the imaginary phallus. As idealizing phantasm of totalizing wholeness, the imaginary phallus resists the truth of symbolic castration, that is, the truth of a sexed body which cannot be self-sufficient and of a desire which cannot be fulfilled. But the resistance of the imaginary phallus remains restricted to the psychic life of the individual. It is not only incapable of undermining the quasi-transcendental status of the symbolic phallus as privileged signifier of sexual difference. Because of its very status as an individual fantasy enabled by the symbolic phallus, the resisting imaginary phallus does indeed, as Butler suggest, maintain the status quo and prop up the power of the symbolic phallus.

By consistently using the notions of the social and the psyche instead of the symbolic and unconscious, Butler indicates her distance to established psychoanalytical theory and, at the same time, establishes the cornerstones of her own account. Though this is a useful and even necessary move, it also makes for a certain slipperiness and vagueness. This is especially apparent in her use of the notion of the psyche. Though one often gets the impression that the (soul of the) Foucaultian subject relates to psyche as ego to id, or conscious reflexivity to unconscious desires, attachments, identifications, and abjections, this parallel breaks down at certain points, raising the question of how exactly the psyche *does* relate to the Foucaultian subject. Sometimes Butler's notion of psyche seems to consist of ego and id; sometimes it seems to only refer to a sort of unconscious. However that may be, in the following I will discuss Butler's own answers to the two questions – concerning passionate attachment and resistance – she addresses to Foucault. Taken together, the answers provide key elements of the new psycho-political account she puts together.

Passionate Attachments

Butler introduces the notion of passionate attachment with the help of Freud. "For Freud an infant forms a pleasure-giving attachment to any excitation that comes its way, even the most traumatic, which accounts for the formation of masochism and, for some, the production of abjection, rejection, wretchedness, and so on as the necessary precondition for love" (Butler, 1997, p. 61). Abstracting from the Freudian account of (infant) sexuality, Butler defines passionate attachment as "the formation of primary passion in dependency" (ibid., p. 7). Utterly dependent on its care-takers, the infant must attach to the care-takers it gets, whether they abuse or nurture it. Because "if the child is to persist in a psychic and social sense, there must be dependency and the formation of attachment: there is no possibility of not loving, where love is bound up with the requirements for life." (ibid., p. 8) Attachment, in Butler's interpretation, becomes a general condition of psychic and social survival because the desire to survive, "to persist in one's own being", necessitates attachment (ibid., p. 28). The necessity of attachment entails the inevitability of alienation because "the desire to persist in one's own being requires submitting to a world of others that is fundamentally not one's own" (ibid.). It means "to be given over from the start to social terms that are never fully one's own" and to be "vulnerable to terms that one never made" (ibid.). Therefore, one "persists always, to some degree, through categories, names, terms, and classifications that mark a primary and inaugurative alienation in sociality" (ibid.).

The point Butler wants to make, however, is not about alienation but about the exploitability of (unconscious) attachments by the regulatory regimes of the social.[1] Taking shape in the discursive field of the social, an identity and sense of self require social recognition. Growing up, we form passionate attachments to terms and practices that promise or confer social recognition. Originating in the need to survive psychically and socially, these attachments are the linchpin of the psychic life of power. They are the unconscious conduits by which the social regime of heterosexual binary gender recycles itself, conferring social recognition at the price of a thorough disciplining of most aspects of human life. Even when we become aware of the price we pay, the attachments will be next to impossible to give up. Social rejection or psychic breakdown is something we do not often take upon ourselves willingly.

With this fusion of Foucaultian and psychoanalytical insights, Butler offers an acute and convincing diagnosis of the very common, yet paradoxical, phenomenon of tenacious and passionate attachment to demeaning and hurtful practices and identities.[2] Contemporary gender identity offers abundant empirical evidence exemplifying the paradox. Starting with feminine gender identity, whether it is burkas or string bikinis, extreme make-over or cliterodectomy, vows of virginity or prostitution, they all have their passionate female defenders whose passion derives from, I am afraid, a very real sense of what conditions social and psychical survival for women, namely, the body. Feminine identity is largely based on a stupendous variety of social regimes and sanctions regulating the female body, its appearance, availability,

[1] As noted before, Butler avoids using the term "unconscious". From the way she makes her argument it is clear, however, that she assumes that attachments at least partially elude the purview of reflection and calculation.

[2] My discussion of this point is indebted to Amy Allen's excellent assessment of the strengths and weaknesses of this particular fusion of Foucaultian and psychoanalytical insights in Butler's work (Allen, 2006).

and use by men and by women themselves. The intensity of these regulatory regimes does not show any sign of decreasing. On the contrary, in modern Western society the regimes regulating female bodies appear to have shifted and increased. If a century ago women's bodies were still largely the private property of men, nowadays they appear to have become public and commercial property. Women's bodies sell not only cars, mobile phones and insurances, but also, increasingly, moral and political ideologies. In the case of masculine gender identity it is not the body but status which conditions social and psychical survival. Here, one of the most important examples of the paradox is the regime of competition which, in Western countries, invades every sphere of masculine life, from the market to the bedroom, from professional life to leisure, and from art and science to morality and religion, turning men into winners or losers with little in between. Though it is a regulatory regime from which men and women suffer, competition is naturalized economically, politically, scientifically, morally and maybe in other ways as well.[3]

In short, there is ample empirical evidence that people in the affluent and relatively free societies of the West stick to gender practices that are restrictive and one-sided at best, hurtful and demeaning at worst. What Butler suggests is that the pervasive submission to these gender regimes might be explained by unconscious passionate attachments to the terms and practices of binary gender as that which guarantees social and psychic survival.

Arguing with the Real

The second question Butler hopes to solve by adding a psychoanalytical perspective to the Foucaultian account of power is the question of resistance. This question proves to be much stickier, mainly because it involves a re-interpretation of the notoriously difficult Lacanian notions of the real, foreclosure, and symbolic law. In order to demarcate Butler's transformation of these notions, I will first give a short outline of the Lacanian conceptualization of foreclosure. Then, I will analyze Butler's discussion with Žižek on the status of the real and the symbolic law, which provides the main context of her transformation of these notions.

[3] Neo-liberalism does a good job, of course, in naturalizing capitalist competition as the only possible way of arranging economical and social life. As already indicated above, the most popular scientific naturalization of competition is provided by evolutionary psychology (male competition over sexual access to females). And, finally, a very common moral naturalization of competition is the conviction that it will spur the development of one's talents.

Lacan introduces the term *forclusion* (foreclosure) as a translation of the Freudian *Verwerfung* which is rendered as "repudiation" in the English Standard Edition of Freud's work. In Freud, a systematic use or a clearly established meaning of repudiation does not yet exist. It is Lacan who develops the notion in a more systematic way, focusing on one sense of repudiation in particular, namely "the sense of a specific defense mechanism which is distinct from repression (*Verdrängung*)" (Evans, 1996, p. 65). In Lacan, *Verwerfung*, foreclosure, is differentiated from repression "in that the foreclosed element is not buried in the unconscious but expelled from the unconscious" (ibid.). Foreclosure comes to refer to the specific mechanism underlying psychosis in which a fundamental signifier (the Name-of-the-Father, the phallic signifier) is foreclosed, that is, excluded from the symbolic. Psychosis is triggered by the reappearance, in the real, of the excluded signifier because the subject is unable to assimilate it. Thus, foreclosure is connected to another Lacanian notion that is of importance for Butler, the notion of the real. As I mentioned before, Lacan, in his work of the 1950s, defines the real as "that which resists symbolization absolutely" and as "the domain of whatever subsists outside symbolization" (ibid., p. 159). The real "is impossible to imagine, impossible to integrate into the symbolic order, and impossible to attain in any way" – which lends it "its essentially traumatic character" (ibid., p. 160).

As one of the most productive Lacanian theorists who provide new political applications of Lacanian theory, Žižek has, of course, attracted Butler's attention. Despite the common ground they share, Butler takes issue with Žižek's use of the notion of the real. She agrees with Žižek's emphasis on the real as the threatening force of the law which, through the threat of punishment, induces the foreclosure that is constitutive of the subject. Both Butler and Žižek subscribe to the view that the subject "is produced in language through an act of foreclosure (*Verwerfung*)" and that the subject continues to be determined by what is refused or repudiated (Butler, 1993, p. 190).[4] Butler disagrees with Žižek, and per implication with Lacan, on two counts: the status of the real and the law, and the function of the law. Not surprisingly, Butler questions the freezing "of the real as the impossible 'outside' to discourse" (ibid., p. 207). She objects to the conceptualization of the real as a permanent and traumatic outside inasmuch as it concerns "the excluded and threatening possibility that motivates and, eventually, thwarts the linguistic urge to intelligibility" (ibid., p. 192). She also questions the assumption, entailed by the Lacanian notion of the real, of "an invariant

[4] Note that the term "subject" here is taken in a – broadly – psychoanalytical sense and not in the Foucaultian sense.

law that operates uniformly in all discursive regimes to produce through prohibition this 'lack' that is the trauma induced by the threat of castration" (ibid., p. 205).

As a follow-up to these objections, Butler introduces the notion of the social, based on a re-interpretation of the Lacanian notions of the real and the symbolic, mixing aspects of both. The lens of the re-interpretation is the Foucaultian concept of power. As it condenses much of the work of transformation, it is important to note the specific features of the social in Butler's work. Its first feature concerns the status and function of the law. Instead of an invariant law that, among other things, confers quasi-ontological status on a hierarchical version of sexual difference – where one sex represents the phallus and the other castration – Butler introduces a variable law that is part of contingent relations of power. In addition to the term "law" she, therefore, uses terms like "demands, taboos, sanctions, injunctions, prohibitions, impossible idealizations, and threats" (ibid., p. 106). The contingent and variable status of the law implies that "there may be several mechanisms of foreclosure that work to produce the unsymbolizable in any given discursive regime" (ibid., p. 205). The second important feature of the social is that it is structured by discursive power. Discursive power in Butler refers to the power of normative regimes – laws, prohibitions, idealizations etcetera – that split the social field, including the subjects who shape their lives and identities in accordance with the normative regimes, excluding the "abjects" who fail to do so and therefore fail to attain full subject status, that is, social recognition. Hence, by dividing the social field into an inside and an outside, discursive power constitutes subjects and "abjects".

The issue of subject constitution brings us to the third and decisive feature of the social, namely, foreclosure as the central element of the psychic life of power. The introduction of foreclosure is a crucial step in Butler's account, for this is the point where Foucault and Lacan are welded together. Foreclosure is the process or act that initiates the psychic life of power, and, hence, links the social and the psychic. Triggered by compelling normative regimes, foreclosure splits the subject and institutes the psyche in the sense of the unconscious. Instead of reappearing in the absolute-outside of the real, the foreclosed reappears in the social outside, or, rather, as the social outside, as those abject creatures who fail to embody the prescriptions and prohibitions of hegemonic normative regimes. Thus, foreclosure, in Butler, joins the Foucaultian concept of discursive power with the Lacanian concept of the symbolic law, transforming both. Through its investment in the symbolic law, discursive power not only organizes the social field, it also shapes the subject.

The symbolic law triggers foreclosure, thereby instituting what Foucault's subject lacks: a psyche. By simultaneously dropping the Lacanian notion of the real in the sense of the absolute outside, Butler embeds the symbolic law, the process of foreclosure and the foreclosed in the newly conceptualized domain of the social.

Conclusion

Though extremely suggestive, this account of the relation of the political and the psychic also remains deeply inconclusive. On the one hand, the symbolic law is transformed into a changeable formation, the status and content of which depend on historical context and contingent power relations. If, for instance, Butler argues that society is structured by the symbolic law of heterosexuality, and, in its wake, binary gender, it is implied that this law of sex is not only a modern formation of discursive power but also of variable force and intensity. That is, it may or may not include a strict prohibition of homosexuality that triggers the foreclosure of early homosexual identifications with and attachments to the same sex parent, producing a subject with a rigid sexual and gender identity. Whereas the re-interpretation of the symbolic law seems to imply that the subject may or may not be constituted by foreclosure, Butler, on the other hand, repeatedly insists that the subject is always constituted by foreclosure.[5] The reason for this insistence seems obvious. Without foreclosure, Butler loses the dimension of the psyche, and more in particular, the unconscious, and would be left with merely a Foucaultian subject. For it is unclear what could constitute the unconscious (the psyche) in Butler's account, if it is not foreclosure.

More seriously, Butler fails to formulate a clear answer to the question of resistance. If foreclosure is constitutive of the subject, it is hard to see what psychic sources the subject will draw upon to resist the symbolic law that triggers foreclosure. Far from being sources of resistance, the foreclosed homosexual identifications and attachments – returning from the outside in the form of a perception of homosexuals as abject creatures, a perception which threatens the subject's sense of self – will install a rigid, homophobic identity that confirms and strengthens the law of heterosexuality. Nor will unconscious desire provide a source of resistance, for, as Butler herself

[5] See, for instance, Butler (1993, p. 243; 1997, p. 212; 2000, p. 140). In *Bodies That Matter*, Butler uses various terms – repudiation, abjection and disavowal – which she links to foreclosure.

concedes, "desire will aim at unravelling the subject, but be thwarted by precisely the subject in whose name it operates ... for desire to triumph, the subject must be threatened with dissolution" (Butler, 1997, p. 9). Even if we take the term "subject" in its reductive Foucaultian sense, as it is, indeed, intended here, subject dissolution will, I am afraid, qualify less as resistance against normalizing power than as existential breakdown.

References

Allen, A. (2006). Dependency, subordination, and recognition: On Judith Butler's theory of subjection. *Continental Philosophy Review, 38*, 199-222.

Butler, J. (1990). *Gender trouble: Feminism and the subversion of identity*. London/New York, NY: Routledge.

———. (1993). *Bodies that matter: On the discursive limits of "sex"*. London/New York, NY: Routledge.

———. (1997). *The psychic life of power*. Stanford, CA: Stanford University Press.

———. (2000). *Antigone's claim: Kinship between life and death*. New York, NY: Columbia University Press.

———., Laclau, E., & Žižek, S. (2000). *Contingency, hegemony, universality: Contemporary dialogues on the left*. London/New York, NY: Verso.

Copjec, J. (1994). *Read my desire: Lacan against the historicists*. London/Cambridge, MA: MIT Press.

Evans, D. (1996). *An introductory dictionary of Lacanian psychoanalysis*. London/New York, NY: Routledge.

Foucault, M. (1979). *Discipline and punish: The birth of the prison*. (A. Sheridan, Trans.). New York, NY: Vintage. (Original work published 1976).

Lacan, J. (1988). *The seminar. Book I: Freud's papers on technique. 1953-1954*. (J. Forrester, Trans.). Cambridge/New York, NY: Norton/Cambridge University Press.

Mitchell, J. (1974). *Psychoanalysis and feminism*. New York, NY: Penguin Books.

Moore, H. (2007). *The subject of anthropology: Gender, symbolism and psychoanalysis*. Cambridge: Polity Press.

Van Haute, P. (2006). De antropologische betekenis van het Oedipuscomplex: een lectuur van Freuds teksten over de vrouwelijke seksualiteit. In P. Van Haute & P. Verhaeghe (Eds.), *Voorbij Oedipus. Twee psychoanalytische verhandelingen over het Oedipuscomplex* (pp. 75-125). Amsterdam: Boom.

Foucault, Lacan, and the Question of Technique

Cecilia Sjöholm

As is well known, Michel Foucault was a stern critic of psychoanalysis. In the final chapter of *La volonté de savoir*, he situates the practice of psychoanalysis between the technologies of bio-power and the disciplining of the body that marked modernity. In Foucault's writing, it was precisely the conjunction of these two phenomena that had such catastrophic consequences for the twentieth century. Although well aware that psychoanalysis was consciously resisting fascism, Foucault saw psychoanalysis as using the same strategy as the technologies of bio-power: targeting the family in order to control the population. Through its focus on the Law of the father and incest taboo, psychoanalysis submits sexuality to a certain order of the family that will, in the end, naturalize a repressive order of "normality".[1] For that reason, psychoanalysis has not only contributed to a heteronormative arrangement of family life, as argued by Judith Butler in *Antigone's Claim*, for instance (Butler, 2000, pp. 65-71).[2] More importantly, psychoanalysis has remained impotent in the face of the racism, the violence and the suicidal culture of the totalitarian orders of Nazism, fascism and communism that were to be the historical result of the technologies of bio-power. To Foucault, the question of sexuality is situated at the crossroads between bio-power and the disciplinary technologies of the body. In this way, the question of sexuality is one of the most sensitive political issues of our time.

In *La volonté de savoir*, psychoanalysis is made reducible to the obligation to confess. However, it would be a mistake to summarize the relation between Foucault and psychoanalysis in that way. In his biography, Didier Eribon depicts Foucault's first encounter with Lacan as respectful, even enthusiastic. Foucault attended the first public seminar of Lacan held at St. Anne's in 1953.[3] This biographical fact is certainly of interest. In 1953-54, Lacan gave his first seminar on Freud's writings on technique. And if we look at

[1] See the final chapter of Foucault (1988).

[2] Butler argues that the Lacanian reliance on Levi-Strauss' structuralist view on the incest taboo has also prevented it from recognizing other forms of kinship than those normalized from the point of view of the "law of the father", where the father really is a father rather than a symbolic position.

[3] Although Foucault later played down the Lacanian influence, claiming not to have understood much – see: Eribon (1989, p. 93).

Foucault's ideas on the technologies of the self together with Freud's and Lacan's writings on technique, we may well consider the relation between Foucault and psychoanalysis in a new light. Both psychoanalysis and Foucault work with the notion of different possibilities of subjectivities. It is precisely the term of technique, or technology, that offers the key to such multiplicity. Both Foucault's technologies of the self, and the technique of psychoanalysis as described by Lacan, are operating at the junction where the concept of technology allows for the self or the subject to adhere to various possibilities of truth, rather than a particular truth.

Freud first reflected on the notion of technique in psychoanalysis in *Studies on Hysteria*, published in 1895. Fifteen years later, he began writing *Allgemeine Technik der Psychoanalyse*, a work that was supposed to be a general account of psychoanalytical technique. It was never completed. Instead, in 1918, Freud published six papers under the title *The Technique of Psychoanalysis*.[4] As James Strachey points out in his introduction to these papers, Freud's writings on technique do not make up a system and there seems to have been a great deal of reluctance on his part to systematize these writings in particular. As a practicing analyst, he did not want the patients to know in advance what was going to happen in the analytic sessions.[5] The reluctance against any systematic account of technique is thereby inscribed in the history of analysis, due to the particular relation between clinic and theory. Psychoanalysis is irreducible to theory alone, and must be passed on through experience. In order to learn a technique, experience is necessary; not just of patients but of a personal analysis. On the other hand, it is necessary to know the grounds of psychoanalysis before any technique is developed. Therefore, the papers on technique attempt to tie together certain theoretical assumptions with reflections based on clinical experience. But the relation between theory and practice is not one of simple transposition. The notion of technique implies a complicated relation to psychoanalytical theory. Freud considered psychoanalysis to be a new science. As such, however, it was never reducible to a set theory with a method; it was a science under construction. The writings on technique show Freud's fear that the theory of analysis could be creating a resistance against the cure.

What, then, does the term "technique" imply in the discourse of psychoanalysis? Lacan begins his 1953-1954 seminar on Freud's papers on technique

[4] These papers are: *The Handling of Dream-Interpretation in Psychoanalysis*, *The Dynamics of Transference*, *Recommendations to Physicians Practicing Psychoanalysis*, *On Beginning the Treatment*, *Remembering, Repeating and Working-Through* and *Observations on Transference-Love*.

[5] See James Strachey's introduction to *Papers of technique* (Freud, 1911-1913).

with a reflection on the master, referring in particular to a master of the technique of Zen Buddhism: "[T]he students [are supposed] to find out for themselves the answer to their own questions. The master does not teach a ready-made science: he supplies an answer when the students are on the verge of finding it" (Lacan, 1988, p. 1). However, as analysis develops, its theory becomes increasingly hypostasized. In his reading of Freud, Lacan observes the analyst becoming more and more uncomfortably aware of his role as a master. Thus, the papers on technique mirror a theoretical development, based on Freud's own experience as an analyst. Famously, Lacan's conclusion is that theoretical tools need to be continuously renegotiated in the clinic. Breaking with the analysis of the ego that was dominant in the psychoanalytical discourse in the fifties, Lacan works with the concepts of the imaginary, the symbolic and the real, and their impact in the clinic, mainly in the experience of transference. Arguing against Michael Balint that the technique and the theory of psychoanalysis amount to the same, Lacan uses these concepts less as theoretical tools and more as technical aids. The question of how we are to conceive of the unconscious in relation to the ego is a theoretical issue. The question of how we are to work our way beyond the ego, however, is one of technique. The imaginary, the symbolic and the real are terms that acquire a meaning in the experience of analysis, and more particularly in the experience of transference. In the seminar, Lacan insists continuously on the singularity of the experience of analysis, on the one hand in order to assure respect for the person engaging in analysis, and on the other in order to assure its efficiency, since every attempt at systematization will help to build the resistance of the patient. The factor *x* in analysis, or the "truth" of the subject towards which "master" Freud was leading his students, is, thus, a singularity which can never be fully theorized or systematized. It can only be encountered through the experience of analysis itself, and the phenomenon of transference through which every analysis must be performed. Therefore, Lacan insists that the crucial questions of analysis have to do with technique rather than theory.

Technology and Memory According to Stiegler

What, then, is technique? Technology and technique share the same etymological root. In the Greek etymology of the word, *tekhne* means craft, and *logia* means saying. The relation between technology and technique is not clear-cut. Technology may appear to refer to a craft, involving tools; technique may seem to have more to do with systems and organization. If we look at the way the word "technology" is used in Foucault, however, it appears interchangeable with that of "technique" in psychoanalysis. Both concepts refer to a manner of doing things, a skill involving a great deal of creative capacity. In *Technics and Time I*, Bernard Stiegler does not indicate there to be a crucial difference between the concepts of technique and technology. What is interesting, rather, in his philosophy of technology, is the relation between technics, as the English translation will have it, understood both as technique and technology, and life. As a process of exteriorization, technology (if we decide to stick with this term for the sake of simplicity, remembering that it is interchangeable with technique in this context) "is the pursuit of life by means other than life" (Stiegler, 1998, p. 17). There is a distinct similarity between the Greek notion of production as *poiesis* and technology. Art, according to Heidegger, is, on the one hand, a form of *poiesis*, or, a making of something out of nothing, and, on the other, a form of knowing or skill – *tekhne* – that helps bring something into being.

Stiegler's concept of technology is close to Heidegger's concept of art in general, and to the way he uses the word *tekhne* in particular. The question of technology is that of production, but its most important aspect lies not in the thing that is produced, but rather in the potential that is uncovered. According to Heidegger, *tekhne* has a revelatory power that is not simply secondary to *poiesis*. *Tekhne*, or, the skill that uncovers the potential of art, is an important aspect of the very essence of art. Art is the highest form of *tekhne* since it has the capacity to reveal the truth of that which *tekhne* as *poiesis*, as a form of making something out of nothing, brings forward. To Heidegger, the question of technology, as well as that of art, is deeply embedded in the question of *Dasein* (ibid., p. 95). The true question of *tekhne*, therefore, has to do with the capacity of making, with the producer and not with what is produced. In this sense, the analysis of technology is close to the analysis of art. Technology is production in the sense of *poiesis*; it is a way of bringing into being what is not. Technology, therefore, is similar to the notion of art in Heidegger's philosophy.

According to Stiegler, there is no way to properly distinguish the historicity of the human from the historicity of technology. Therefore, one must overcome an opposition that is often assumed to exist from an anthropological point of view, where human beings are defined through technical knowledge or skills on the one hand and through their intellect on the other. The idea that humanity is defined through its intellectual capacities presumes the human subject to be a form of interiority. However, in Stiegler's philosophy, humanity is defined through forms of exteriorization rather than interiorization. Exteriorization is the origin of technology, as well as the origin of the human. Exteriorization is a kind of rupture through which the human and the tool come into being at the same time. The process through which they come into being does not merely represent two sides of the same thing, but a process of differentiation.

Stiegler considers the sign as something which introduces the rupture that lies at the very heart of the process of exteriorization. Technology is the invention of human memory through rupture. The most prominent tool of technology, in Stiegler's thought, is the sign. What we talk about as humanity is produced through technologies that are coextensive with the production of signs. Technology, thereby, is never reducible to the use of tools. It involves a process of exteriorization produced both through gesturing and through tools that, in turn, will produce traces – traces of memory. Human history is the continuous production of ruptures that, in turn, produce traces or forms of inscription. Humanity cannot be conceived beyond these traces. What defines humanity, then, is not the capacity of memorization, but, rather, the capacity to produce traces through the process of exteriorization. We cannot conceive of what is human as lying beyond technology. Neither memory nor history can have an existence of its own, outside of the rupture that takes place through the technologies of signs. The creation of memory is simultaneous with the making of signs and inscriptions: "[I]t is by freeing itself from genetic inscription that memory at once pursues the process of liberation and inscribes thereupon the mark of a rupture — on stones, walls, books, machines, madeleines, and all forms of supports; from the tattooed body itself to instrumentalized genetic memories, disorganized, and inert as it were, then reorganized, manipulated, stored, rationalized, and exploited by the life industries named 'biotechnologies'" (ibid., p. 169). The invention of the human is thereby ambiguous in the philosophy of Stiegler; humanity is both coextensive with its history and defined through the technologies that exceed it, pointing to something that is still to evolve.

The question of what is to be considered human singularity (or, the question of the *who*) is always intertwined with the metaphysical question of what helps produce such singularity (or, the question of the *what*). As Stiegler puts it, the question of the *who* and the *what* are two sides of the same phenomenon: "If the individual is organic organized matter, then its relation to its environment (to matter in general, organic or inorganic), when it is a question of a *who*, is mediated by the organized but inorganic matter of the *organon,* the tool with its instructive role (its role *qua* instrument), the *what.* It is in this sense that the *what* invents the *who* just as much as it is invented by it" (ibid., p. 169). Stiegler, in reading Heidegger, argues that the *who* and the *what* are tied to each other through the rupture of the sign that is coextensive with the human. The Heideggerian term *Dasein* was created to avoid the notion that the question of being is posed by an ego, or a subject reflecting on itself, isolated from its environment. In tying the question of the *who* and the *what* together – through assuring us that human singularity can never be a question of sheer spirituality or interiority – Heidegger shows that there is an element of uncanniness attached to the question of the *who*. When we ask the question of the *who*, we are always thrown outside of the notion of the self. Since the *who* is tied up with the *what*, it introduces an element that makes it impossible for the self to coincide with itself. The unitary consistency of the human self, argues Stiegler, is always to come, but it never appears to be set in place (ibid., p. 259). The relation between the *who* and the *what* is determined by traces produced through technology, or the sign system. Moreover, the technology of the sign system is also present in the individual's relation to himself. An individual reflecting on himself can never ask himself "who am I"? in a way that would reduce him to a question of sheer interiority. The question of the *who* is entangled with an element that forbids the self to coincide with itself, with the sign.

In Stiegler's philosophy, exteriorization is reminiscent of Lacan's theorization of the signifier. Exteriorization is described as rupture in Stiegler, just like the inscription of the signifier in Lacan's thought. According to Lacan, the signifier introduces a foreign aspect into the subject; it is the Other, challenging every conceivable idea that the subject be something self-contained or some kind of unity. Therefore, the *ego* cannot be the aim of the analysis. It is perhaps not by coincidence that Lacan's seminar on the technique of psychoanalysis is dedicated, primarily, to the deconstruction of the analysis of the ego. Like Heidegger's *Dasein*, the Lacanian subject was created in order to avoid the notion of a human subject reflecting on itself in an isolated manner, beyond the process of exteriorization that takes place through the sign. The history of the technique of psychoanalysis shows that the more the ego affirms itself, the more it is alienated. Lacan's question becomes: who then, beyond the ego, is it that seeks recognition (Lacan, 1988, p. 51)? In Lacanian discourse, just as in Heidegger, the question of the *who* is entangled with the *what*. The subject of psychoanalysis is one of speech, or discourse, and is marked by a signifier that will continue to have its effect not only on the unconscious, but on the constitution of the ego. Arguing against the old school of ego-analysis where the task of analysis is to enlarge the level of consciousness, Lacan argues for a technique of analysis where the cure is achieved through a series of displacements. The task of analysis is to work through the process of displacements and to arrive at the junction where the *who* meets the *what*, where the singularity of the subject can be identified through the mark of the signifier. That mark, however, will pursue the process of displacement in which it is already caught. The subject is inconceivable beyond the function of speech and the function of transference, both variables that constitute the focus for the question of technique.

Lacan's reflections on Freud's papers on technology are more than a critique of ego-analysis. They are a critique of the notion that analysis should be theorized in a certain fashion once and for all. The technique of psychoanalysis is irreducible to theory alone since the ruptures and displacements that appear in the work with the signifier, beyond the ego, can never be fully determined.

Technologies of the Self

Foucault came to consider the most important human practices as "technologies". Rather than the use of tools, technology denotes the use of crafts. In his text *Technologies of the Self*, Foucault names four kinds of technologies, which are all means through which man comes to understand himself: the technologies of production, through which man produces or changes artefacts; the technologies of sign systems, which make it possible to create discursive meanings through the use of signs and symbols, the technologies of power, which shape and dominate the individual according to certain goals, and, finally, the technologies of the self, through which the individual elaborates his intellect, body and emotions (Foucault, 2000a, p. 225). All these technologies were regarded as interwoven by Foucault.

Foucault defines the self as a striving towards knowledge. But it is not a striving that has always looked the same.[6] For Aristotle, a natural link exists between sensation, pleasure, knowing and truth. The self, in Aristotle, is a unity where the discovery of truth also becomes enjoyable, where knowledge becomes something one should strive for. Researching the tradition of the care of the self in classical philosophy, however, Foucault became less and less interested in the idea of discourse as regulative for the individual, and more interested in the individual's relation to himself. The technologies of the self, therefore, occupied a particular place in the system of technologies: representing a position through which the individual was able to formulate

[6] See: *History of the systems of thought*, in: Foucault (2000b).

a productive conception of the self, and a productive conception of truth in relation to the systems of discourse that were regulative representatives of power:

> Perhaps I've insisted too much on the technology of domination and power. I am more and more interested in the interaction between oneself and others, and in the technologies of individual domination, in the mode of action that an individual exercises upon himself by means of the technologies of the self. (ibid.)

Foucault separates the technologies of the self, or, the care of the self, from a hermeneutics of the self. The injunction "know thyself" has dominated Western philosophies for a long time. The care of the self, however, has been forgotten and obscured. The care of the self is a technique linking the subject to truth in a way different from the notion of uncovering a truth, independent from and beyond one's corporeal existence. The aim is not to discover *the* truth, as in the hermeneutics of the subject, but, rather, to link the subject to a truth, one that is learned and memorized and progressively put into practice. To progressively apprehend a relation to truth is to establish a relation to the external world.

The ancient "care of the self", however, has been forgotten. In the third volume of the history of sexuality, *Le souci de soi*, Foucault describes how the philosophy of late antiquity could be described as an ethos rather than a science, a way of life in which body and soul participate on equal terms. The ethos of the care of the self aims toward certain achievements, through which you become true to yourself. As these practices evolved, the body was lost. In late antiquity, the care of the self was aiming towards a freedom of the flesh. The techniques of asceticism were developed in order to win a freedom from bodily needs. Rather than winning such freedom, however, the care of the self was eventually overshadowed by the injunction of "knowing" oneself (ibid., pp. 95-109). The art of writing, which is tied to introspection, was instrumental in this development. Marcus Aurelius, for instance, shows how a new freedom may develop through the nuances of introspection. In this, the experience of the self evolves in writing; a whole new field of possibilities is allowed to develop (ibid., pp. 207-221). The achievement of this development is Nietzsche, whom one can always discern in Foucault's writings. In Nietzsche, the self is set in play as a deceitful will striving for advantage and survival. The quest for knowledge of the self is displaced by technologies that are created to define, hide or create truth. In Nietzsche, also, the technologies that help create truth-concepts, such as the technologies of the self, are more important than the philosophical question of the truth. We have, then, come full circle, back to an ideal where the truth of the self is never discovered, but, rather, attained.

Foucault's use of the term "technology" refers to the ways in which a conception of the self has arisen through distinct corporeal and discursive practices. Foucault's point, then, is that the self is developed through different goals and aims, through experiences that allow for the self to change, and also through discursive technologies that influence one's conception of the self. While new technologies develop, the care of the self will also develop. Losing track of the changes that the self has undergone in relation to different truth-concepts, an important insight has been lost to Western philosophy; namely, the insight that there are different ways of creating knowledge, and that there are different forms of self. When the relation between *tekhne* and *poiesis* is lost, philosophy ceases to be a technology of becoming in which the body is taken care of as well as the education towards philosophical truth. When philosophical life is detached from *eros*, or appetite, or the desire to prove one's strength in other ways, then all those aspects of life that belong to the body are taken over by institutions. When that occurs, the body instead becomes the focal point of disciplinary technologies that go hand in hand with the technologies of bio-power, aiming to control the body in order to control the population. The contemporary philosophical neglect of the fact that there are different kinds of self and different kinds of truth, and the scientistic ideals which rule philosophy as well as psychoanalysis, go hand in hand with the rise of bio-power.

Freud's use of the concept "technique of psychoanalysis", and, also, Lacan's in the seminar on *Freud's Papers on Technique* make possible new forms of subjectivities at the junction between *tekhne* and *poiesis*. However, to Foucault, in his work on the history of sexuality, psychoanalysis is born out of a practice of confession and governed by an aspiration to a universal form of truth. In Foucault's critique, psychoanalysis is governed by modern scientistic ideals. These ideals have replaced the notion that truth is something you achieve, with the notion that truth is something you discover. Psychoanalytical therapy is a form of confessional subjectivation. In this sense, psychoanalysis, in the writings of Foucault, is a form of technology that shapes a certain relation of the self to itself, but it is a technology that has lost the aspect of *poiesis*, or the possibility of becoming. Instead, the therapy of psychoanalysis is based on scientistic ideals, while being developed through practices of confession. The patient will ask, "Who am I", or perhaps, "What am I?" The only question that is valid to Foucault, however, would allow for multiple answers: "What can I become?"[7]

Lacan and the Problem of Resistance

It is, however, not certain that Foucault would have detached himself from psychoanalysis had he looked closer at the question of how the self is argued in Freud and Lacan; after all, to both of them, the question of the subject displaces the idea of the self as central to human identity. Is there not, after all, a certain allowance for a variety of truth-concepts both in the ancient technology of the self and in psychoanalysis? According to Foucault, there is a correlation between confession and subjectivation. However, in reflecting on the way in which the concept of technique is used, we may well show that psychoanalysis is not prone neither to reductive scientism, nor to the obligation to confess. Like the practices informing the care of the self, psychoanalysis creates a truth-concept produced through the techniques that are employed. What is at stake here is a notion of psychoanalysis as a kind of process, set in motion through forms of technology, or techniques, that help create *a truth-concept* rather than discover *the truth* about the subject. In other words, psychoanalysis is a practice that helps produce forms of truth, rather than a practice that discovers a particular truth. It is not a science, using a method applied to a theory, but a technique. We may consider psychoanalysis within a framework where the very notion of the practice of psychoanalysis or the technique of psychoanalysis is inseparable from the truth-concept that is created. Thus, it is precisely in looking at the way in which the concept of technique is used, in Foucault and in the psychoanalytical writings of Freud and Lacan, that we may trace the truth in relation to the subject. In other words, the concepts of "technique" or "technology" seem to replace the idea of method, or the idea that psychoanalysis is a science that may be theorized, and then applied through a distinct method that will remain the same.

Psychoanalysis is always concerned with the particular, with the singularity of the subject, or what Heidegger would call the question of the *who*. Freudian analysis is always concerned with the singular. Therefore, it cannot

[7] Butler has a lengthy discussion of this in her book on ethics and selfhood, *Giving an Account of Oneself.* To Foucault in his later days, the subject can never be formatted outside of the norms of society, but it can take shape in relation to these norms in forms that also define its freedom. Therefore, Foucault's question "what can I become?" implies a greater freedom than "who am I?" (Butler, 2005, p. 31).

be a science in the narrow sense of the word. The scientist possesses a system of knowledge through which the objectal world is reflected, a system with a coherent theory and a method through which such theory may be applied. The subject of psychoanalysis, however, is not one of knowledge, but one of speech, or discourse. "Where the id was, the ego must be", Freud said, and the ego-analysts all mistook that sentence to refer to the task of analysis being the creation of a self capable of forming a coherent view of the world. But the task of analysis, according to Lacan in his early seminar on Freud, is not to enlarge the ego or the level of consciousness. It is, rather, to work through the displacements that will place the ego at a great many places (Lacan, 1988, p. 51). If we are to follow Foucault's critique of psychoanalysis, we must assume that the patient of psychoanalysis will ask: "Who or what am I" rather than the question of *poiesis* – "What can I become?" The latter would allow for a multiplicity of answers. The *who* of psychoanalysis is never reducible to the self. The Foucaultian mistake lies precisely in failing to recognize this fact, and indicates that Foucault has failed to see the importance of the fact that psychoanalysis is a practice. The question of the *who* in psychoanalysis is not a simple one to answer. It is crossed with the question of the *what*, situated at the junction at which the singular quality of the subject manifests itself as something foreign to the ego, beyond the imaginary aspects of a self capable of coherence.

As we have seen, the reason for psychoanalysis to resort to the concept of technology, for Freud as well as of Lacan, is the need to create a clinic where no theory is developed that will submit the practice of analysis to a demand for finding *the* truth. Whereas Freud's own writings show a wariness against there being any "master" of truth, Lacan's seminar begins with the teachings of the master of the Buddhist: what he can teach is that the answer, or the truth, cannot be taught. Moreover, he remarks that no one knows the full scope of the psychoanalytical technique of Freud himself, who seems to have applied it in various ways: "As the best authors, and those who knew Freud, have admitted, one cannot gain a complete conception of the way in which he applied the technique" (ibid., p. 20). Lacan, in turn, is particularly interested in tracing the lacunas and the inconsistencies in Freud's own theory in relation to his technique. In the case of Dora, for instance, Freud's theory regarding the interpretation of her symptoms was clearly wrong. His technique, however, was allowed to develop precisely through his mistakes. The phenomena of transference and counter-transference were observed *après-coup*, in reflecting on those aspects of the treatment that did not appear to fit with the theory of unconscious sexual desires that Freud was relying on at first.

The relation between theory and technique is filled with lacunas in the history of psychoanalysis. These lacunas will determine the way in which the clinic is theorized in Lacan's own writings on technique. To Lacan, the most important question in Freud's writings on technique is that of resistance. As we have seen, Freud developed his writings on technique in order to *avoid* the creation of a fully developed psychoanalytical theory. If the patients were to be knowledgeable in the theory of analysis, new forms of resistance against the cure would develop.

The question of resistance is linked to the ego, Lacan argues. To some extent, the ego is a creation of resistance, at least in the situation of analysis. It is a well-known fact that Lacanian analysis began as a challenge towards the ego-psychology developed after Anna Freud. It is perhaps less discussed that the challenge was made through a discussion of psychoanalytical technique. Lacan remarks that, to Freud, the ego was a "technical necessity" – that is, that it had a functional role (ibid., p. 24). That functional role, in turn, had to do with the question of resistance that was very much at heart of the Freudian discussion of technique. The technique of psychoanalysis aims at the reconstruction of the subject with regard to its history. But history is not simply the past. History is what is "historicized in the present because it was lived in the past" (ibid., p. 12). The technique of psychoanalysis, therefore, is aiming at a sort of restitution of the subject's history. What matters is not the remembrance of formative events but their reconstruction, the rewriting that takes place in the situation of analysis. In the process of such a rewriting or restitution, the technique of analysis is working both with and against the resistances of the ego. In order to avoid ideas that would simplify notions such as desire, the unconscious, sexuality, etc., and, thereby, immobilize the process of such a rewriting, Lacan targets some concepts that dominate the analytic discourse at the time of writing. Among these problematic concepts one can count the ego in particular, but also Melanie Klein's theory of the object. In the seminar on technique, Lacan introduces the imaginary and the symbolic as relational concepts rather than aspects of a certain theory of the unconscious. He gives a discursive account of the process of analysis, seen from the viewpoint of technique, rather than theorizing the subject.

Psychoanalytical technique is a question of restituting the past as an ongoing process. If one looks at Freud's writings, one sees what techniques are specifically involved in such a rewriting: the creation of transference, the interpretation of dreams, and processing the past through remembering, repeating and working through. The restitution of the past, then, is never a question of finding the truth about the history of the subject. The technique of analysis restructures how the subject relates to the past. In analysis, truth is always "the truth of the subject", which "must be detached in its distinctiveness in relation to the very notion of reality" (ibid., p. 21). In restructuring the past, psychoanalysis does not work through the Foucaultian question of "What can I become?" In that sense, its technique is not a *poiesis*, aiming at a creation or recreation of the self. In restructuring and restituting the past, however, psychoanalysis displaces the very question of the self. The question "Who am I?" is never the right one to ask, and neither is "What am I?" In psychoanalysis, the *who* is tied up with the *what*, the signifier making it impossible for the self-reflective subject to coincide with itself. The subject of discourse is always marked by the signifier, which is precisely what prompts the process of analysis to be attached to the question of technique. As we have seen, the presence of the signifier in human life is precisely what attaches the human subject to the question of technique, according to the writings of Stiegler. Lacan, in turn, argues that the impact of the signifier on the human subject implies that the question of technique must always be present in psychoanalysis, thereby avoiding that theory to take its place.

Both psychoanalysis and Foucault work with the idea of different forms of self, both in the historical and the futural sense. There is not one right answer to the Foucaultian question of "What can I become?" and there is not one right answer on how the past is to be restituted or restructured in analysis. The technologies of the self, and the technique of psychoanalysis, operate at the rupture where technologies imply a form of becoming, through indicating the possibilities of truth-concepts rather than pointing towards a particular truth. Both Foucault and Lacan use the term "technique" in order to unravel the singularity of the subject, while indicating several possibilities of subjectivity at the same time. In this sense, one must assume that there is a great deal to be learnt through reading Foucault, Freud and Lacan together, precisely through the concepts of technique and technology.

References

Butler, J. (2000). *Antigone's claim*. New York, NY: Columbia University Press.

———. (2005). *Giving an account of oneself*. New York, NY: Fordham University Press.

Eribon, D. (1989). *Michel Foucault*. Paris: Flammarion.

Foucault, M. (1988-1990). *The history of sexuality*: *Vol. I-III*. (R. Hurley, Trans.). London: Vintage Books.

———. (2000a). *Essential works of Foucault, 1954-1984. Vol. 1: Ethics: subjectivity and truth.* (P. Rabinow, Ed. and R. Hurley and others, Trans.). New York, NY: Penguin.

———. (2000b). *Essential works of Foucault, 1954-1984. Vol. 2: Aesthetics.* (P. Rabinow, Ed. and R. Hurley and others, Trans.). New York, NY: Penguin.

Freud, S. (1911-1913). Papers of technique. *Standard Edition 12.*

Lacan, J. (1988). *The seminar. Book I: Freud's papers on technique. 1953-1954.* (J. Forrester, Trans.). London: Norton.

Stiegler, B. (1998). *Technics and time. 1: The fault of Epimetheus.* (R. Beardsworth & G. Collins, Trans.). Stanford, CA: Stanford California Press.

Section IV
Sexuality and Aesthetics

Between Signifier and Jouissance – Lacan with Teresa

Ari Hirvonen

"It's like for Saint Teresa – you need but to go to Rome and see the statue by Bernini to immediately understand she's coming [*qu'elle jouit*]. There's no doubt about it" (Lacan, 1975, pp. 70/76).[1] With these words, Jacques Lacan introduced Saint Teresa in *Seminar XX: Encore*, held on 20 February 1973.

The statue Lacan refers to is Gian Lorenzo Bernini's marble baroque statue *L'estasi di Santa Teresa* on display in the Cornaro Chapel of the church of Santa Maria della Vittoria. The Venetian Cardinal Federico Cornaro had commissioned the transformation of the left transept of the Church into a sepulchral chapel for himself and his family. The statue of Teresa (1515-1582, a Spanish nun, the leader of Carmelite Reform, canonized in 1622) was completed in 1652 during the Pamphili papacy of Pope Innocent X.

Gian Lorenzo Bernini,
L'estasi di Santa Teresa,
Santa Maria della Vittoria,
Roma.

[1] When a citation features two page numbers separated by a slash, the first number refers to the French text, and the second one to the English translation.

Bernini's statue shows Teresa at the moment of her transverberation and Lacan asks "What is she getting off on?" (*Et de quoi jouit-elle?*) (Lacan, 1975, pp. 70/76) It may or may not be a coincidence that Lacan asked this question just two years after Teresa was elevated as the first woman ever to the rank of Doctor of the Church by Pope Paul VI.

Law and Phallic Jouissance

In the beginning of *Seminar XX*, Lacan argues that analytic experience attests to the fact that everything revolves around the phallic *jouissance* (Lacan, 1975, pp. 13/7). "*Jouissance*, qua sexual, is phallic" (Lacan, 1975, pp. 14/9). The masculine-phallic-sexual *jouissance*, a semiotic *jouissance*, is universal (Lacan, 1974, p. 178). This seems to be in accordance with Freud for whom there was only one libido, which, in Lacan's vocabulary, would be a phallic one and subject to the signifier and the symbolic order. All sexual *jouissance* is mediated in the symbolic order.

However, the image of the statue on the cover of *Seminar XX* already hints that this is not all. To show how this is not all, I will first turn from the notion of baroque excess to the minimalism of formal logic – that is, to the diagram of sexuation (Lacan, 1975, pp. 73/78):

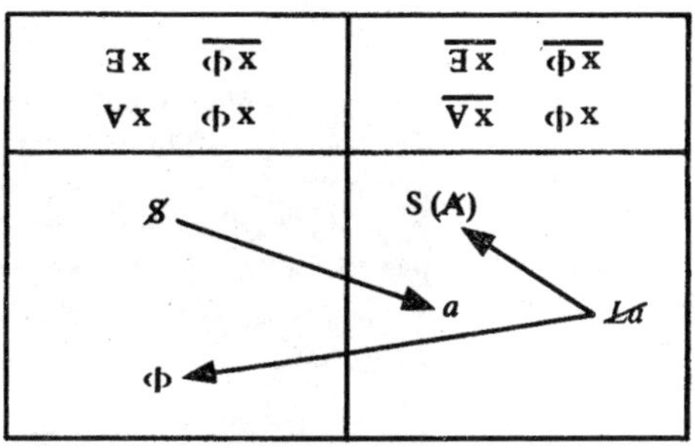

The left hand side is the male side; the right-hand side, the female one. According to Lacan, "Every speaking being situates itself on one side or the other" (Lacan, 1975, pp. 74/79). In *Seminar XI*, where Lacan turns from the subject of desire to the subject of drive, he argues that there is nothing in the psyche that would make the subject situate itself as male or female. The decisive factor is the subject's situation in relation to the Other (Lacan, 1973a, p. 186). Hence, sexual difference is based neither on anatomical, chromosomal and hormonal differences, nor on cultural-constructivist models of gender

On the male side, in the upper part of the table, two propositional formulas are written. The lower line reads: "All men [a universal quantifier, or, what Lacan called 'quantor'] are subjected to the phallic function". This affirmation of the phallic function refers to a symbolic castration, the appearance of the *Le Nom-du-Père/Non-du-Père* (the Name-of-the-Father/No-of-the-Father), access to the paternal metaphor and the symbolic register, and the primordial symbolization of the law. All men are subject to the phallic law and alienated into language. The phallic signifier marks the place for *parlêtre*, the speaking being. Therefore, a signifier represents a subject for another signifier.

This universal proposition is negated by another proposition: "There is one subject [a particular quantifier] who is not submitted to the phallic function". These two formulas, which seem to be in contradiction, should be read together. First, as a precondition for the existence of the universality and closed totality of men, there must be something that transgresses its limits. The universal community of brothers subjected to the law is defined, not by some common nature or sameness, but by what it is not: by the primal and omnipotent father. The existence of *the* man is hence based on the difference of all the brothers from the primal father – and also from woman. The exception is the limit that produces the whole, of which the logic is finite. This, beyond the law, is the ultimate foundation of the law. Second, the two formulas signify that the unlimited *jouissance* must be given up so that the desire and the social being-together can come forward. The plenitude of *jouissance* and being is barred. As Charles Shepherdson says, the phallic *jouissance*, as the law of the symbolic order, "appears only when the unlawful jouissance of the primal father has been expelled … as 'impossible'" (Shepherdson, 2003, p. 145). Third, the unlimited *jouissance* remains a masculine fantasy of *jouissance* beyond castration and lack. It is the fantasy of the subject beyond the law, of someone having the complete *jouissance*, but also the fantasy of some object being able to give full *jouissance*.

The lower side of the table connecting the male side to the female side indicates that man has only one libidinal position and is unable to attain his sexual partner except inasmuch as the partner is the cause of his desire. In other words, the man has a relation only to object *a*, which is not any object of desire, but the object cause of the desire. For Bernard Baas, object *a* is beyond and behind experience, a non-objectified object, that which in the body cannot be symbolized (Baas, 2008, pp. 18-19).

However, the phallic *jouissance* is doomed to fail. There is a barrier between the desire for something as articulated in signifiers and what can satisfy the subject. Since the satisfaction that the subject obtains when realizing his desire is subject to the bar, that is, the phallus, between signifier and signified, it always fails to fulfil the subject and thus leaves something more to be desired: "Just as one cannot take lack out of Lacan, one cannot take the failure out of the phallus" (Fink, 2004, p. 160). The phallic *jouissance* is "the obstacle owing to which man does not come [*n'arrive pas*], I would say, to enjoy woman's body, precisely because what he enjoys is the *jouissance* of the organ" (Lacan, 1975, pp. 13/7). This *jouissance* of the One is "located, limited, and outside the body" (Soler, 2006, p. 39). Moreover, the phallic signifier is an obstacle between male and female and the possibility of unmediated relationship between them.

For Lacan, there is no sexual relationship (*rapport sexuel*), that is, what exists is the failure of the sexual relationship. This is Lacan's version of Freud's failure of the pleasure principle, as Paul Verhaeghe points out (Verhaeghe, 2002, p. 115). The reality of sex and sexual relationships are based on semblance, on the fantasy of sexual complementarity, which functions as a defence against the real. Beyond the support of the fantasy of reality, "botching [failing, *ratage*] is the only way of realizing that relationship" (Lacan, 1975, pp. 54/58). In opposition to Freud, Lacan argues that it is man who approaches woman, but what he approaches is the cause of his desire, object *a*, which is *l'acte d'amour*, which differs from *faire l'amour*, which is poetry (ibid., pp. 67-68/72). The sexual relationship comes up short and fails because one encounters object *a* in another subject and because it reduces the Other to a partial object that serves as the cause of desire. Moreover, the object, its essence, is a failure, *un raté* (Lacan, 1975, pp. 54-56/58; also see: Salecl, 2000, p. 178). Likewise, the phallic *jouissance* fails in establishing the One of the sexual relationship, the One as Aristophanes' spherical beings without lack, the One as the harmony between being and Supreme Being.

Not-All and Other Jouissance

According to Lacan, there is a male way of revolving around the fact that there is no such thing as a sexual relationship, and "then the other one", "the female way" (Lacan, 1975, pp. 54/57). To encounter this other one, Lacan has to go beyond Freud: "What I am working on this year is what Freud expressly left aside: *Was will das Weib?* 'What does woman want?'" (ibid., pp. 75/80). He has to challenge Freud's claim that there is only one libido, which is masculine: "What does that mean if not that a field that certainly is not negligible is thus ignored. That field is the one of all beings that takes on the status of woman – assuming that being takes on anything whatsoever of her destiny" (ibid., pp. 75/80).

In a 1958 lecture, Lacan, on the one hand, underwrites Freud's thesis about sexual difference being based on the castration complex and the opposition between having or not having a penis. On the other hand, instead of speaking of the penis, Lacan speaks of the phallus, which is a signifier (Lacan, 1966, pp. 694/582). Lacan's formulations made woman a partner of the masculine subject: as the phallus, she was the representative of what man is missing; as the object, she served as the cause of his desire; as his symptom, he could fixate his *jouissance* upon her (Soler, 2002, p. 102). In a 1960 presentation, Lacan concentrated on the question of female sexuality. In relation to female homosexuality, he argues that female sexuality appears as "the effort of a *jouissance* enveloped in its own contingency ... in order to be *realized in competition* with the desire that castration liberates in the male in giving him the phallus as its signifier (Lacan, 1962, pp. 735/619). In *Seminar X*, Lacan developed the idea that those who experience *jouissance* are women (Lacan, 2004). However, it is in *Seminar XX* that Lacan defines the feminine *jouissance* as a qualitatively different form of *jouissance*. The Other now designates the Other sex, that is, woman. Hence, Lacan's diagram of sexuation illustrates that what is crucial in the sexual difference is no longer the position in relation to the phallus (having or being the phallus), but the position in relation to *jouissance*.

Let us look at the two formulas for femininity. On the upper part of the right-hand side the upper line reads: "There is no subject [a particular quantifier] that is not subjected to the phallic function" or "there exists no jouissance that is not phallic". This double negation means that there is no one who is not subjected to the symbolic law and determined by the phallic signifier. There is no exception to the law and no sovereign in whose name the law is founded, which would be needed for the universal of women (Ragland, 2004, pp. 142, 187).

The lower line signifies the negation of the universal: "Not all of a woman is subject to symbolic law". Woman is not totally subjected to the phallic law of the signifier or inscribed fully into the signifying net. She is defined by a position that Lacan indicates as not-all or not-whole (*pas-tout*). Law is not all for her and "there is always something in her that escapes discourse" (Lacan, 1975, pp. 33/34). Woman does not identify predominately with the symbolic order and social conventions but with the real of affect, loss and trauma (Ragland, 2004, p. 179). Being not One is an answer not just to the question of feminine being, but to being as such. As Joan Copjec says, "It is not only feminine being, but being in general that resists being assembled into a whole". The proposal from which Lacan's ethics takes off is that "being is not-all or there is no whole of being" (Copjec, 2003, pp. 18-19).

Here, one confronts the logic of the particular that negates the universal. If, on the masculine side, there is the logic of the signifier that implies lack by representing a subject for another signifier, the barred S ($), the subject succumbed to castration, on the female side there is the barred definite article *La (La̸)* of *La femme* (Ragland, 2004, pp. 8, 61). "There is no such thing as *The* woman" (*Il n'y a pas La femme*). There is neither an essence of the feminine nor a signifier of Woman in the unconscious. Women do not constitute a universal, a closure, a class or a collective entity. As Shepherdson says, there is no universal proposition on the side of woman. The universal quantifier "all" is replaced with the quasi-existential "there is", that is, *il y a, es gibt,* in which "a massively complex meditation on the 'givenness' of Being can be found" (Shepherdson, 2003, p. 139). According to Etienne Balibar, women constitute a paradoxical class, a collection under a single name of subjects bound to one another by nothing except their singular way of being an exception (Balibar, 1995, p. 190). If for man the infinite is placed in the service of producing the totalizable and finite One, for woman, it is a relation to the contingency and failures of the law that produces something new that both exhorts from and returns to the law a certain corporeality (Barnard, 2002, pp. 178-179).

Two arrows are drawn on the lower part of the female side. One points at the phallic symbol, which, for Lacan, is the phallic signifier. The other points at the signifier of the barred Other (S(A̸)), the signifier of the void or lack in the Other, of the radical incompleteness, which evokes the real and the beyond of the phallus. This one indicates woman's other relation to the Other and the feminine *jouissance*. Woman has two possibilities, two libidinal positions: the phallic function and the *jouissance* beyond the phallus. If not all of a woman's *jouissance* is phallic *jouissance*, there is an excess on her side. Woman, as she is excluded by the nature of things, that is, the nature of words, as a not-all has "a supplementary *jouissance* compared to what the phallic function designates by way of *jouissance*" (Lacan, 1975, pp. 68/73). While any speaking being whatsoever is allowed to inscribe itself in the feminine part, if it "inscribes itself there [under the banner of woman], it will not allow for any universality, it will be a not-whole" (ibid., pp. 74/80).[2]

[2] According to Bruce Fink, there is a difference between structurally defined men and women, in that women do not have to renounce the phallic *jouissance* to have the Other *jouissance*. They can potentially have both. For men, it is either/or – or at least he thinks he can have the other by giving up the one (Fink, 2004, p. 163).

Re-Subversion of the Subject: Teresa

For Lacan, mystics, such as Teresa, Hadewijch d'Anvers and Saint John of the Cross, are paradigmatic examples of this Other *jouissance*. Hence, Teresa's *jouissance* is not just the mimesis of the phallic *jouissance*, but *en plus*, an extra. Teresa's *jouissance*, which is enveloped in its own contingency, does not "fall under the bar of the signifier, knows nothing about the phallus, and is therefore not caused by an object *a*" (Soler 2006, p. 40). Teresa "exposes the real void place in the symbolic set of ensembles" (Ragland, 2004, p. 185).

It "exists" as something that cannot be expressed, articulated, subjected to the law, brought into the register of truth, as something that does not belong to the symbolic predication. If a discourse aims at meaning and if it indicates the direction toward which it fails, then we may have reached the failure or limit of meaning. The unconscious knows nothing about this unforeseeable and unexpected real *jouissance*, which has not passed into a signifier. Its condition is exactly the fact that it can neither be spoken and expressed nor measured and evaluated by any normative criteria. It is *jouissance* that woman hides and steals (*dérober*) (Lacan, 1973b, p. 23). The essential testimony of Teresa consists in saying that she has experienced it, yet "know[s] nothing about" it (Lacan, 1975, pp. 71/76).

This is exactly what her autobiography says. She writes of her rapture (*arrobamiento*), "which is also called ecstasy", which differs from the union. In the union, we are on our own ground, but raptures, which one cannot resist, have "a great many operations" and the effects they produce are both interior and exterior (Teresa, 1565, p. 147). Bernini's sculpture was based on Teresa's experience following a confrontation with one of the highest kinds of angels, a cherub: "In his hands I saw a long golden spear and at the end of the iron tip I seemed to see a point of fire. With this he seemed to pierce my heart several times so that it penetrated to my entrails. When he drew it out, I thought he was drawing them out with it and he left me completely afire with a great love for God. The pain was so sharp that it made me utter several moans" (ibid., p. 244). This is spiritual pain, but, as Teresa confirms, the body has a share, a great share, in it. At the same time, it is the blackest darkness, a lacuna without any light. "[T]he glory which I felt within me at that time cannot be expressed in writing, or even in speech, nor can it be imagined by anyone who has not experienced it" (ibid., p. 368). Her elliptical and paradoxical writing, her long breathless sentences and turnings from inside to outside and vice versa, does not offer definite meanings and grounds for self. Her wandering writing worries even herself. It is writing beyond the laws of theological and philosophical discourses.

Philippe Lacoue-Labarthe described Lacan's *Seminar VII* on the ethics of psychoanalysis as a journey to the limits of knowledge and towards non-knowledge (with Bataillean resonance). To cross this line is to cross the limits of *Savoir* or *Science* (with a capital "S", as the terminology of speculative idealism is written in French), since what is to be crossed is what Heidegger called the barrier or the enclosure of metaphysics, that is, philosophy (Lacoue-Labarthe, 1991, pp. 24-25).

As Lacan moves around Teresa, it is evident that he, once again, designates the line (of knowledge, ontology, subject, truth) and tries to gain access to the beyond of it. This happens in multiple ways. The feminine mode of being is not-whole. As such, women, who are part of the symbolic order, are also always already beyond the phallic order of knowledge. As singular beings, they subvert the ontology of womanhood. In women, the foundation is lacking, since there is a lack of the Woman and lack of the primal lawgiver Mother. Woman is connected to the Other as lacking, to the void in the Other.

Teresa thus testifies that "the apparent necessity of the phallic function turns out to be mere contingency" (Lacan, 1975, pp. 87/94). The experience of the feminine *jouissance* takes place beyond the normative operations of the symbolic order. It *ex-sists* as something not subjected to the law.

As Ellie Ragland says, the feminine *jouissance* is of a piece with the feminine epistemology, which differs from the masculine logic of the law. On the female side are "the unbounded open sets that make room for the place(s) of equivocation, the *logic* of inconsistency, and an ungraspable vacillation that Lacan lovingly named the *not all*", which contains the coexistence of two contradictory positions – being in the phallic function and not being in it – which cannot be united into one (Ragland, 2004, p. 61).

According to Verhaeghe, Lacan opposes the traditional form of knowledge, which belongs to the Other of the signifier, determined completely by the phallic One to another form that is guaranteed by the supreme Other of the Other who keeps the final Knowledge. But Lacan leaves behind this binary structure: also the other form of knowledge belongs to the Other, but it belongs to that part in the Other where the Other is not-whole, the gap in the Other in which something else of this Other makes an appearance. This is where the Other *jouissance* belongs (Verhaeghe, 2002, pp. 110-111, 124). Hence, it is outside of the symbolic order, albeit from within, since there can be no beyond the phallus, if one understands this as something being beyond differentiation, society, language, law, and reality (Ragland, 1986, p. 305).

As Lacan puts it, the Name-of-the-Father is not all, since there are two faces of the Other: the Other, *Autre*, as the symbolic order, as the locus of signifier, as the law, as that in which the father function is inscribed, insofar as castration is related to the father function, and then this other face: the Other *jouissance*, the God face. While "that does not make two God's (*deux Dieu*)", "it doesn't make just one either" (Lacan, 1975, pp. 71/77). Now we can understand – in a less theologico-religious way – why, concerning the mystics, Lacan asks, why not interpret "one face of the Other, the God face", as based on the feminine *jouissance*?: "Doesn't this *jouissance* that one experiences and knows nothing about put us on the path of ex-sistence?" (ibid.) Lacan argues that "[i]t is insofar as her *jouissance* is radically Other that woman has more of a relationship to God" (ibid., pp. 77/83).

The Other *jouissance* implies a knowledge that is acquired by the body through experiencing it, and this experiencing causes its inscription on the body (Verhaeghe, 2002, pp. 110-111, 124). Even if the unconscious knows nothing of this *jouissance*, this is not an objection to analysis, since one analyzes the subject and not *jouissance* itself (Soler, 2002, p. 107). In analysis, one can study the subjective consequences of this Other *jouissance*, that is, the commandments of encounter with *jouissance*. This encounter can be brought back to life and aroused without being made into a signifier (Lacan, 1973b, p. 23). Therefore, the feminine *jouissance* is neither something nor nothing. It only exists in a conditional mode, as a possibility, and, hence, falls outside the grasp of propositions such as "it is" or "it is not" (Shepherdson, 2003, pp. 139-140, 146). Perhaps Bernini's angel is nothing but a reminder of this fact. As Lacan speaks of the strangeness of the feminine being, he refers to angels: *étrange*, strange, is a word that can be decomposed: *l'être-ange*, to be an angel or angel being (Lacan, 1975, pp. 14/8).

The position of woman and the feminine *jouissance* do not offer any new kind of guarantee for wholeness, coherence and consistency of the being of the subject. Actually, Lacan had said earlier that "the path toward death [let me add: death of the subject] is nothing other than what is called *jouissance*" (Lacan, 1991, pp. 18/18), which is close to what Georges Bataille had said about Teresa, who dies because she cannot die: what "she did was to live more violently" in "a swift movement of loss within" her (Bataille, 1987, pp. 239-240).

The non-totalizable dialectic between the symbolic and the real, desire and drive, signifier and body, outside and inside, universal and particular, transcendent and immanent make the possibility of Hegelian sublation (*Aufhebung*) impossible. A philosophical hero – especially the hero of the speculative idealism – creating a coherent system without aporias, voids and excesses turns out to be a fantasy (of pairing), which is condemned to failure. Lacan shows how, in the tradition of philosophy, the consistency of being and the Supreme Being enshrouds the lack and the not-whole, and, thus, how philosophy lacks the lack (see: Nancy, 1991, p. 203). Therefore, Lacan's *Seminar XX* can be seen as a deconstruction of the subject, the metaphysical tradition and knowledge-systems of One and All, the onto-theology of beings and the Supreme Being as the ultimate foundation of truth and being.

However, is Lacan's discourse, which attempts to throw itself outside of the ontological closure, still rigorously inscribed within this closure? This is what Lacoue-Labarthe and Jean-Luc Nancy argue in their deconstructive reading of Lacan's "L'instance de la lettre" in *Le titre de la lettre* (1973). They do not deny the Lacanian subversion of the subject: the subject is seen as lack, as divided and split. As the locus of the signifier, it cannot assert a position from which to recapture itself in the transparency of meaning; it is no more the master of meaning, it is decentred and excentred, and its speech is marked by split and alienation. But the locus of the Lacanian signifier is, nevertheless, the subject, which is presupposed. The structure of the signifying chain is the subject. It is in a theory of the subject that the logic of the signifier settles. After all, the subject maintains itself through its subversion, that is, the subject is reinscribed as lack, which centres Lacan's discourse. Hence, Lacan's negative discourse of subject (discourse of negativity, lack and hole) does not destroy the metaphysics of subjectivity and truth, but, instead, inverts and displaces it. All the essential features of the metaphysical ontology are here, and one could call it *onto-théo-sémio-logie*. This *negative* ontology opens onto and is founded, that is, closed, on "a gaping hole whose bottom is hidden but whose outline can be discerned" (Lacoue-Labarthe & Nancy, 1973, pp. 167/127). Hence, Lacan's discourse turns out to be a repetition of negative theology.

In *Seminar XX*, a lecture held on 20 February 1973, Lacan answered Lacoue-Labarthe and Nancy by saying that their book was "a model of good reading" ("I have never been read so well – with so much love"), even if they had "assumed that I have an ontology, or, what amounts to the same thing, a system" (Lacan, 1975, pp. 62/65, 66/70). Lacan was also more and more critical towards the concept of being, as it is sustained in the philosophical tradition, and which gives rise to the Supreme Being: the Other of the Other.

This is the very same lecture in which Lacan introduced Teresa, and one cannot avoid considering her as an answer to Lacoue-Labarthe and Nancy's book. The feminine *jouissance* – and also the feminine mode of being not-all and being that concerns *jouissance* – may be seen as a radicalization of Lacan's subversion of the subject. In other words, Lacan's answer is a turning from the being of the speaking subject of desire to *jouissance* and the "being" of not-all. His discourse seems to be a rigorous attempt to de-inscribe itself from the metaphysical ontology. *Encore*, the subversion of the subject. Perhaps this means nothing but the deconstruction of his supposed negative ontology of the subject. Two short remarks before returning to *Seminar XX*. First, Lacan's subversion of the subject may be more "fundamental" than Lacoue-Labarthe and Nancy state.[3] Second, already from the *Seminar XI* onwards, the real becomes a genuine concept, which changes Lacan's discourse on the subject, as Verhaeghe has shown. In that seminar, Lacan introduced the second lack: the first one was the lack in the chain of signifiers (related to the desire and discourse of the Other, the movement from signifier to signifier, the advent of the subject, law and science); the second one was the anterior and real lack (related to death, drive, the advent of the living being, the real that cannot be assimilated by the chain of signifiers) (Verhaeghe, 1998).

Between Ontology and Deconstruction (of Jouissance)

Lacan's "answer" to his critiques is one more step away from the subject of ontology (and of law and predictability). However, it should be questioned *à la* Lacoue-Labarthe and Nancy. Therefore, I will still address the question of whether Lacan's *Seminar XX* is, not merely a deconstruction of the subject, meaning and knowledge, but also a construction of the ontology of the being of *jouissance*, the onto-theology of Teresa. To do this, I will take up two topics: figure and image.

(1) *Figure* – Why does Lacan characterize the feminine *jouissance* in terms of the mystical ecstasy of a saint? The figure of a saint raises two questions.

First, one could argue that Teresa's body is enjoyed by God (why Lacan in general takes up God). In other words, Teresa's *jouissance* is the *jouissance* of the Other, that is, of God. This would be nothing but religious-psychotic *jouissance*. As a result, the transcendental Other would be the ultimate and non-lacking ground for the subject. Perhaps one cannot avoid undecidability between this invasive *jouissance* and the feminine *jouissance* as the *jouissance* of the body, since signifying and interpreting it are doomed to fail because of the lack of a signifier.

[3] For what Lacan understands by the subversion of the subject and how this goes together with the dialectic of desire, see: Van Haute (2002).

Second, is Lacan – in spite of everything – enchanted by the brilliance of Saint Teresa's ecstasy? In *Seminar VII*, Lacan confronted Antigone as a tragic hero or figure, not as theatre, as Lacoue-Labarthe says (Lacoue-Labarthe, 1991, p. 21). Lacan also read *Antigone* as Heidegger did, that is, in the light of the problematic of the truth of (desire of) subject/*Dasein*, as Philippe Van Haute says (Van Haute, 2003, p. 205). Therefore, Lacan – once again – introduces a heroic being of psychoanalysis – the figure of Teresa – who has the courage to be authentic in her solitude and incorporation of the feminine *jouissance*, who transgresses the limits of the phallic law and order, who is beyond the Good and goods of the socio-political order. Even if both the ontology of the subject and being are deconstructed in *Seminar XX*, even if Teresa's *jouissance* does not correspond any kind of ideal, idealization of *jouissance* or ideal identity of being, this figure may function as a model or type, not of the truth of the desire of the subject, but of the truth of the *jouissance* of the body.

(2) *Image* – Lacan turned to modal logic and combined it with the existential quantors of the universal and the particular to explain the sexual difference. He saw that the modern science of the letter (number theory, set theory, topology, quantum physics), a move from the science of reality to the science of the real, would open ways for psychoanalysis and would make possible a non-imaginary approach to the question of the subject. His "mathemes", which he uses to summarize and formalize psychoanalytical theory, are a way beyond fantasy: "Mathematical formalization is our goal, our ideal" (Lacan, 1975, pp. 108/119; also see: Fink, 2004, p. 153). In *Seminar XX*, he continues to develop his new topology of Borromean knots, which he had started in *Seminar XIX*. In spite of this, Lacan refers to Bernini's Teresa as a representative of the feminine *jouissance*.

Does this representation of the feminine *jouissance* in Bernini's theatre of ecstasy lead woman into exile in the masculine imaginary? Does Lacan submit the feminine *jouissance* to the visual and specular, to the phallic gaze? Does this lead to the logic of identification: we identify with what we see (ego and imaginary processes) or with the seeing subject? Or, even more fundamentally, does Lacan, in spite of all, introduce Teresa as the representation or model of the subject of *jouissance* and does he thus found a (more positive) ontology of the subject?

The statue is of the register of the symbolic and also of the imaginary. However, we have to see what "is" at the limits or beyond this imaginary and/or symbolic image and meaning. For Lacan, works of art do imitate the objects they represent, but their end is not to represent them, since they make something different out of that object. They always involve encircling the Thing (*la Chose*) (Lacan, 1986, pp. 169/141). Moreover, in art, which followed from the effects of Christianity, "everything is exhibition of the body evoking *jouissance*". Lacan says that in this sense he coincides with "baroquism". "It's not without reason that people say that my discourse has something baroque about it" (Lacan, 1975, pp. 102/113). (Moreover, let us not forget the gaze as a stain of the real, as the invisible that returns from the world back to the subject and opens a space of visibility for it, as something that interrupts the symbolic coherency and consistency of the image).

Keeping all this in mind, we have to take seriously when Lacan invites us to see the baroque statue. We see her coming, but we are not able to get anything out of her, not a word (see: ibid., pp. 69/75). The marble does not speak and we should not try to subject it to the master's discourse, which emphasizes the verb *être* and the ontology of "it is what it is" (ibid., pp. 33/31). Perhaps we should look at the statue almost like we look at the Borromean knot, which offers us an access to the real and which figures something beyond the logic of discourse and of metaphorical representation.

The statue represents no-thing. But it presents the event of *jouissance*, which takes place both in and beyond the imaginary and symbolic order, and, hence, evokes the real and being as ex-sistence. It is animated by the throbbing and palpitation of *jouissance*. There is the silence of signifiers as the marble writhes so that it turns into a fluid movement and thus renders visible Teresa's inexpressible being-in-ecstasy by presenting the body-in-*jouissance* as *jouissance* inscribes itself on her body. Bernini's Teresa brings forth an intimate exteriority, *extimité*. See how her body contracts violently at the abdomen in a kind of solar paroxysm of the solar plexus, because the arrow did not just pierce her heart but penetrated to her entrails (Lavin, 1980, p. 109). In it we confront, not the speaking being, but the body. The body, to which *jouissance* belongs, does not refer here to the signified and imaginarized body, but to another body, that is, organism and organs (Verhaeghe, 2001, p. 79). There is a shift from the subject as the subject of discourse, as the effect of signifiers, to substance, which is, neither the essence of the subject nor the pre-symbolic real, but something different: the excess or the surplus that is both in and beyond the symbolic. Bernini's Teresa brings forth the substance of *jouissance*, the body-in-*jouissance*. That is why we have to go to Rome.

Finally, if we were to go to Rome, we would see a piece of paper attached to the bar which separates the spectators from the statue. In it there are some lines of Teresa's autobiography. Why does Lacan refer to Hadewijch d'Anvers' texts but pass over Teresa's writing, which not only decentres the subject, but also leads to the limits of the law and the symbolic? Why not see her writing as related more to *jouis-sens* than *sens* or read it in relation to Joyce's writing?

(Not) all in (not) all, *Seminar XX* radicalizes Lacan's subversion of the subject. It brings forth the failure of the symbolic and the law. They are not all. Beyond both the knowledge of science/idealism and the truth of desire, there "is" *jouissance*, which is unpredictable, incalculable, unknowable. The feminine *jouissance*, not-all of woman and Teresa mean a deconstruction of the subject. However, one cannot avoid the risk that one's discourse grounds a new ontology, even if this were a grounding of the groundlessness of the subject (of *jouissance*). Perhaps Lacan's subversive discourse itself calls, in turn, for deconstructive questioning.

References

Baas, B. (2008). *Asia, ääni ja aika.* (K. Sivenius, Trans.). Helsinki: Loki-Kirjat.

Balibar, E. (1995). Culture and identity (Working notes). In J. Rajchman (Ed.), *The identity in question* (pp. 173-196). New York: Routledge.

Barnard, S. (2002). Tongues of angels: Feminine structure and other jouissance. In S. Barnard & B. Fink (Eds.), *Reading seminar XX: Lacan's major work on love, knowledge, and feminine sexuality* (pp. 178-179). Albany, NY: State University of New York Press.

Bataille, G. (1987). Mysticism and sensuality. In *Eroticism* (M. Dalwood, Trans.). London: Marion Boyars. (Original work published 1957).

Copjec, J. (2003). *Imagine there's no woman: Ethics and sublimation.* Cambridge, MA: MIT Press.

Fink, B. (2004). *Lacan to the letter: Reading Écrits closely.* Minneapolis, MN: Minneapolis University Press.

Lacan, J. (1962). Propos directifs pour un congrès sur la sexualité féminine. In *Écrits.* Paris: Seuil, 1966 / Guiding remarks for a convention on female sexuality. In *Écrits.* (B. Fink, Trans.). New York, NY: Norton, 2006.

———. (1966). La signification du phallus (Die Bedeutung des Phallus). In: *Écrits.* Paris: Seuil. / The signification of the phallus. In *Écrits.* (B. Fink, Trans.). New York, NY: Norton, 2006.

———. (1973a). *Le séminaire XI: Les quatre concepts fondamentaux de la psychanalyse. 1964.* Paris: Seuil.

———. (1973b). L'étourdit. *Scilicet, 5*, Paris: Seuil.

———. (1974). *Le séminaire XXI: Les non-dupes errent. 1973-1974.* 11 June 1974. Retrieved from http://www.ecole-lacanienne.net

———. (1975). *Le séminaire XX: Encore. 1972-1973.* Paris: Seuil. / *The seminar. Book XX: Encore: On feminine sexuality, the limits of love and knowledge. 1972-1973.* (B. Fink, Trans.). London/New York, NY: Norton, 1999.

———. (1984). *Le séminaire IV: La relation d'objet et les structures freudiennes. 1956-1957.* Paris: Seuil.

———. (1991). *Le séminaire XVII: L'envers de la psychanalyse. 1969-1970.* Paris: Seuil. / *The seminar. Book XVII: The other side of psychoanalysis. 1969-1970.* (R. Grigg, Trans.). New York, NY: Norton, 2007.

———. (2004). *Le séminaire X: L'angoisse. 1962-1963.* Paris: Seuil.

———. (2005). *Le séminaire XXIII: Le sinthome. 1975-1976.* Paris: Seuil.

Lacoue-Labarthe, P. (1991). De l'éthique: à propos d'Antigone. In N. Avtonomova (Ed.), *Lacan avec les philosophes* (pp. 21-36). Paris: Albin Michel.

Lacoue-Labarthe, P., & Nancy, J. (1973). *Le titre de la lettre: Une lecture de Lacan.* Paris: Galilée, 1990. / *The title of the letter: A reading of Lacan.* (F. Raffoul & D. Pettigrew, Trans.). Albany, NY: State University of New York Press, 1992.

Lavin, I. (1980). *Bernini and the unity of the visual arts.* Text volume. London/New York, NY: Oxford University Press.

Nancy, J. (1991). Manque de rien. In N. Avtonomova (Ed.), *Lacan avec les philosophes (pp. 201-206).* Paris: Albin Michel.

Ragland-Sullivan, E. (1986). *Jacques Lacan and the philosophy of psychoanalysis.* Urbana/Chicago, IL: University of Illinois Press.

Ragland, E. (2004). *The logic of sexuation: From Aristotle to Lacan.* Albany, NY: State University of New York Press.

Salecl, R. (2000). *(Per)versions of love and hate.* London: Verso.

Shepherdson, C. (2003). Lacan and philosophy. In J. Rabaté (Ed.), *The Cambridge companion to Lacan* (pp. 116-152). Cambridge: Cambridge University Press.

Soler, C. (2002). What does the unconscious know about women? (F. Raffoul & D. Pettigrew, Trans.). In S. Barnard & B. Fink (Eds.), *Reading seminar XX: Lacan's major work on love, knowledge, and feminine sexuality* (pp. 99-108). Albany, NY: State University of New York Press.

———. (2006). *What Lacan said about women: A psychoanalytic study.* (J. Holland, Trans.). New York, NY: Other Press.

Teresa of Ávila (2004). *The life of Teresa of Jesus: The autobiography.* (E. Allison Peers, Trans.). New York, NY: Image. (Original work published 1565).

Thurston, L. (1998). Ineluctable nodalities: On the Borromean knot". In D. Nobus (Ed.), *Key concepts of Lacanian psychoanalysis* (pp. 139-163). London: Rebus Press.

Van Haute, P. (2002). *Against adaptation: Lacan's "subversion" of the subject.* New York, NY: Other Press.

———. (2003). Antigone, psykoanalyysin sankaritar? (K. Kurki, Trans.). *Tiede & edistys, 28(3),* 195-207.

Verhaeghe, P. (1998). Causation and destitution of a pre-ontological non-entity: On the Lacanian subject. In D. Nobus (Ed.), *Key concepts of lacanian psychoanalysis* (pp. 164-189). London: Rebus Press.

———. (2001). *Beyond gender: From subject to drive.* New York, NY: Other Press.
———. (2002). Lacan's answer to the classical mind/body deadlock. In S. Barnard & B. Fink (Eds.), *Reading seminar XX: Lacan's major work on love, knowledge, and feminine sexuality* (pp. 109-139). Albany, NY: State University of New York Press.

Painting as Hysteria – Deleuze on Bacon

Tomas Geyskens

Great clinicians are artists. When the French psychiatrist Lasègue first isolated and defined exhibitionism in 1877, he did not begin his article with a description of cases of manifest exhibitionism, but, rather, with a story about a man who followed a woman in the streets each day. In order to introduce a new syndrome, it seems necessary to write a short story first and only then to describe cases of manifest pathology (Deleuze, 2004, p. 275). During a discussion in the Wednesday Circle, Freud, too, argued that case studies are pointless if they are merely objective reports of what has been said during the analytical sessions. Something of the unconscious can only be conveyed by case reports when they are presented in an "artistic" way, says Freud.[1] The unconscious is a matter of style. On this point, *le point littéraire*, the clinical encounters the artistic (Deleuze, 1989, p. 14; 1969, p. 273).

But also the other way around: great artists are clinicians. Whoever reads the works of Sacher-Masoch discovers a symptomatology of masochism that is far superior to the later attempts by Krafft-Ebing, Freud and the DSM. Pleasure in pain, for example, which plays such an important role in the psychoanalytical idea of masochism, is of secondary importance for Sacher-Masoch and must be understood as following from elements which *are* essential to masochism, such as the contract, the fetish, the education of the woman into the ideal cold mother, and the suspension of sexuality (Geyskens, 2006). One finds the same clinical acumen in Sade on sadism, in Dostoevsky on epilepsy, in Burroughs on toxicomania, and in Bukowski on alcoholism. That these artists themselves may have suffered from one or another of these pathologies is less important than the fact that they are its finest symptomatologists: "For authors, if they are great, are more like doctors than patients" (Deleuze, 2004, p. 273).

This critical-clinical project is continuously elaborated and purified in the development of Deleuze's thought. In *Présentation de Sacher-Masoch* (1967) he still argued for a fruitful collaboration between literary criticism and psychiatric or psychoanalytical clinical work (Deleuze, 1989, p. 14). More than ten years later, in his 1981 work *Francis Bacon: Logique de la sensation* (Deleuze, 2003),

[1] "Eine gewissenhafte, aber 'künstlerische' Darstellung wie in der Dora" (quoted in Lavagetto, 2002, p. 225).

this project has not been abandoned, but rather, transformed. Deleuze now aims at a purely aesthetical clinic, which is independent of both psychiatry and psychoanalysis.[2] Therefore, his *Francis Bacon* is not only a book about painting, but also about the clinical essence of painting, namely, hysteria.[3] But how must we understand this clinical/aesthetical relation between painting and hysteria? And why is the work of Francis Bacon so appropriate to elucidate hysteria as the clinical essence of painting? And what is wrong with, for example, the psychoanalytical theory of hysteria, that it must be replaced with an aesthetic clinic that should remain totally independent of psychoanalysis and psychiatry? We shall try to answer this last question first, even though in his book on Bacon Deleuze does not treat this question himself. Aside from some sneering remarks, psychoanalysis – along with criticism of it – no longer plays a role in Deleuze's thought after 1980.

According to Freud, the hysterical body tells a story. The hysterical symptoms, the convulsions, the anaesthesias and hyperaesthesias, the paralyses, the disorders of sensory activity, etc., are symbolic representations of traumatic memories or repressed fantasies. The most remarkable symptom of hysteria, the *grande attaque*, was also analyzed by Freud and Breuer as the expression of a psychic representation: "The constant and essential content of a (recurrent) hysterical attack is in the return of a psychical state which the patient has already experienced earlier – in other words, the return of a memory. We are asserting, then, that the essential portion of a hysterical attack is comprised in Charcot's phase of the attitudes passionnelles. In many cases it is quite obvious that this phase comprises a memory from the patient's life and frequently, indeed, that memory is always the same one" (Freud, 1893a, p. 152). When such psychic content is missing, and the attack is limited to corporeal phenomena – epileptic convulsions or cataleptic sleep – Freud nevertheless finds a psychic representation to which the somatic symptoms seem to correspond: "Even in such cases examination under hypnosis provides definite proof of a psychical mnemic process such as is usually revealed openly in the phase passionnelle" (ibid., p. 152). Freud's article is a beautiful illustration of the famous transition

[2] "It is true that there are numerous dangers in constructing a clinical aesthetic (which nonetheless has the advantage of not being a psychoanalysis)" (Deleuze, 2003, p. 51). "… under the rubric of a purely aesthetic clinic, independent of any psychiatry and psychoanalysis" (Deleuze, 2003, p. 54). "Masoch is neither a pretext for psychiatry or psychoanalysis" (Deleuze, 1998, p.53).

[3] "Can we speak of a hysterical essence of painting? … This problem concerning the essence of each art, and possibly their clinical essence, is less difficult than it seems to be" (Deleuze, 2003, p. 54).

from the diagnostic *looking at the body* of Charcot, to the therapeutic listening to the psychic content in Freud's *talking cure* (see: Didi-Huberman, 1982).

Freud's emphasis on "psychic content" was certainly the beginning of psychoanalysis, but not the key to the world of hysteria. By isolating the level of psychic representations, Freud neglected the corporeal and affective madness of hysteria: "Freud 'neurotified' hysteria. … By interesting himself exclusively with the theatrical fantasizing in hysteria, Freud abandoned at the same time the pole of passion – which one called hysterical madness (*folie hystérique*) which left its trace in the 'attack'. In fact, these hysterics were no more neurotic than psychotic. They were 'mad'" (Green, 1972, p. 220). It is this madness of the body in hysteria, the ridiculous "acrobatics of the flesh"[4] neglected by psychoanalysis, that Deleuze has in mind in his discussion of Bacon's paintings. For Deleuze, hysteria should not be understood from the perspective of literature or the narrative procedures of psychoanalysis, but from the perspective of painting.[5] Hysteria is the clinical essence of painting, but this only becomes visible in painting because the painter succeeds where the hysteric fails. Painting adds to hysteria precisely that which it fatally misses: *un peu d'art*.[6] By adding "a little art" to it, painting shows what is at stake in hysteria: not the symbolic expression of a psychic content, but the "pure presence of the body" (Deleuze, 2003, p. 52).

Deleuze's aesthetic clinic of painting as hysteria has gained clinical importance now that hysteria has become more and more resistant to psychoanalytical therapy and, as borderline-personality disorder, increasingly disposes of Freud's "psychic content". In anorexia, bulimia and self-mutilation, contemporary hysteria only shows the excessive presence of the body, the quivering of the flesh that does not speak, but works directly on the nerves. In contrast to psychoanalysis, painting can reveal the sense of this hysterical body in a positive manner. For contemporary psychoanalysis this pure corporeality is, after all, merely the symptom of a deficient "mentalization" or symbolization. In this, psychoanalysis shows its affinity with psychiatry: it can only determine pathology in a negative way, as deficiency (Deleuze, 2006, p. 24).

[4] "The athleticism of the body is naturally prolonged in this acrobatics of the flesh" (Deleuze, 2003, p. 23).

[5] One could argue that, in Deleuze's earlier works on Masoch, Sade, Carroll and Lasègue, literature has a specific clinical affinity with perversion, while in his later works after *Anti-Oedipus* he relates American literature to schizophrenia. Maybe Freud could understand hysteria only as a "negative perversion" because he approached it from the perspective of literature?

[6] "With painting, hysteria becomes art. Or rather, with the painter, hysteria becomes painting. What the hysteric is incapable of doing -a little art- is accomplished in painting" (Deleuze, 2003, p. 52).

In a way, Deleuze returns to Charcot, who was not only a great clinician of hysteria but also a great artist of psychiatry.[7] Freud writes of him: "He was not a reflective man, not a thinker: he had the nature of an artist – he was, as he himself said, a 'visuel', a man who sees, … who bubbled over with vivacity and cheerfulness and who always had a joke on his lips" (Freud, 1893b, pp. 12/18). Charcot made hundreds of sketches and photographs of hysterics in outrageous poses and positions, and he kept a painting studio throughout his entire life.[8] However, he probably did not distinguish clearly enough between the eye of the camera and that of the painter, as a result of which his clinic of hysteria remained captive to the spectacular and the illustrative. According to Deleuze, one can avoid the trap of the spectacular and the illustrative, not by turning from Charcot's "looking" to Freud's "listening", but by turning from photography to painting. But *how* does painting succeed in making the pure *présence* of the body visible in a positive manner? And why is Francis Bacon the painter of hysteria *par excellence*?

To make the presence of the body visible, painting must first enter into a combat with the figurative. Painting is not photography. It has been claimed, even by Bacon himself sometimes, that the rise of photography made it possible for painting to detach itself from the task of representing, narrating or illustrating. In the course of the nineteenth century, then, photography is thought to have taken over this task from painting, whereby the latter obtained its freedom from the figurative. But this view presents two striking weaknesses: first, it underestimates the power of photography and of our visual culture on the whole; second, it establishes a radical break between (classical) painting before photography and (modern) painting after the advent of photography.

Photography, and, by extension, our whole culture of images, is not just a way of representing things; it has become the way in which we see things. Before the painter begins to paint, the canvas is already virtually filled with all sorts of images, clichés, representations and phantasms.[9] The gaze of

[7] "If we look at the 'picture' of hysteria that was formed in the nineteenth century, in psychiatry and elsewhere, we find a number of features that have continually animated Bacon's bodies" (Deleuze, 2003, p. 49).

[8] "He brought an artist's eye to the study of hysterical bodies. Charcot had planned to become an artist and always maintained a studio in his home where he could paint. He and his interns sketched hysterical patients during their attacks, and he even installed a full photographic studio, with a professional photographer, Albert Londe, to record the women's movements and expressions" (Showalter, 1997, p. 31).

[9] "Modern painting is invaded and besieged by photographs and clichés that are already lodged on the canvas before the painter even begins to work" (Deleuze, 2003, pp. 10-11).

modern man is subjugated to these photographic representations.[10] Painting is the attempt to neutralize this tyranny of virtual representations in view of something completely different, what Deleuze, with Cézanne, calls "la sensation". But is this not a lot of strain for nothing? Is not sensation the most simple, spontaneous given, the "data" that we always already have at our disposal when we perceive? Deleuze completely reverses this schema of classical psychology. Sensation is not that which is most immediate or most subjective, but the end result of a very specific procedure, namely, painting.

In his analysis of sensation, Deleuze depends heavily upon phenomenology, especially the work of Henri Maldiney. In *Le devoilement de la dimension esthétique dans la phenomenologie d'Erwin Strauss* (1966), Maldiney distinguishes between two aspects of sensation: the representative and the "pathic". Sensation is not just the material for, or the announcement of, perception.[11] In sensing, we relate, first of all, to the world in a pathic, non-representational way. Or, better, we are *affected* by the world before we *relate* to it.[12] Subject and object do not stand against each other here; "I" and "World" are only two indissolubly interconnected sides of this being-affected.[13] The yellow of Van Gogh's sunflowers is not just one of the "secondary qualities" of these flowers; for Van Gogh the yellow is in the first place "la haute note jaune de cet été" (Maldiney, 1966, p. 137). Yellow *sets the tone* before it is identified as the quality of a specific object: "Van Gogh does not refer to a descriptive colour that helps him to identify a field of sunflowers. When he uses the musical term "note", it is because the world resonates in this yellow (*dans ce jaune, le monde sonne*); and it resonates in so far as in this yellow Van Gogh inhabits a world which is not yet crystallized into objects" and in which Van Gogh is not yet crystallized into a subject (ibid., p. 137; my translation). But this pathic dimension is not logically or chronologically prior to that of representation; it is *brought about* by painting. For this reason, a phenomenology of "sensation" remains abstract so long as it does not begin with the concrete experience of

[10] "They are not only ways of seeing, *they are what is seen, until finally one sees nothing else.* The photograph 'creates' the person or the landscape in the sense that we say that the newspaper creates the event (and is not content to narrate it). What we see, what we perceive, are photographs" (Deleuze, 2003, p. 91; italics in the original).

[11] "Avec le percevoir, qui est le premier niveau de l'objectivation, nous sommes déjà sortis du sentir" (Maldiney, 1966, p. 136).

[12] "Le rapport moi-monde, lié par le 'et', lié par le 'dans' ou par le 'avec' n'a pas la structure de l'intentionnalité" (Maldiney, 1990, p. 205).

[13] "Sensation has one face turned toward the subject (the nervous system, vital movement, 'instinct', 'temperament' – a whole vocabulary common to both Naturalism and Cézanne) and one face turned toward the object (the 'fact', the place, the event). Or rather, it has no faces at all, it is both things indissolubly" (Deleuze, 2003, p. 34).

painting. This is why Deleuze will not so much describe *what* "sensation" is, but *how* a painter like Bacon brings about this "sensation".

The *deformations* of the figurative, the violent spasms of the sunflowers, show how, in Van Gogh's later works, the representative moment can hardly hold the enormous power of the pathic moment. So also does Bacon deform the figurative in a variety of ways, beyond representations, clichés and phantasms, to paint the pure presence of the body. The first deformation Bacon carries out in his canvases is that of the relationship between figure and background. Figurative painting and photography establish the relationship between figure and background in such a way that it inevitably opens a space for the narrative and the illustrative. No matter how vague or *claire-obscure* the background is, the painting becomes a kind of window or a scene. To break with the figurative – without making the leap into abstract art or *action painting* – it is crucial that this relationship between the figure and the background will be deformed. Bacon does this through a number of rather simple interventions.

First, he places the figure in an oval or a circle, in a ring, an oval bed or a chair. Sometimes the figure is also surrounded by a parallelogram, or sitting in a glass cube. In this way Bacon isolates the figure from the background. But this only works because the background is also deformed. Bacon's backgrounds are not landscapes or interiors. By rubbing out large fields in bright colours and through the addition of meaningless spots and circles, a flat field emerges that no longer stands *behind* the figure, but beside or around it. Because of this, the "background" comes as close as the figure itself. As a result, the background and the figure stand next to each other and no room is left where a story could slip into the painting. The figure, therefore, is surrounded by a completely closed space, which seems to turn or to be able to revolve like a pedestal. The inaccessibility of Bacon's spaces is, remarkably, not the result of obscurity or depth, but caused by their being so flat, bright and simple. Everything is equally close.[14]

These deformations completely isolate the figure. Through the isolation of the figure, the figurative disappears. Bacon's paintings do not tell a story; they are not pictures or illustrations of any pre-given reality. The figures are freed from the figurative. This does not mean that nothing happens in the painting, but this happening is not representational. It is not a spectacle. For this reason, Bacon sets out to remove all references to a spectator from his paintings. In the second version of *Study for Bullfight nr. 1,* for instance, the stands where

[14] "What concerns us here is this absolute proximity, this co-precision, of the field that functions as a ground, and the Figure that functions as a form, on a single plane that is viewed at close range" (Deleuze, 2003, p. 6).

the audience sits are painted over. Only the bull and the bullfighter remain (Deleuze, 2003, p. 13). The figure does sometimes need a second figure, but as a witness rather than as a spectator, and functioning as an "equal", a "standard weight" against which the figure will vary.[15] In this way, the witness shows what happens to the figure. The figure becomes the "anomaly" of the witness.[16] The figure undergoes a series of deformations. A first deformation comes about as a result of the impact of the field ("background") on the figure. Because the space around the figure seems to turn or to be displaced, and because each trace of the spectator is eliminated, the figure becomes enclosed in the surrounding space. This forces the figure to an incredible effort, "a derisory athletics, a violent comedy" (ibid., p. 15).

The convulsive effort of the body is not only the effect of the movement of the field. The body takes over this movement in an attempt to escape from itself. In *Figure Standing at a Washbasin* (1976) we see a figure at a washbasin. But this figurative scene is being deformed into a Figure that puts its efforts to the limit to escape through its mouth into the drain of the washbasin. Hysteria is not about me escaping from my body, but about the body trying to escape from itself through one of its openings, in an immobile spasm: "It is a scene of hysteria. The entire series of spasms in Bacon is of this type: scenes of love, of vomiting and excrement, in which the body attempts to escape from itself *through* one of its organs, in order to rejoin the field or material structure" (ibid., p. 16). This interpretation also makes sense of the specific role that the shadow and the mirror play in Bacon's work. The shadow of the figure in Bacon's work is always just as full and solid as the figure itself. As the duplicate of the figure, it has liberated itself from the figure's spasm and now spreads or runs out into the background (ibid.). The mirror accomplishes the same remarkable function as the shadow. For Bacon, the mirror is not a reflecting surface, but a mostly black, dark space. The figure sits *in* the mirror, where it becomes stretched out and flat after the body, in an extreme, spastic effort, has escaped from itself through its mouth, anus, throat or through the toilet or into the drain of the washbasin (ibid., p. 50).

According to Deleuze, Bacon's paintings always show the spasm of a body that wants to escape from itself through some little hole that is always much too small. It is this spasm that leads Deleuze to an aesthetic clinic of hysteria:

---

[15] "We will see that, in his paintings and especially in his triptychs, Bacon needs the function of an attendant, which is not a spectator but part of the Figure. … They are attendants not in the sense of spectators, but as a constant or point of reference in relation to which a variation is assessed" (Deleuze, 2003, p. 13).

[16] "An anomaly is a fact of individual variation which prevents two beings from being able to take the place of each other completely" (Canguilhem, 1966, p. 77).

the hysterical spasms in Bacon's paintings form a series with the hysterical hyperesthesias, hysterical pity, the hysterical scream, the hysterical smile, and the hysterical fall. It is important to note that this series is not a mere enumeration of pathological traits, as in psychiatry, or a displacement of symptoms, as in psychoanalysis. Deleuze holds a Jungian or Szondian rather than a Freudian conception of psychopathology.[17] Hysteria is not so much a pathological state or syndrome as a moment of crisis and passage, a transition from the spasm to the smile and the fall. How, then, must we understand the sense of this series?

In *Studies on Hysteria* (1895), Breuer warns his readers (and his co-author?) that the cathartic method is limited to the representational or ideogenic aspect of hysteria. This warning is subsequently disregarded, but it nevertheless shows that Breuer had a greater feeling for the somatic side of hysteria than Freud: "Let us consider an everyday instance. A woman may, whenever an affect arises, produce on her neck, breast and face an erythema appearing first in blotches and then becoming confluent. This is determined by ideas and therefore according to Moebius it is a hysterical phenomenon. But this same erythema appears, though over a less extensive area, when the skin is irritated or touched, etc. This would not be hysterical. Thus a phenomenon which is undoubtedly a complete unity would on one occasion be hysterical and on another occasion not" (Freud & Breuer, 1895, p. 188). Breuer's doubts concerning the exclusive importance of representation in the clinic of hysteria show themselves at another level as well. In the introduction of his theoretical contribution to *Studies on Hysteria*, he emphasizes that he will only speak in psychological terms: "Psychical processes will be dealt with in the language of psychology" (ibid., p. 185). But only a few of pages later, he develops a theory of affects in the language of electromechanics: "We ought not to think of a cerebral path of conduction as resembling a telephone wire which is only excited electrically at the moment at which it has to function (that is, in the present context, when it has to transmit a signal). We ought to liken it to a telephone line through which there is a constant flow of galvanic current and which can no longer be excited if that current ceases. Or better, let us imagine a widely-ramified electrical system for lighting and the transmission of motor power; what is expected of this system is that simple establishment of a contact shall be able to set any lamp or machine in operation" (ibid., p.

[17] For this distinction between Freud, Jung and Szondi, see: Szondi (1963, pp. 43-54). For the connection between Deleuze and Leopold Szondi, see: Deleuze and Guattari (2004, pp. 318-320). For Deleuze's Jungianism, see: Kerslake (2007).

193). Etcetera. When Breuer – in spite of his earlier proclamation – makes the transition from a psychology of representations to an electromechanics of affects, he anticipates Deleuze's conception of hysteria. The bodily sensations that characterize hysteria are not expressions of representations or meanings; they are primarily *vibrations* (Deleuze, 2003, p. 45). An electrical current goes through the flesh, and works *directly* on the nerves.[18] It is well-known that such vibrations or forces that affect the body do not obey the organic unity or the anatomical structure of the body. However, that does not mean that they are imaginary. What the hysteric feels and painting reveals is how the body as pure vitality and thus as pure pathos puts the organic-organized body under pressure.[19] In the hysterical body, forces are at work that are too powerful for the organic organization of the organs, "like the forces of the cosmos confronting an intergalactic traveller immobile in his capsule" (ibid., p. 58). Because of this, a convulsive disorganization and re-grouping of the organs takes place. Freud says: "Certain regions of the body, such as the mucous membrane of the mouth and anus, seem, as it were, to be claiming that they should themselves be regarded and treated as genitals" (Freud, 1905, p. 153). But, the other way around, sexual organs can also function as mouths or anuses (Deleuze, 2003, p. 47). For what is at stake is not a deformed expression of the sexual instinct, but the experience of the body *under* the organism: "The body is felt *under* the body, the transitory organs are felt under the organization of the fixed organs. Furthermore, this body without organs and these transitory organs are themselves *seen*, in phenomena known as internal or external 'autoscopia': it is no longer *my* head, but I feel myself inside *a* head, I see and I see myself inside a head; or else I do not see myself in the mirror, but I feel myself in the body that I see, and I see myself in this naked body when I am dressed… and so forth" (ibid., p. 49; italics in the original). The hysteric feels and *sees* the way in which the body becomes detached from the organism.

According to Deleuze, the hysterical body painted by Bacon cannot be recuperated by le corps vécu of phenomenology.[20] When Deleuze speaks about the body as flesh, he does not refer to "la chair" but to "la viande". To understand this idea, we must look at the paintings of Bacon. Deleuze

[18] "First of all, there are the famous spastics and paralytics, the hyperesthetics or anesthetics, associated or alternating, sometimes fixed and sometimes migrant, depending on the passage of the nervous wave and the zones it invests or withdraws from" (Deleuze, 2003, p. 49).

[19] "There is a special relation between painting and hysteria. It is very simple. Painting directly attempts to release the presences beneath representation" (Deleuze, 2003, pp. 51-52).

[20] "The phenomenological hypothesis is perhaps insufficient because it merely invokes the lived body. But the lived body is still a paltry thing in comparison with a more profound and almost unlivable Power (*Puissance*)" (Deleuze, 2003, p. 44).

remarks that, even when Bacon paints portraits, he does not paint a face, but a head. The face is a more or less independent, structured organization that, for this reason, hides the head. On the other hand, the head is only one end of the body (ibid., p. 20). The face belongs to the bones, but the head is meat. In Bacon's paintings the meat and the nerves are detached from the bones. The quivering flesh falls from the bones and the "fleshy" head is set free from the face (ibid., p. 22).

When Bacon reveals the head beneath the face, it does not mean that he deprives his portraits of their soul by reducing them to mere bodies. Bacon's portraits do have a soul, but that soul is bodily through and through. The soul in Bacon's work is the sighing of the beast.[21] This hysterical *rapport* with the cries and moans of beasts is not, however, based on a hysterical identification with, or an excessive sympathy for, animals. When, in Turin, the mad Nietzsche embraced a moaning horse, this historical, hysterical scene is not about pity for a horse, but about mercy for the meat, where the distinction between human and animal recedes into the background.[22] Nietzsche's "pitié pour la viande!" is a hysterical pity for life as a slaughterhouse (ibid., p. 23). Bacon's red-green-bluish butcher's meat is not – as has sometimes been claimed – an expression of the painter's sadism, but of hysterical pity. For Deleuze, this pity for the meat is also the kernel of all hysterical religiosity: "Bacon is a religious painter only in butcher shops". Deleuze quotes Bacon: "I've always been very moved by pictures about slaughterhouses and meat, and to me they belong very much to the whole thing of the Crucifixion. … Of course, we are meat. If I go into a butcher shop I always think it's surprising that I wasn't there instead of the animal" (ibid., p. 24). Bacon's interest in meat is not the sadism of the surgeon but the mercy of the nurse. It is not without good reason that even militant atheists like Charcot and Freud, at the end of their careers, have bowed their heads before the great Mercy of Lourdes.[23]

This pity for the meat reaches its crisis in the hysterical scream. Bacon always tried to paint this scream. The problem is not so much how to paint a sound, but how to make visible forces that otherwise remain invisible. That is, after all, the task of painting for Deleuze: making invisible forces visible.

[21] "It is not that the head lacks spirit; but it is a spirit in bodily form, a corporeal and vital breath, an animal spirit. It is the animal spirit of man" (Deleuze, 2003, p. 20).

[22] "Bacon does not say, 'Pity the beasts', but rather that every man who suffers is a piece of meat. Meat is the common zone of man and the beast, their zone of indiscernibility" (Deleuze, 2003, p. 23).

[23] "In the late 1880s and early 1890s Charcot himself sent patients on a pilgrimage to Lourdes" (Showalter, 1997, p. 32). "I do not think our cures can compete with those of Lourdes" (Freud, 1933, p. 152).

In the case of the hysterical scream, this means that the scream cannot be a response to an already visible spectacle, a spectacle before which – or about which – one screams. If this were the case, we would relapse into the figurative. The hysterical scream that Bacon has in mind, is something totally different. Bacon's scream is not just an expression of pain, nor is it merely a reaction to some horrible event. The scream is the result of something greater than the pain one is capable of feeling, and greater than the spectacle about which one screams.[24] What then is this invisible and intangible force? Deleuze is very brief on this "more profound and almost unliveable Force" (ibid., p. 44). He seems to leave to painting the task of tracing this force and making it visible.[25]

Maldiney – Deleuze's *companion de route* in the whole Bacon book – seems to go further. In his *Penser l'homme et la folie*, he invokes the scream in his description of the "pathic". Sensation relates to perception as the scream relates to speaking. The scream belongs to the dimension of the pathic, just as speaking belongs to the dimension of representation. It is this pathic dimension of sensation that Deleuze aims at when he speaks about the vibrations of the flesh, where the difference between humans and beasts recedes into the background. However, that humans suffer like beasts ("every man who suffers is a piece of meat"), does not erase the distinction between humans and animals, and that distinction, according to Maldiney, is discovered in the scream. The human being who screams, says Maldiney, screams the world (crie *le monde*): "The world that is disclosed in this scream is not the one that is expressed by language, but neither is it simply the sound of a living creature" (Maldiney, 1990, p. 203). In the scream, nothing is perceived or expressed; in the scream, the body discovers its excessive presence, "la pure presence du corps". Maldiney writes: "The wondering about the miracle of the 'there is' is absolutely contemporaneous with the scream" (ibid., p. 204). But Maldiney's description remains rather pious. When it concerns an event that affects us before we intentionally relate to it, the astonishment is more like a wound than like wonder. The hysterical scream does not reveal the world of being-in-the-world, but the "world" as pure affect. It is only this excessive presence (*cet excès de presence*)[26] that breaks with the "photographical" world

[24] "If we scream, it is always as victims of invisible and insensible forces that scramble every spectacle, and that even lie beyond pain and feeling" (Deleuze, 2003, p. 60).

[25] "The task of painting is defined as the attempt to render visible forces that are not themselves visible" (Deleuze, 2003, p. 56).

[26] "The hysteric is at the same time someone who imposes his or her presence, but also someone for whom things and beings are present, *too* present, and who attributes to every thing and communicates to every being this excessive presence" (Deleuze, 2003, p. 50; italics in the original).

of representations, clichés and phantasms.[27] The hysterical scream as the pure pathos of presence.

But this excessive presence not only shows itself in screaming and suffering: "Bacon suggests that beyond the scream there is the smile" (Deleuze, 2003, p. 28). Bacon calls this smile hysterical and adds, modestly, that he never succeeded in painting this smile (ibid., p. 28). Since Leonardo da Vinci, the mysterious smile of hysterical girls has always been the highest goal in painting. Art historians and psychotherapists seem to believe that such a hysterical smile *hides* something, but for Bacon and Deleuze the smile is what *remains when the body disappears* (ibid., pp. 28-29). To clarify this bizarre idea, Deleuze discusses Bacon's 1953 triptych, *Three Studies of the Human Head*. Bacon's triptychs are not comic strips; they should not be read from left to right; they do not tell a story.[28] The bringing together of the three panels does not tell a story, but initiates a *rhythm*.[29] Only with this rhythm Bacon's work really comes into its own, because rhythm is the essence of sensation. In a strict sense, one cannot perceive a rhythm, one can only feel it.[30] Hence, it is only in this rhythmic movement that Bacon's work frees itself from the figurative and the representational, without becoming abstract.[31] According to Deleuze, we can differentiate three rhythms in Bacon's triptychs (ibid., p. 71). First there is the witness-rhythm (*le rythme témoin*). In the triptych of 1953, this witness is located in the smile of the figure in the left panel. As a result of its horizontality and relative stability, this smile forms a more or less fixed element in the rhythmic movement of the triptych.[32] In opposition to this stable, horizontal element, the two other figures move in opposite directions.[33] In the central panel, one sees a man who is screaming, which gives the rhythm an upward movement. In the right panel, we see a figure that falls and disappears. According to Deleuze, all of Bacons triptychs are characterized by this triple movement that connects the three panels in a bizarre trapeze act or an acrobatic dance. Bacon's 1953 triptych is experienced as a rhythmic series

[27] "La prise de l'étant comme tel a lieu dans la surprise de l'être. Dans le sentir il y a et j'y suis. E. Straus a raison de l'assimiler au cri" (Maldiney, 1990, p. 204).

[28] "The triptych does not imply a progression, and it does not tell a story" (Deleuze, 2003, p. 69).

[29] "The coexistence of all these movements in the painting is rhythm" (Deleuze, 2003, p. 33).

[30] "Un rythme n'est pas objectivable dans l'espace. Il ne saurait au sens propre être perçu. Il prend fond dans le sentir" (Maldiney, 1990, p. 207).

[31] "Le rythme dépasse toute espèce de perception figurale" (Maldiney, 1967, p. 157).

[32] "This horizontal can be presented in several Figures. First there is the flat hysterical smile" (Deleuze, 2003, p. 75).

[33] "What matters in the two opposable rhythms is that each is the 'retrogradation' of the other, while a common and constant value appears in the attendant-rhythm" (Deleuze, 2003, p. 80).

from the scream, to the smile, to the fall. The fall is the active moment that pushes the scream in the opposite direction. The horizontality of the hysterical smile forms the point of reference against which this double movement varies. When Deleuze says that in hysteria the body tries to escape from itself, this does not mean that the body wants to transcend itself into a state beyond the body, but that the body frees itself from itself in the *rhythm* of its movement.[34] In painting and hysteria, however, this rhythm remains entangled in a combat with the weight of the flesh or with the materiality of the paint. That is why music begins where painting ends, because, unlike painting, music "strips bodies of their inertia, of the materiality of their presence: it disembodies bodies. … This is why music does not have hysteria as its clinical essence, but is confronted more and more with a galloping schizophrenia" (ibid., pp. 54-55).

Psychoanalysis has domesticated the hysterical body by considering it to be a corporeal expression of unconscious representations. Its therapy, which is based on the narrative procedures of literature,[35] neglects the pure presence of the body, its rhythms, vibrations and paroxysms. It takes a painter like Bacon to see in hysterical postures the pure presence of the body at the mercy of invisible forces. To see the presence of the body instead of its representations, one needs the eye of the painter, not the ear of the psychoanalyst or the gaze of the psychiatrist-photographer. Painting turns the eyes into organs of touch: "One might say that painters paint with their eyes, but only insofar as they touch with their eyes" (ibid., p. 155). Of course, such an aesthetic clinic does not involve a therapy of hysteria in any medical-psychiatric sense of a cure or a return to "normality". On the contrary, it produces a more radical change of perspective.[36] Bacon's aesthetic-figural approach to hysteria reveals why the hysterical poses and spasms are the most natural of postures *in view of the forces they confront*: "The body seems to enter into particularly mannered

[34] "'Ruthmos' désigne la forme dans l'instant qu'elle est assumée par ce qui est mouvant, mobile, fluide" (Maldiney 1967, p. 157).

[35] "It still strikes me myself as strange that the case histories I write should read like *short stories* and that, as one might say, they lack the serious stamp of science. I must console myself with the reflection that the nature of the subject is evidently responsible for this, rather than any preference of my own. The fact is that local diagnosis and electrical reactions lead nowhere in the study of hysteria, whereas a detailed description of mental processes such as we are accustomed to find *in the works of imaginative writers* enables me, with the use of a few psychological formulas, to obtain at least some kind of insight into the course of that affection" (Freud, 1895, pp. 160-161, my italics).

[36] "Abjection becomes splendor, the horror of life becomes a very pure and very intense life" (Deleuze, 2003, p. 52)

postures, or is weighed down by stress, pain, or anguish. But this is true only if a story or a figuration is reintroduced: figurally speaking, these are actually the most natural of postures, as if we caught them 'between' two stories, or when we were alone, listening to a force that had seized us" (ibid., p. 161).

References

Canguilhem, G. (1978). *On the normal and the pathological.* (C.R. Fawcett, Trans.). London: D. Reidel. (Original work published 1966).

Deleuze, G. (1989). *Masochism: Coldness and cruelty.* (J. McNeil, Trans.). New York: Zone Books. (Original work published 1967).

———. (2004). *The logic of sense.* (M. Lester & C. Stivale, Trans.). London: Continuum. (Original work published 1969).

———. (2003). *Francis Bacon: The logic of sensation.* (D.W. Smith, Trans.). London: Continuum. (Original work published 1981).

———. (1998). *Essays critical and clinical.* (D.W. Smith & M. A. Greco, Trans.). London: Verso. (Original work published 1993)

———. (2006). *Two regimes of madness.* (A. Hodges & M. Taormina, Trans.). Cambridge, MA: MIT Press. (Original work published 2004).

Deleuze, G., & Guattari, F. (2004). *Anti-Oedipus.* (R. Hurley, Trans.). London: Continuum. (Original work published 1972).

Didi-Huberman, G. (1982). *L'invention de l'hystérie: Charcot et l'iconographie photographique de la Salpêtrière.* Paris: Macula.

Freud, S., & Breuer, J. (1895). Studies on hysteria. *Standard Edition 2*, pp. 1-321.

Freud, S. (1893a). On the theory of hysterical attacks. *Standard Edition 1*, pp. 151-153.

———. (1893b). Charcot. *Standard Edition 3*, pp. 11-23.

———. (1905). Three essays on the theory of sexuality. *Standard Edition 7*, pp. 125-245.

———. (1933). New introductory lectures on psycho-analysis. *Standard Edition 22*, pp. 1-182.

Geyskens, T. (2006). Gilles Deleuze over Sacher-Masoch: Literatuur als symptomatologie. *Tijdschrift voor Filosofie, 68(4)*, 779-801.

Green, A. (1972). *On private madness.* London: Rebus Press.

Kerslake, C. (2007). *Deleuze and the unconscious.* London: Continuum.

Lavagetto, M. (2002). *Freud à l'épreuve de la littérature.* Paris: Seuil.

Maldiney, H. (1973). Le dévoilement de la dimension esthétique dans la phénoménologie d'Erwin Straus. In *Regard parole espace* (pp. 124-146). Lausanne: L'age d'homme. (Original work published 1966).

———. (1973). L'esthétique des rythmes. In *Regard parole espace* (pp. 147-172). Lausanne: L'age d'homme. (Original work published 1967).

———. (1990). *Penser l'homme et la folie*. Grenoble: Million.
Showalter, E. (1997). *Hystories*. London: Picador.
Szondi, L. (1963). *Schicksalsanalytische Therapie*. Bern: Huber.

Epilogue – Sexuality and the Quarrel between Philosophy and Psychoanalysis

Eran Dorfman

Who's afraid of psychoanalysis? More than a century after the publication of Freud's *The Interpretation of Dreams* and *Three Essays on Sexuality*, the answer still seems to be: philosophers.

Why is it so? Although psychoanalysis was founded by Freud as a scientific and rational theory, its investigation has always focused on the irrational aspects of human life, whether their name was "the unconscious", "sexuality", "drives", etc. This paradoxical meeting point of the rational and the irrational marks the difference between psychoanalysis and philosophy. And yet, if we look at it more closely, we will find that philosophy, too, is a rational enterprise which, sooner or later, meets the irrational aspect of reality. Philosophy acknowledges the realm of irrationality but remains suspicious of it. In what follows, I shall argue that it is this ambiguous attitude which leads to many of the hostilities and misunderstandings that exist between philosophy and psychoanalysis.

It was Freud himself who compared the unconscious to the Kantian "thing in itself". But for Kant, at least in his first *Critique*, the thing in itself is the limit of philosophy: it is beyond our reach, and therefore should, after its preliminary demarcation, be kept out of the philosophical investigation. Freud, on the other hand, takes the Kantian discovery as the starting point of his theory:

> Just as Kant warned us not to overlook the fact that our perceptions are subjectively conditioned and must not be regarded as identical to what is perceived though unknowable, so psycho-analysis warns us not to equate perceptions by means of consciousness with the unconscious mental processes which are their object. (Freud, 1915, p. 171)

Freud admits that the unconscious cannot be reached as such, but, contrary to Kant, he adds that it cannot be set aside either, since it is the secret object of all conscious perceptions. Therefore, the entire psychoanalytical enterprise is devoted to seeking phenomenal and circumstantial evidences for what can never become evident itself. Whereas Kant's project remained critical and aimed to set the limits of human understanding by discovering its *a priori* conditions, Freud's project, on the other hand, aimed to bypass these conditions by facilitating the entrance of unconscious material into the scope of conscious reflection.

Both philosophy and psychoanalysis, then, acknowledge the existence of an irrational core within (human) reality, but they do not agree upon its bounds and effects within the phenomenal world. Psychoanalysis claims that the unconscious has a crucial influence upon the conscious sphere, such that it turns the structure of human understanding upside down. The Freudian discovery of what secretly motivates consciousness goes hand in hand with the wish to shake the traditional picture of the human being, and, interestingly, this wish corresponds to the very nature of the unconscious: it is a dynamic agency which does not acknowledge limits, and, therefore, needs a special theoretical and practical treatment.

This leads us to a second difference between psychoanalysis and philosophy: the unconscious not only poses problems for theory, but has practical effects on human life and creates symptoms which psychoanalysis aims to cure. Psychoanalysis is thus a theory which, at the same time, is a therapeutic practice. Whereas philosophy has traditionally posed itself as a detached and remote reflection upon the world and the self, psychoanalysis is forced to constantly draw from clinical findings, engaging in a dialogue between the theory and the clinic.

But Freudian psychoanalysis has not simply seen itself as a mere hybrid of thought and praxis. The dialogue which Freud initiated between the empirical world and its theorization soon led him to the notorious assertion that psychoanalysis is a new science: like the scientist, the psychoanalyst proposes a hypothetical theory, puts it to an empirical test, adjusts the theory to the results, goes back to the laboratory, and so forth. But can we justify Freud's pretension to scientific status?

Most contemporary scholars would agree that psychoanalysis is not a science in the rigorous sense. Every first year psychology student, for instance, reads in her textbook that no distinct scientific evidence is to be found for psychoanalytical hypotheses such as the Oedipus Complex, the Structural Model or the Theory of Drives.[1] Does this mean that one should dismiss the entire psychoanalytical enterprise, ban it from universities, and leave its treatment to non-academic psychoanalytical societies, as is more and more the case today? Instead of carelessly doing so, we must recall that psychoanalysis

[1] The recent neuro-psychoanalytical movement is an exception to this, but its future and scope are yet to be determined.

has set for itself the paradoxical task of investigating the irrational domain. Hence, the question of its scientific status should not concern psychoanalysis exclusively, but any discipline which deals with irrationality.

In this sense, it is interesting to note the ambiguous position that philosophy holds towards both science and irrationality. Modern philosophy often distinguishes itself from the empirical sciences, looking for universal *a priori* truths, in opposition to the particular *a posteriori* truths of science, which are subject to constant changes and updates. Philosophical truth is eternal, while scientific truth is ephemeral. But this does not mean that philosophy is not interested in science. On the contrary, philosophy has always maintained – secretly or openly – the fantasy of becoming the queen of sciences, supplying them with the logical foundations upon which they would flourish. The imagined relationship between philosophy and science is thus supposed to be unidirectional, going from the former to the latter, keeping philosophy pure and conferring the dirty work onto empirical science alone.

Philosophy may hold itself superior to science, but, nonetheless, it respects it. On these grounds, why is it that philosophy seems so often, at least in the analytical tradition, to despise psychoanalysis? The reason for this is not psychoanalysis' obstinate interest in irrationality *per se*, but rather its pretension to be a science: the science of the Irrational. This obliges psychoanalysis to make hypotheses and speculations, which, by their very nature, cannot be verified or confirmed. Philosophy, as the queen of sciences which checks and controls their logical basis, is thus inclined to harshly reject any pretension of scientifically dealing with irrationality. But what method, then, should confront and explore this domain? Could it be philosophy itself?

We should note that the more a certain philosophy lays claim to a logical validity, wishing to found itself as the firm basis of science, the more it tends to overlook irrationality. As we saw earlier, Kant discovered the thing in itself beyond reason, but he was content to point out its formal existence, warning us not to investigate it philosophically. In this way, he doomed the thing in itself to remain outside the limits of rational knowledge. The same applies to numerous philosophers, from Plato to Wittgenstein, who all acknowledged the irrational as the opaque domain of life, but delegated its further treatment to methods and disciplines such as religion, mysticism and art. Other philosophers, still worse, have pretended to rationalize, control and eventually refute and abolish irrationality, claiming that it can always be reduced to rational factors. We should, therefore, conclude that most philosophers do not wish to bother themselves with, or even admit the existence of something which, by definition, resists theory, that is, resists philosophy.

This is where sexuality comes into the picture. Indeed, it may seem easy to dismiss such a vague and amorphous notion as the unconscious, but it is more difficult to ignore the concrete and evident aspect of human life which constitutes sexuality. Freud's ingenuity lies not only in his insistence upon finding rational explanations for that which must remain irrational, but also in concretizing this exact presupposed irrational core, locating it within a specific domain of human life, namely, sexuality. In this way, Freud gave body to his theory. And it is precisely this body which philosophy still looks for and still seems to lack.

Western philosophy, I claimed earlier, prefers to remain pure, but purity seems to go hand in hand with the negation of the body. This negation leaves philosophy, after more than 2500 years of investigation, floating in a world of ideas. Psychoanalysis, on the other hand, has a tradition of barely more than a hundred years, but it is remarkable to note the solid foundations it has developed, at least partly due to its choice to locate its investigation of the unconscious in the domain of sexuality.

Indeed, this choice was at the centre of numerous polemics, but these, too, eventually helped psychoanalysis to grow and to flourish. Moreover, sexuality has contributed to the lively character of psychoanalysis not only by its provocative aspect, but also and principally because it has allowed us to situate abstract instances in a tangible domain. It has allowed a variety of physical symptoms to be understood in light of psychical forces, which are, in return, influenced and altered by bodily behaviours. Sexuality stands at the intersection between the rational and the irrational, between causality and what necessarily eludes any causal explanation. As such, sexuality permits us to extract the irrational domain from the obscurity and opaqueness of the ineffable. Sexuality does, indeed, have a dark element in it, but this element is always in interaction with others. It takes place within the body and expresses itself in words and signifiers that call for explanations, models and speculations. These may never be fully illuminated, but nonetheless become a solid body of knowledge for further investigation.

Here, psychoanalysis can contribute to philosophy, but at the same time, it is here that philosophy can contribute to psychoanalysis. Unarguably, bodies tend to change, to grow old, hence requiring different forms of treatment as the years go by. Philosophy can help psychoanalysis renovate itself precisely through its criticism of sexuality. As we have seen, philosophy has always prevented itself from becoming contaminated by empirical investigation or clinical therapy.[2] Now, on the one hand, this distance helped it to develop sophisticated conceptual and analytical tools, and, on the other hand, to avoid an over-institutionalization, as often is the case with psychoanalysis, quickly becoming divided into self-enclosed guilds. As such, philosophy can examine psychoanalysis' premises regarding sexuality (and other domains), and retrace the ways it has developed its theory, suggesting alternative solutions when necessary.

However, in order to engage in such a critical project, philosophy must accept assistance from psychoanalysis in return. More concretely, it must first of all cease to fear psychoanalysis, that is, the body and the irrational forces which it encapsulates. Indeed, central twentieth-century philosophers such as Sartre, Merleau-Ponty, Foucault, Deleuze, Althusser, and, more recently, Irigaray, Butler, Žižek and others, who dared to transgress the limits of the comfortable field of logical, *a priori* truths, soon confronted the question of the human body and its sexual status. And it is no coincidence that these thinkers have all shown a great interest in psychoanalysis, even though often in a critical manner. For them, psychoanalysis has filled the lacunas left by classical philosophy. It has supplied them with insights, clinical findings and numerous hypothesis concerning the human body and sexuality. Indeed, they did not always agree with them, and sometimes severely judged the psychoanalytical method itself, but they never overlooked psychoanalysis or dismissed it without further ado, and this, in itself, is already a tacit acknowledgment of its importance to their own investigation.

To conclude, psychoanalysis' pretension to be a science, combined with its insistence on the irrational domain of sexuality, is the reason that philosophy tends to reject psychoanalysis. At the same time, however, this constitutes a strength from which philosophy can benefit, too. The domain of sexuality can be profoundly understood neither by the natural sciences, nor by analytical philosophy, but only by a method which adjusts itself to sexuality's peculiar, irrational nature; a method which would explore the human body and its

[2] In the last decade we see, however, the rising of movements which call themselves practical or therapeutic philosophy. The focus in such therapies is on the rational, although often hidden premises of the patient's behaviour. For instance, when the patient complains about problems that he or she has with having friends, the therapy would consist of discussing the definition of friendship, drawing on numerous philosophers who touched on this question, from Aristotle to Heidegger and Wittgenstein, passing through Montaigne and Nietzsche. Interesting as this method may be, it is important to remark that it fails to confront and profoundly question the irrational motives of human behaviour, and, in this sense, it is basically a more intellectual version of cognitive psychology.

irrational drives, such as love and hatred, affection and aggression; a method which would dare to speculate upon these concepts, and yet which would ceaselessly check and correct these speculations by means empirical and clinical findings. And this method, it goes without saying, is psychoanalysis. If philosophy wishes to regain its relevance to human life, to initiate a fruitful dialogue with a more embodied method, inspiring it and letting itself be inspired by it, then psychoanalysis offers a promising starting point. In order for this to happen, good will is needed from both sides, philosophers and psychoanalysts alike. We hope that the present book will amount to a way-marker on the path towards a mutual dialogue and investigation, leading to a better understanding of the human being and the forces which rule it and are ruled by it in turn.

References

Freud, S. (1915). The unconscious. *Standard Edition 14*, pp. 161-215.

Notes on the Contributors

Jens De Vleminck is a junior researcher at the Institute of Philosophy (KU Leuven, Belgium). He is a member of the Center for Psychoanalysis and Philosophical Anthropology (RU Nijmegen, The Netherlands – KU Leuven) and the Belgian School for Psychoanalysis. His PhD thesis is on human aggression in Freud.

Eran Dorfman is an Alexander Von Humboldt Fellow at the Freie Universität Berlin, and a Program Director at the Collège International de Philosophie, Paris. He completed his PhD on Merleau-Ponty and Lacan at the University of Paris XII, which was elaborated into a monograph in Springer's Phaenomenologica series (*Réapprendre à voir le monde: Merleau-Ponty face au miroir lacanien*, 2007). He has published numerous articles on phenomenology and psychoanalysis and is currently preparing a book on the foundation of the everyday, drawing on philosophical and psychoanalytical theory.

Tomas Geyskens has a PhD in Philosophy. He has published on Freud and Deleuze and, with Philippe Van Haute, he has co-authored *Confusion of Tongues* (Other Press, 2004), and *From Death Instinct to Attachment Theory* (Other Press, 2007).

Ari Hirvonen is Adjunct Professor in Philosophy of Law at the Faculty of Law at the University of Helsinki. He is a Senior Researcher at the Centre of Excellency in Foundations of European Law and Polity Research funded by the Academy of Finland. He has published texts on tragedy, continental philosophy, moral and legal philosophy, political theory, psychoanalysis, critical criminology, the Greek idea of justice and evil in law. He has edited *Polycentricity: Multiple Scenes of Law* (Pluto Press, 1998) and, with Janne Porttikivi, *Law and Evil: Philosophy, Politics, Psychoanalysis* (Routledge, 2009).

Adrian Johnston is Assistant Professor in the Department of Philosophy at the University of New Mexico at Albuquerque and an assistant teaching analyst at the Emory Psychoanalytic Institute in Atlanta. He is the author of *Time Driven: Metapsychology and the Splitting of the Drive* (Northwestern University Press, 2005), *Žižek's Ontology: A Transcendental Materialist Theory of Subjectivity* (Northwestern University Press, 2008), and *Badiou, Žižek, and Political Transformations: The Cadence of Change* (Northwestern University Press, 2009).

Elissa Marder teaches French and Comparative Literature at Emory University where she served as Director of the Emory Psychoanalytic Studies Program from 2001-2006. Her book *Dead Time: Temporal Disorders in the Wake of Modernity (Baudelaire and Flaubert)* was published by Stanford University Press in 2001. She has also published essays on diverse topics in deconstruction, literature, feminism, film, photography and psychoanalysis. She is currently completing a book entitled *The Mother in the Age of Mechanical Reproduction: Psychoanalysis, Technology and Literature.*

Paul Moyaert studied Philosophy in Leuven and Paris and is a trained psychoanalyst and member of the Belgian School for Psychoanalysis. He teaches Philosophy at the Institute of Philosophy in Leuven and is the author of books on the ethics of Lacan (*Ethiek en Sublimatie,* 1994), neighbourly love, mystic love, the sense for symbols in Christianity (*De mateloosheid van het Christendom,* 1998) and praying with images as a symbolic practice (*Iconen en beeldverering,* 2007). All books were published by Boom/Sun in Amsterdam.

Ruth Ronen is Professor of Philosophy at Tel Aviv University. She teaches and writes about crucial junctions of psychoanalytical thought with philosophy, and is the author of *Possible Worlds in Literary Theory* (Cambridge, 1994), *Representing the Real* (Rodopi, 2002), *Aesthetics of Anxiety* (SUNY, 2009) and *Art before the Law* (forthcoming).

Vladimir Safatle is Professor at Universidade de São Paulo (Department of Philosophy and Institute of Psychology), invited professor at Université de Paris VII and Paris VIII, and a scholar in the Erasmus Mundus project (2009). He is the author of *The Passion of Negative: Lacan and Dialectics, Cynicism and the End of Criticism, Introducing Lacan* and *Fetishism: To Colonize the Other* (all in Portuguese). He is responsible for the Brazilian translation of Theodor Adorno's *Gesammelte Schriften* and one of the coordinators of the *International Society of Psychoanalysis and Philosophy.*

Charles Shepherdson is Professor of English at the State University of New York. He has held fellowships with the Henry Luce Foundation, the Pembroke Center for Teaching and Research at Brown University, the Commonwealth Center at the University of Virginia, and the Institute for Advanced Study in Princeton. In 2006 he was appointed by the United States Department of State to the Senior Specialist Roster in American Studies for 2006-11, and from 2006-08 he was National Science Council Professor at Tsinghua University and National Taiwan University. He is the author of several books on psychoanalysis and philosophy including *Vital Signs: Nature, Culture, Psychoanalysis* (Routledge, 2000) and *Lacan and the Limits of Language* (Fordham University Press, 2008). He is currently working on aesthetics and emotion.

Cecilia Sjöholm is Professor of Aesthetics at Södertörn University. She has a PhD in both Philosophy and Comparative Literature. Her research is concerned with the intersection between literature, art, and philosophy, above all the tradition of phenomenology. Her current project is entitled *Making Sense of Aisthesis: The Return of Sensibility*. Her latest books are *Kristeva and the Political* (London: Routledge, 2005) and *The Antigone Complex: Ethics and the Invention of Feminine Desire* (CA: Stanford University Press, 2004). Her latest articles include "Arendt at Colonnus: Naked Man", a contribution to the anthology *Interrogating Antigone: From Philosophy to Performance*, Oxford University Press, ed. Steve Wilmer and Audrone Zukauskaite (forthcoming) and "Margarethe von Trotta: *Leviathan in Germany*", in *Cinematic Thinking: Philosophical Approaches to the New Cinema*, ed. James Phillips (Stanford UP, 2008, pp. 109-128).

Philippe Van Haute is Professor of Philosophical Anthropology at RU Nijmegen and a practicing psychoanalyst (Belgian School for Psychoanalysis). He is the author of *Against Adaptation: Lacan's Subversion of the Subject* (Other Press, 2002), (with Tomas Geyskens) *Confusion of Tongues: The Primacy of Sexuality in Freud, Ferenczi and Laplanche* (Other Press, 2004), and (with Tomas Geyskens) *From Death Drive to Attachment Theory: The Primacy of the Child in Freud, Klein and Hermann* (Other Press, 2007).

Veronica Vasterling is an Associate Professor at the Department of Philosophy and the Institute for Gender Studies (RU Nijmegen). Her research interests range from philosophical anthropology and feminist philosophy to psychoanalytical and gender theory.